Six Mountain Hikes from around the world

Paul Carpenter

Six mountain hikes from around the world

Published by Lulu.com

ISBN 978-1-4466-1230-9

Copyright © Paul Carpenter 2011
www.mtn-m.co.uk

Cover image – An Teallach Highlands of Scotland
Back cover image – A view across Loch Morlich in the Cairngorms

Six mountain hikes from around the world

To Mum and Dad,
Where would I be
Without you.

Six mountain hikes from around the world

Contents

List of Photos - 7
List of route Maps - 8
Introduction - 9

New York State – The Adirondacks
Mountains of snow and Winds of dreams – 11

Austria - Stubaier Alpen
Peaked to Perfection –59

New Zealand – Arthurs pass and Lake Sumner
Into Nature's untouched kingdom –105

Norway – Jotunheimen National Park
Where the giants still reign –153

Scotland – Monadhliath and Cairngorm Mountains
Guardians of speyside –193

California – Yosemite National Park
Hidden Treasure –233

Six mountain hikes from around the world

List Of Photos

The Adirondacks
Towards the high peaks
Heart Lake
Typical woodland
Mt Colden
Lean-to by lake Colden
Sign post under 6ft snow
Lean to by Indian pass brook
Avalanche pass
Avalanche pass
Fellow gatherer
View from Mt Jo
Heart Lake
Algonquin Peak from the cabin
Frozen river

Austria, Stubaier Alps
Innsbrucker Hutte
Towards Hohes Tor
Path to Nurnburger Hutte
Grunausee
Nurnburger Hutte
Sulzenau Hutte
Sulzenau Ferner
Dresner Hutte
View from Mutterberger see
Grabagrubernieder
looking back to ridge
Neue Regansburger Hutte
Franz Senn Hutte
Looking back from Schlicker Seespitze
Starkenburger Hutte

New Zealand
Bridge over Boyle river
Looking towards woods
Cabbage tree
Hope Halfway Hut
Spooky bush
Swing bridge over Huruni river
Number 3 hut
Near to pass
View from pass south
View from porch of Locke Stream Hut

Mt Howe
River Avon in Christchurch
Mt cook and its glacier
The high Country

Norway
Bergen
Within the fjord
Raubergstulen
Spiterstulen
Veopallen from Glitterheim
Towards Glitterhind
Gloptind
Gjende lake
High Plateau
Fondsbu

Scotland
Parallel roads within Glen roy
Looking back down the glen
Dog Falls
Loch Roy
Glenshirra Forest
Spey dam
Ruthven Barracks
Early morning view towards Cairngorms
Loch Einich
Track to Glen Luibeg
Ben Macdui summit
Camp at lochan buidhe
Top of alladins crag
Weather station on cairn gorm
View from camp site

Yosemite
El Capitan
Valley view towards el capitan
Royal Arches
Sentinal Rock from Merced river
Half dome
Vernal falls
Half dome
Above Ten Lakes
Half Moon meadow
View from camp at ten lakes
Towards falls ridge
Glen Aulin
Near little devils Postpi

List of route Maps

Adirondacks - 16
Stubaier Alps - 61
Arthurs pass and Lake Sumner - 108
Jotunheimen National Park - 156
Monadhliath and Cairngorm Mountains - 195
Yosemite National Park - 235

Introduction

I've always liked that saying 'watch where you place your feet, cause you never know where they might take you'. It relays a thought of childish adventure rummaging amongst the scrubland at the end of the garden or exploring a woodland or the interior of your house.

Some people know already from year to year where their feet will take them, and that's OK, to get to know intimately the people and surroundings around you is something I'll always miss, but occasionally I get itchy feet and desire pastures new. After all you never know what's around the next corner and if I hadn't been inquisitive enough to find out, I wouldn't have experienced many of the sights and sounds beyond my horizon that I've seen while creating this book.

Such as the realization of hearing the sound of nothing amongst the giants of Norway, or falling asleep to the singing of Maori in New Zealand nor (especially nice for a truck driver like me) sitting 10,000 feet up in the Sierra Nevada's early in the morning drinking my coffee without the sight of a single person or vehicle, although this was the case during most of my wilderness trips.

Of all the countries and mountain area's which I have visited, I could not say that there is one in particular I like, they all have their own unique beauty and character, be it their landscape or human histories and apart from writing about the route I have tried to include remarkable tales of the people who went before me and lived in these wild area's – but less talk and more on with the adventure, so turn the page and allow me to take your feet to far flung and near colourful places!

Paul Carpenter – Scotland 2011

Six mountain hikes from around the world

UNITED STATES of AMERICA

New York State, The Adirondacks

Mountains of Snow and Winds of Dreams

I'm sure there was some apprehension when I first suggestion to the family that we should all go off on one of my ventures but the idea of staying in a cabin in the mountains, by a lake, appealed to them all - especially the kids. Remembering my own childhood make-believe adventures, I knew what their imagination would make of this forest clad mountainous region and the possibility of seeing so many animals.

Towards the high peaks

At dawn on our first morning we surveyed the wonderful scenery that was to be our back yard for two weeks, it was obvious from their reactions that, for once, I had made a right choice – especially as, due to a week-long freak snowstorm just before our arrival, everything lay under a thick blanket of snow. This, apart from being a surprise to the locals, meant that our spring plans of canoeing and horse riding were cancelled but the family didn't complain. Lake Placid and all its winter Olympic venues were just down the road – and we soon took advantage of this winter paradise playground.

Heart Lake

The snow also affected the walk I'd planned but luckily the cabin we'd rented (the Campground Cabin) was on Adirondack Mountain Club land. This encompassed Heart Lake and the grand Adirondack Loj, whose property was in an area of the park called High Peaks, one of the most popular hiking areas in the park. What originally was to be a 5-day excursion became a 3-day circular route from our cabin (staying in lean-to`s) with a few single day trips. I'd hoped to use skis, but unfortunately my skill didn't match the amount of trees I would have to evade! Consequently this meant using snowshoes, on which I was less skilled on then skis, but was easier to master (so the guides said)...

Fortunately snow is more forgiving than rock, when fallen onto; tales of my considerable experiences of this will follow but first, a little history...

The Adirondacks, despite being one of the largest parks in the USA (6 million acres of Government and privately-owned land) is not that well-known for its hiking potential outside the USA; this I found very unusual. Visitors in earlier days, especially those suffered from an illness, went there for healing effects of the surrounding trees, to breathe in the fresh, fragrant air, absorb the peaceful and presumably soothing view. Fortunately we had no illness, only two very active kids, but even during their noisy play my wife and I could feel the calming effects of our surroundings. Time - and life - seemed somehow slower there than anywhere else I have been. Some would say it was due to being there with my family but the fact there was nobody else sharing the woods with us, probably helped. In the summer there would be masses of campers using the tent pitches and lean-tos, which the snow presently hid. For now, we saw only squirrel's, chipmunks and heard only birds.

As in other areas of wilderness that the white man has invaded with his modern inventions, it was as easy for us to sit back and enjoy the tranquillity of the mountains as it was for the first paying visitors a few centuries ago: artist, writers and the well-to-do. But to the first inhabitants several millennia ago this area, with its animals, trees and mountains, was not seen as scenic wonders – it meant food, clothing and shelter. They didn't affect or change the look of the mountains, nor really did the first white hunters and pioneers who penetrate them, but it is *their* presence you feel along the banks of clear rivers, in the early morning mist and in the rustling of trees.

They were the Algonquin Indians, who hunted and lived in these mountains, along with the Mohawks; they used the waterways for transport and ate the bubs and bark off trees; from their name derived the Adirondack, meaning bark eaters in the Iroquois language.

For centuries the tribes of North Eastern America and Southern Canada fought battles between one another, moving periodically to better hunting or farming grounds (the Iroquois were mostly farmers, living in timber houses); or to move deeper into the vast forest to escape from a stronger enemy. Eventually between 1400 and 1600 A.D, two wise or holy men called Deganahwideh and Hiawatha travelled amongst the Tribes reminding them of the teachings of the Great Spirit and his dislike for war. They were sent to establish the great peace, spread the great laws, but mostly to bring together the tribes into one Long house (sort of government house) under a tree of peace. The branches of this tree would protect those under it and the roots would spread to others who would wish to join. Five tribes first agreed to this peace, the Mohawks (people of the flint), the Oneidas (people of the upright stone), the Onondaga (hill people), the Cayugas (people of the muck lands) and the Senecas (people of the great mountains) with the Tuscarora nation joining in 1715. Making what had been the five nations into six, collectively called the Iroquois or Haudenosaunee. Together they ended the bloodshed and starvation that had threatened the Indians futures and grew into one mighty and powerful tribe, with a government system that was fair to all, a system that may of influenced the forming of the Declaration of Independence, fitting in with the Anglo Americans idea of a free and independent country. The Iroquois helped many during the French–English and Revolutionary conflicts.

The first record of a European seeing the Adirondacks and encounter the Iroquois was a French explorer in 1609, called Samuel de Champlain. Unfortunately, this meeting was not planned and in the fight that ensued, he used a harquebus (long barrelled gun) which unknown to him broke one of the Indians cardinal rules, which is to never use a weapon that the other side does not know about. Subsequent actions like this, and the fact that the French made friends with the Iroquois arch enemies, the Huron, meant that they lost a strong ally to the British. Most of the land that surrounded the more mountainous and impenetrable parts of the Adirondacks was populated well before the interior. After the wars, trappers (who later become the first guides), settlers, landowners, then logging and mining companies took their share of the Iroquois land, who were already slowly dwindling through disease, involvement in the wars and by encroachment of their land. They, in time were put onto reserves and the Adirondacks started to see towns, business, and tourism develop. Naturally after this rush of development, it did not take long until the Adirondacks saw its first opportunity to becoming a park, especially when the logging companies had nearly completed their aim of clearing the area of timber. Not only did they leave a landscape bare and ugly, but also the run off of rainwater down the Hudson River was starting to threaten the big cities to the south. So in 1892 the park was created, and after a bit of magical forest management and time, the mountains and the trees that had covered them were brought back for all to enjoy.

Six mountain hikes from around the world

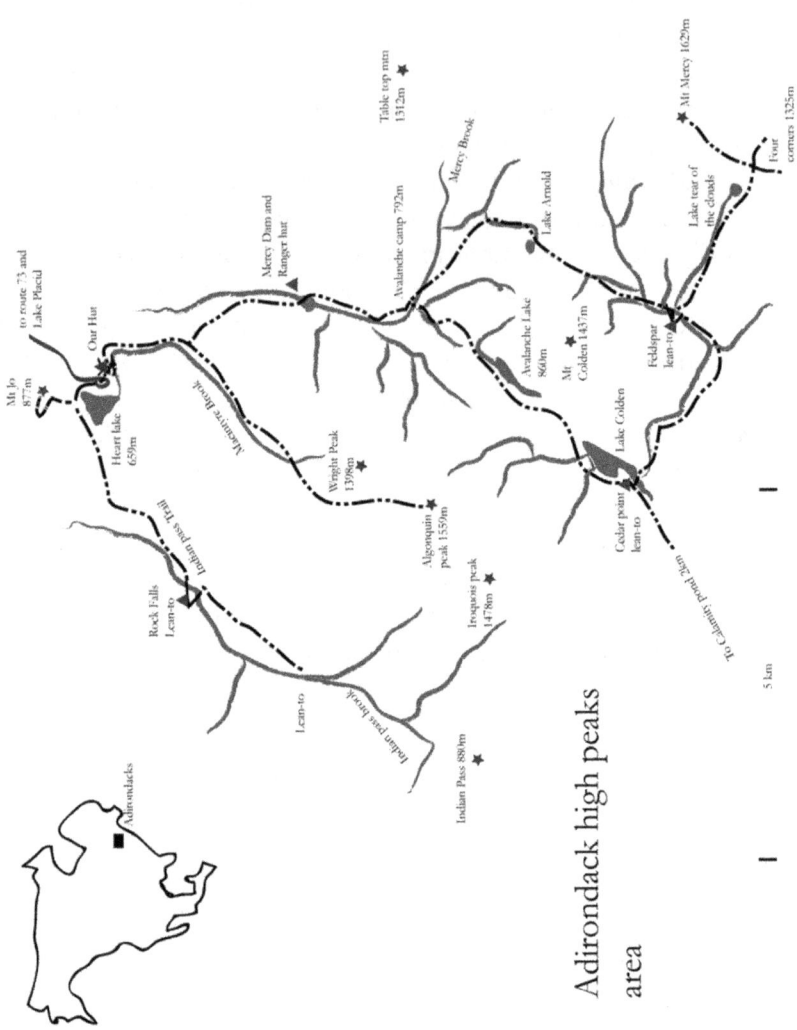

Three day Circular Hike

Day 1   Our Cabin – feldspar lean-to

+450m   10.9km

For the first couple of days, I just mellowed out with the family, exploring our surroundings, building up my energy; on American cuisine i.e. steak, steak and more steak, gathering my rations for the trip and getting to grips with the snowshoes. I think the kids had more fun with then most, watching our youngest in a size 12 shoe was hilarious. Since our arrival the weather had been wonderful; freezing during the night, but bright and clear during the day, it was no different upon my departure. It felt quite weird leaving the family behind this time; usually it's to a busy airport. However, today as I waved, it was to my wife standing outside our little cabin with the kids messing around in the deep snow. The whole scene looked like something out of the little house on the prairie and in a way, made me feel better during this trip, knowing that they would be not far away.

I left early, walked the short distance to the trailhead at the start of my walk and signed the 'Intentions book'. Then I was off, waddling along like an overburdened penguin, firstly through a dense patch of fir trees then out into a much more open, mixed wood of firs and, mainly, birch; their smooth cream-coloured bark carpeted the floor of the forest. This was to be my scenery for most of the trip, except on the high peaks, where trees finally gave way to the weather. But I was happy with what lay ahead of me and surprised to realise how far I could see into the forest - beyond the naked trees to an endless carpet of white. Another reason to slow down was the chance to train the binoculars on a wide variety of birds.

Typical woodland

The Iroquois have an interesting explanation of how birds acquired their songs, which they told their children, to show them that it is preferable to be honest than to cheat. Long, long ago the only songs and music heard in the forest of North America were the drums and voices of the Indians. The Great Spirit loved a good song and was often found listening to the tunes. Then he discovered that the birds longed to sing like man. He gathered all the birds to his council stone and told them that at sunrise the next day they must all fly; the higher they went, he said, the better the song they would achieve. One particular bird felt quite jealous of the eagle perched next to him, knowing the eagle could fly much higher. So in the morning, just before all the birds took flight, he hid amongst the eagle's feathers.

During the first day quite a few birds reached their limit and returned to earth possessing the commonest of songs. Only the larger birds soared higher, the eagle with his large, powerful wings going furthest. Then, just as he reached his limit, the bird hiding in his feathers flew out and upwards as the eagle descended. Eventually the little bird saw a hole in the sky, went through it and found himself in the spirit world - or the happy hunting grounds; there he heard a beautiful song. He stayed long enough to memorise it, then flew back to earth - eager to show off his new talent. But his arrival was less then welcoming. All the other birds knew he had cheated and, in shame, he hid in the thickest wood. He can still be seen there today, only singing occasionally; but when he does the other birds fall silent, for they too wish to hear the sweet song of the hermit thrush.

Back on the trail, I had my own problems. Unused to walking on deep snow and snowshoes, I realised that if I wanted to reach my destination on two limbs, not four, I must adopt a completely different speed and stride. The path was compacted by the hordes who had preceded before me but, if I ventured just a few inches off it, would sink into the soft snow and possibly fall headlong into, not an attractive option. This happened a few times but not enough to discount the obvious advantage of snowshoes for walking on snow. On the style I wore my boots were strapped on to a larger base in the same way as a tele-mark binding is to a ski, thereby enabling me to lifted the back of my feet, with the base and the support under the boot having crampon like metal spikes. Their lovely bright red colour also made them easier to find if thrown in anger - so I was told!

Along the trail I saw many reason to justify the use of the snowshoes - deep holes (called 'postholes' locally), caused by those who thought just boots would do. As for the metal spikes, their advantage on steep ground is obvious and as they are all facing downwards are all hidden away during a fall - unless you end up contorted into all sort of weird positions, as I did, a few times. Generally I regarded them as a new toy to play with at the outset, then later appreciated the energy they saved on the lesser-used trails. For the first few miles, I found the trails easy to follow and walk along, but as I distanced myself from the cabin and on to lesser-used trails the depth of the snow (times up to 12 foot) hid half of the circular markers used in this area (positioned 8 ft. above ground level). Also, whereas the trees had been trimmed a certain height above the ground, I was constantly amongst their dense, higher branches due to the depth of the snow and in some places occasionally became entangled in branches hidden just below the snow.

On the first leg of today's trip to Marcy dam none of these potential annoyances caused problems; I was left with my thoughts as I occasionally passed hikers/skiers enroute to and from the dam. You could call the Dam the gateway to these mountains, due to the numerous trails verging on to it, the many lean-tos and campsites around the lake and a Ranger Station. Most of the walk was in solitude and silence, after the birds stopped singing for the day; only the scraping and crunching of the snowshoes kept me company as the trail led me past the trail to Algonquin peak, halfway to the dam.

Within these wonderful forests there are also maple trees, which in spring are used by the locals for what is affectingly called 'sapping time' - the time-honoured tradition of gathering maple sap, which is then boiled to make the syrup. It may sounds simple but there many conditions that determine the quality of the end product: - which tree is best to sap, how much sugar it contains, how much sap can be drained from a particular tree... Then, once you have the sap, you have to know how to heat it properly. I've no idea if, with time and patients, the gathering and making of maple syrup becomes easier; but for a beginner like me the end product probably wouldn't compare with what my wife likes to pour over her morning pancake! I *might* perhaps be able to make one by-product I know my kids would like - something called 'jack-wax'; namely a ladle full of hot sap poured onto the snow and left to cool until hard - then eaten. And the extra bonus of a few snow fleas (which virtually littered certain areas) would surely add to its energy content!

Late March and April are regarded as 'sapping season' due to the spring thaw, when the frozen roots of the maple thaw and once more absorb water. The sugars present in the roots dissolve into this, in turn causing more water to be absorbed into the roots and this forces the sap up into the branches. The best times to gather the sap is after cold, freezing nights - when the sap in the trunk freezes and stops flowing, while water is still being absorbed by the roots; this causes an excess of sap that is released the next day, up the trunk, once the trunk thaws. No trees under 10 ins. in diameter are sapped and, on average, one gallon of sap can be made from two trees 18 ins. diameter. Or, you can buy a gallon from local producers for $20 - 30 dollars a gallon...

Apart from making jack-wax, I soon realised the unique advantages of snow and ice - they made travel over obstacles a lot easier, especially the watery ones. Although the big thaw had begun, most of the rivers I met were still piled high with snow. As I descended the last rise towards Marcy dam, I could hear its outlet flowing, but saw only snow all around - except on a timber bridge crossing the dam, which was partly visible. The lake was wonderfully - piled high with snow and some ski tracks across it; but even with this evidence of the ice's strength and the potential easy short cut, I was wary of using it. Apart from the usual film-induced horror of falling under the ice, I had an inkling that the recent new snow - combined with a drop in temperature – had slightly decreased the thickness of the underlying ice.

Although the Adirondacks lie on the same latitude as Northern Spain, the winter brings severe drops in temperature; this helps form thick icy crusts on all the areas 3,000+ lakes. The only element that can stop the ice thickening is a good layer of snow, which acts as a blanket. On certain lakes their ice cover is used as a winter short cut for vehicles, particularly logging trucks. The snow is cleared constantly to enable the ice to reach a thickness sufficient to take the weight. It seems unbelievable that a 10-ton truck can cross over ice, but 18 ins. of ice is all that is needed – providing it has no cracks. On one occasion, on Raquette Lake near the Needles, a fully laden truck went under; the driver escaped, the cargo, once released basically took care of its self and the truck, was fitted with a steel air tank and raised that way.

With evidence like this of what the ice's strength might be on Marcy Lake, some might not hesitation to use the short cut but there were several signs around the lakes edges which made my decision for me, i.e. slight darkening of the snow (which I considered meant areas were turning to slush and unlikely to take the weight of a 32 oz. Steak, let along my bulk). So this time it was off along the bridge for me!

Just across the bridge I signed another 'intentions book' - you can't have too many people knowing of your whereabouts. I could have visited the Ranger Station nearby to register too, but carried on – enroute to Avalanche camp about 1.5 km`s away - past a few lean-tos and the junction for the Van Hoevenberg trail to Mt Marcy.

It's difficult to look back and remember particular parts of trails I used on the trip, other than the particularly testing ones. Most streams were silent, small bridges hidden, boulders just another pile of snow; even some lean-tos were hidden, like Kagel lean-to. I'd intended using it as an indication of my proximity to Avalanche Camp but, before I knew I 'd missed it, I'd arrived at my destination. From here my circular route began, returning via the well-used trail I could see coming down from Lake Colden. My trail, going off on the left, looked slightly less used and much narrower; I gave up using the poles at one point and packed them away because they kept sinking into the snow, unbalancing me. On this new trail I became acquainted with the annoying situations mentioned earlier. So far I'd been going slow to conserve energy but now had no choice.

Even though the trail I'd been using thus far had been well trodden, I was constantly looking out for trail markers, mostly out of habit, but as I progressed further along my present trail, that practise seemed futile. If tangled branches didn't hide them, they were hidden by the snow line; so I had no choice but to trust my compass and the tracks left by those who had preceded me in checking my general direction. According to the map, I should go in a straight line roughly S/E over a constant climb towards the next trail junction. My only hope was that, like all the other junctions thus far, the signpost would be visible... It wouldn't do to climb any further than was necessary and, luckily for me, the tracks I was following led me straight to a visible signpost and I followed the next track S/S/W up the final climb of the day towards Lake Arnold.

It soon became clear, after waddling through these mountains for just a few hours, why the region was neglected until well after the surrounding countryside was settled. Today it's easy for us to presume that tarmac roads and large stores were always there, but stories abound of the trials and tribulations experienced by the first people who tried to tame this wilderness. Some had to build their own roads from the nearest settlement to their new homes, covering distances of ten's of miles. What they could not farm or make themselves, they had to buy from the few corner shops existing at the time, involving long and difficult journeys over land and water. But one particular character, one amongst many, braved the wilderness and the elements to bring these people a little light entertainment, perhaps news from the outside world and - more importantly - a suitcase (the type called a 'turkey' in those days). Its contents ranged from kitchen utensils to envelopes and harmonicas. He was called a 'pack peddler' and his prosperity was limited only by his ingenuity. Slowly but surely that turkey case would turn into *two* cases, then he might arrive with a wagon and, maybe a few months later, this would be pulled not by him but a horse. Eventually his visit ceased - because he had opened up his own store somewhere in the area. A true example of the American Dream!

Naturally the path to the realisation of this dream wasn't easy and possibly, in some instances, ended in death. The rough roads and wilderness probably claimed their fair share of lives; local ghost stories abound to back this up. One concerns an old, particularly gruesome-looking pack peddler who happened to be visiting a loggers' camp near Indian Lake. For some reason he and the loggers did not get along and that night he was dragged from his bed and killed. Then he and his cart were put in an old cellar, which was set alight. Since then spooky events have occurred in that house and others - strange noises; such as that of a babies cry whose skeleton was subsequently found under the floorboards and given a proper burial. Most noises could be explained but there were no doubts about the old peddler's visits as on some nights his horse was heard coming up the track, followed by the sight of his gruesome face and twisted hands. Locals say he was returning to the last place saw alive.

My thoughts, however, were far from ghosties and ghoulies, being focused on the trail - or lack of one. On reaching Arnold Lake I could see the signpost, but only one set of ski tracks going in the direction I needed; the rest carried on up to the summit of Mt Colden on my right. The best thing about the ski tracks was that I could at least use them, as a guide down to my destination, but that didn't mean the snow wouldn't be as compacted as it would have been by snowshoes. So, after a few hesitant steps (and sinking into the snow past my knees), I decided a rest was in order before descending further into the virgin snow. Arnold Lake was near and convenient for this purpose and was, I am sure, a great place to picnic out in summer, being surrounded on one side by the steep rise of Colden and the remainder by old, unlogged forest. The air was still cold and the lake surface resembled a soup bowl with its thick fluffy layer of snow. The area was peaceful and resembled a Christmas picture post card and after half an hour I felt tempted to stay there the night. But despite the beauty of the lake and the fact that the 3 kms left, all downhill on new snow was starting to feel like much more, I got up and moved on.

To my surprise and relief I found snowshoe tracks just as I passed the lake, which naturally I used. Now and again I lost them among the trees, tried to find them again and on one occasion did not – which led to an amusing (though not at the time) situation. I found a short, steep slope down into a ravine and would have passed it if not for the tracks I saw along its base; during the descent one of my snowshoes got caught under a branch hidden and I spent much time and energy thrashing about to get a foothold in order to pull my leg out.

My other limbs were useless in the deep snow; I was unable to anchor onto anything solid. When I finally manage to escape this trap I fell into another and another until I reached the bottom! I did try sliding down but in the soft snow it was as pointless as the trashing of my arms and legs. On another of my ventures away from the tracks I found a river whose steep banks I'm sure did have a bridge somewhere along it but, instead of walking along the bank to find it, I thought I'd be clever and cross - via what looked like two wide tree trunks. In reality it was just one, with heavy snow build-up on either side - which of course I didn't know until I steeped on it...! The only sense I had shown in this entire fiasco was not putting all my weight on that first step so, instead of crashing down into the snow and ice on the river, I managed to get on to the trunk and crawl across.

Mt Colden

Eventually I found the tracks again; they soon lead me to the next trail junction and on to the lean-to I planned to spend the night in, roughly 6 hours after leaving my family. Before coming here my idea of a lean-to was a small shelter, open at one end, made up of odd branches. The lean-tos here looked like that basically but are larger and much sturdier, more like a log cabin with one missing wall. Each has an 'Intentions Book' (whose entries helped wile away many amusing hours) and an enclosed toilet nearby. This one also produced some very inquisitive birds, including the Black-capped Chickadee and Red breasted Nuthatch. As the evening draw on they occasionally landed on the shelters entrance and walked towards me. As I cooked supper one flew straight towards my head and somehow stopped instantly within millimetres of my eyes, hovered around for a second and was off. If it hadn't stopped when it did I would probably have a large hole in my forehead now! Considering the bird was that close I should have been able to identify it, or at the most recall some distinguishing marks but all I remember is its clear, bright eyes. So I've named it the swift head-butter!

Day 2 Feldspar lean-to – Lake Colden via Mt. Marcy

-1629m +620m, 11.4Km

I knew about the snowstorms before leaving home, so decided to bring my 4-season sleeping bag; it normally keeps me comfortable during hikes in Scottish. But last night the temperature plummeted; I awoke with feet so cold I had to put socks on – and gloves on over them – before I could get back to sleep! This proves how different it can be sleeping in the open air, rather than a tent; I envied the local birds for their insulating layers of feathers; once snuggled up with their beaks in their feathers, the spread of their warm breathe was sufficient to keep them cosy.

Waking up brought a bonus - seeing the clear moonlit sky. The image of the moon and stars was fantastic and very clear, probably due to the clean air here. According to Iroquois tradition, the moon existed before the earth and the face on it is that of an old woman; she, in her divinity, tried to foresee the end of the world – and failed. The stars appeared much later and were created out of mortals and animals, i.e. the 'big dipper' (or 'saucepan' as I call it); they see this as a bear and three hunters. These hunters were pursuing the bear on earth until they were attacked by a giant stone monster and carried up into the sky by invisible spirits. The blood from the injured bear is said to cause autumn leaves to turn red and yellow. Another involves a group of 7 stars called Pleiades situated within the Taurus constellation. In Greek mythology these represent seven sisters and to the Iroquois, seven young Mohawk warriors who, during a particularly energetic dance to a powerful witch song (performed because their parents refusing them food for a secret feast), rose up into the night sky and became seven bright stars that will dance forever. Whenever they are seen directly above the villages of the Iroquois it signifies the beginning of the New Year feast.

Lean-to by lake Colden

Now it was morning. Time for the all-important, delightful moment of emerging from a warm snug sleeping bag into the sharp, crisp cold of the back and beyond – but this would only happen when I saw signs of the temperature being above freezing! This I would know when the ice on the roof began dripping down, these drips would also provided me with a source of water. Apart from being free from snow fleas, it was easier to filter and used less gas to boil then snow would have. But if that method of water collection appears easy and lacking in adventure, try getting it from the occasional patches of river lying clear of snow that might be found nearby, although it could be debatable as to which would get wetter, the inside of the water bottle or your clothes…

Sign post under 6ft snow

I got up, got my boots on and went in search for my food. Despite the cold temperature of both day and night, plus thick layers of snow, I was still warned to tie my food up between trees. I had to venture out into the woods (which I affectingly called 'string gallery' due to the many differing cords hanging from trees) and retrieve my bag. I had to tie it up because the Adirondacks have black bears - with a certain liking to our cuisine and toiletries. It's useful to know that most of them do not hibernate in caves here; providing it is out of the way they might choose a space between boulders or under exposed roots – with sometimes only a layer of snow between them and the elements. This is another reason why I follow visible tracks - I didn't want to step on and arouse a potentially very grouchy bear, perhaps with young.

My plan was to climb Mt. Marcy, return, pick up any equipment left behind and proceed to Lake Colden. Returning to the last trail junction of yesterday, I set off, not actually thinking I'd achieve

Lake Colden. At one point up the trail to the summit I even thought I might be staying at the same hut again. Since early morning the cloud had been down below 1450m, thankfully producing no wind or rain but I found only one set of snowshoe tracks to follow through some of the thickest snow so far encountered. Initially each deep step, through tangled branches and dense tree's either showing or hidden by snow, didn't feel too bad – especially with the light pack on my back. But this first part of the ascent, running parallel with Feldspar Brook, was the steepest and eventually I felt like a child's toy whose batteries were running out, gradually slowing down. When I stopped to regain my breath there was an occasional view but in comparison with my efforts there weren't enough of them.

I was thankful for the cloud as it kept the sun off my back and the glare off the snow (yesterday's problems). When I reached Lake Tear-of-the-Clouds it lived up to its name, with cloud and slight drizzle swirling above it, in and out of the trees, creating a mystifying atmosphere. It is unlikely that few Europeans saw the lake before 1872, when a certain surveyor named Verplanck Colvin and his team found it, and discovered it was the source of the Hudson. It is interesting that the source of the Nile was found before this lake – but it has one claim to fame that the Nile does not. Many famous visitors may have picnicked by its shores on their return from the highest peak in the Adirondacks (Mt. Marcy) but, roughly 30 years after its discovery, one such visitation had local as well as national significance. The visitor was Theodore Roosevelt, Vice-President of the U.S.A., who was on holiday after leaving President McKinley recovering in hospital following an attempt on his life. While Mr. Roosevelt and his party were resting by the lake, a guide appeared with a message for him: the President had taken a turn for the worst. Later, back at the Tahawus Club where he was staying, another message came: the President was dying. So Roosevelt began a 40-mile night journey over rough roads and wilderness to North Creek and the nearest train station.

I decided not to stop at the Lake during my trip. As I was on flatter and firmer snow I could regain my breath and make my way to the next track junction, Four Corners. Positioned on the top of a sort of divide between two rivers, it gave access straight down into Panther Gorge and, on either side, Two Summits. Amazingly, the sign was still just visible so I turned left and began climbing again, through a thinner wood of spruce and balsam. This lasted until halfway up, where many of the rocks and slabs were still visible but partly covered by ice. The snowshoe spikes came into their own and I made good time during the last part of the climb, as I didn't need to raise my legs above my head after every step. There were occasional views down into Panther Gorge and beyond Elk Lake, when the cloud cleared. Just below the summit there is a small rock face, which served as a windbreak for about an hour. There was few view's as the summit lived up to its Indian name of Tahawus – or 'Cloud-splitter'. Information on a plaque records the date of the first ascent (05.08.1837), details that it was named after a governor of that time and lists the surveyors present.

During a cold, cloudy day in the middle of the week such as I was experiencing, this summit might only expect to be visited a couple of times. So it seemed ironic that two hikers, ascending the summit from opposite directions, now arrived within 5 minutes of each other! It had taken me 2 hours from the lean-to to reach the top; then the other hiker told me he had left the Loj (7.5 miles and – 1000m away) 4 hours earlier. I'd felt *my* time was quite an achievement, especially when each kilometre felt more like a mile, but on hearing just how used he was to the conditions and the area, I felt better. For all I knew he could have even been a '46-er' (member of a club whose members have climbed mountains over 4,000ft). From his comments on the unexpected snow conditions I gathered that local businesses were delightful with the financial benefits resulting from the extended snow cover, raising the ski slopes/shops profits by up to 50% compared to the previous year. I remember wondering at the time if that was because my wife was working the Visa card excessively but as he didn't mention toyshops maybe it was OK...

The return trip down to the lean-to went as expected but took more time than if there had been no snow; this finally convinced me, on leaving the lean-to, to take advantage of one of the snow's advantages – walk along the rivers, which I had so far had little opportunity to do. In this case, the Opalescent River – and the trail I *should* have taken down to Lake Colden virtually run parallel with it. Occasionally, and reluctantly, I had to return to the trail when snow cover looked unsafe or on steep, narrow gorges; but that did not spoil my enjoyment. I expect scrambling up this river is a major occupation for some during the summer, but for me it was simply pleasant to see and hear the water tumbling through ice; there would have been good views of the surrounding peaks had the cloud lifted.

Lean to by Indian pass brook

Around Lake Colden and Flowed Lands (another large lake near it) lies a perfusion of lean-tos, hidden around their shores. Full occupation in the warmer months probably turns this area into a kind of camp city, 'humming' from activity and people!.... But there were no such telltale signs or smells as I crossed the river for the last time, via a bridge, and headed towards the river connecting the two lakes. All other tracks I'd been following had taken to their own destinations and I was alone again. Bliss – surrounded by the peace and quiet of empty hills! I was less than a kilometre from my destination and consequently in no hurry; and, as I emerged from the endless cover of the trees into the open space created by the lake, my fatigue diminished.

At one point, before common sense took over, I thought of dropping my gear and heading towards a small lake called Calamity Pond, some kilometres past Flowed Lands. There is a statue there which – when erected (all 1 ton of it) not long after 1845 – was carried in over wild, rough and mostly trail-less country. It was erected in remembrance of David Henderson, an employee of McIntyre Ironworks; he died by the pond from a bullet accidentally discharged from his own gun. In comparison to the lovely, solid-looking bridge ahead of me, getting that stone there must have been some achievement, but they did it – and apparently it's still standing.

I was standing too, but my legs were telling me it wouldn't be for long. Instead of heading for the bridge with its pleasant platform on the other side allowing passage around a rock face, I headed down on to the Lake; it saved much hassle and seemed the much more energy-consuming way. I soon reached the small outcrop of land I was aiming for, arrived at a lovely snug lean-to called Cedar Point, and relieved my legs. Apart from resting on the summit I hadn't had a real break all day so, instead of emptying the rucksack as usual, I just laid there reading the Intentions Book again; helping me to unwind, it also enlightened me on the subject of a particularly large furry animal that enjoyed visiting this particular shelter – a female bear! The hikers had named her Gertrude and she seemed to be quite a character, a dab hand at helping herself from suspended food bags. Thankfully the remarks were written during May/June, around the time another, more ferocious little beastie appears – the 'black fly' or 'buffalo gnat'. Like the Scottish midge, they swarm in their thousands – biting and sucking continuously. They thrive on cold, fast-running rivers and mountain streams and it is probably a good idea to avoid this area during their four-week stay. Mosquitoes, however, arrive around mid-June, so one pest replaces another. They prefer to breed on the calmer, stagnant waters of the lowlands, which explains why the Iroquois wrote a story about them rather than the black fly, though it could apply to either.

On the Seneca River many winters ago, says the story, two giant mosquitoes appeared; they preyed on the Indians who used the rivers for canoe travel. The Indians were forced to move because so many of their people were killed on the water, but the beasties followed and, eventually, two canoes full of warriors were sent to kill them. After a short time the mosquitoes descended on them, almost filling the sky as the Indians continuously fired arrows at them. Half of them were killed. The remainder chanted their war song and lead their enemy into the trees and bushes where mosquitoes could not fly. After many arrows had pierced their skins they dropped to the ground, where the Indians battered them with their war clubs. Once their blood began seeping out on the ground, hordes of smaller mosquitoes erupted from them; and to this day they attack humans as revenge for the death of their grandfathers. Thinking about these two adversaries, whose business is to ruin hiker's waking hours, I considered my two present problems of deep snow and freezing nights. They were heart-warming and superficial compared to the constant hitting of my face, neck, legs and arms due to the little beasties, or running about after a brown bear called Gertrude!

I had not chosen my lean-to by accident; I planned to stay for the view. Later, after supper, I sat looking out over my grand view of Lake Colden, with Avalanche Pass beyond, a narrow steep-sided fault valley. The cloud began descending into it and I hoped it meant the coming night would be warmer than the last. The cloud *did* owe me something for the disappointment of lack of views.

Day 3 Lake Colden – Our Cabin

- 210m   10km

If my family had not been waiting for me just over the next rise there would have been two good reasons for considering venturing out into the wilderness again. One, to avoid wasting time in a hotel room waiting for my homeward flight (as on other trips) and the other – more important – to find and walk around Lake Colby; there I might be lucky enough to trip over an old propeller. It fell off a plane making an emergency landing there and to United Arab Emirates Airlines is worth $5,000 reward. I'm sure I could find what the locals have failed to do in the six years since the incident…..

I woke early, grateful for the cloud that provided me with a warm, peaceful night's sleep but, when ready to set off, the weather closed in and rain followed, the first since my arrival. I'd planned to walk over the lake to cut out slogging through the woods but the combination of a warm night and now rain made it look doubtful so I walked to the next lean-to. There I met a New Yorker who confirmed my suspicions that, until the previous day, everyone had used the lake and not the woods to move around; this meant most trails around the lake would still be thick with virgin snow. But luckily the edge of the ice down from his hut wasn't too bad and I managed to get over to the other side of the lake, as far as the Warden's hut. There I rejoined a reasonably well-used trail, slightly disappointed that I couldn't have taken more advantage of the ice; but at least the trees gave temporary shelter from the rain.

Avalanche pass

Oh what a whinger I am sometimes – a little rain and I'm a grumpy old man! I needed a funny story to make me smile and, as I ventured out on to Avalanche Lake, nicely snuggled in between the two steep cliffs of Avalanche and Colden Peaks, I got one. I was having little trouble crossing the lake and only once had to use one of the walkways bolted into sheer cliffs (built in the 1920's); these provided access along the lake in summer. It's the name of these walkways that's amusing – "Hitch up, Matilda". The name, coined back in 1868, resulted from the sufferings of an unfortunate guide who had to carry a large woman around the cliffs whilst her family urged them on shouting "Hitch up, Matilda!" Whenever she appeared to be slipping off. Imagine the feelings of that poor, breathless guide underneath her!

The level of the long, thin lake has been raised a few times by avalanches from both mountains; it's blocked off at its northern end by a substantial rockslide off Colden, creating Avalanche pass. Here I encountered warning signs of avalanches coming off an area of Colden that was clear of trees. That slope is apparently good for skiing down when safe, if you care to. But I was having far too much trouble negotiating the mangled fallen trees mixed with snow at the bottom to even think about it. But relief came rapidly as I began the short but steep descent to Avalanche Camp, signifying the end of my three-day loop. If it hadn't been for the few hikers I met coming up, my anticipation of reaching the end would have convinced me to do some glissanding or maybe, if they were still around, use something locally called the 'scoop shovel express' to get down. Back in the major logging days the loggers had several methods of moving the timber off the mountains into the rivers, where they would be humanly guided down the rivers to the mills. One method stands out for its 'funtastic' appeal – in essence, a wooden slide. The 'scoop shovel' name comes from one adventurous fire-spotter, as he used the slide and a large shovel as a quick way home every night from the top of Whiteface Mountain. Just imagine what a ride that would be in winter with the ice and snow, but better in summer when you can splash into the river at the bottom and not smash down on the ice…

Due to my source of water and watching the lakes; I'd been aware during my trip that the snow was thawing fast, but not until I reached Avalanche Camp again two days later did I appreciate just how much snow had dispersed during that time. The lean-to I hadn't been able to see before, nearer to Marcy Dam, was now clearly visible and I could get into the lean-to at Avalanche Camp; its entrance had been blocked before. Just as well because, apart from the increasing rain, the thunder and lightning followed – not a time to be out in the open. It's odd how really scared some people are of thunder; my wife would try as hard as possible to get inside me at any hint of thunder, yet would stand in the open and marvel at the split second streaks of lightning flashes. Thunder didn't bother me but if it struck directly overhead I was worried about the strong vibrations I felt going through my body. As for lightning, I wish I had the luck of the Iroquois – who, legend says, will never be struck by lightning providing they burn tobacco during early spring. The Iroquois are friends of the Thunder People; this helps a lot, due to an incident, which occurred many summers ago. Legend states that the Iroquois' acquaintance with the Thunder People occurred on an island, Jo-Ka-ta-ren-re on the St. Lawrence River, during a storm similar to that I was experiencing. One of the small Thunder People descended to earth and took an Indian girl for his wife. They lived together very happily for a year, until she became pregnant and had to return to earth because the Chief wanted her to raise the child amongst her own people. Before she left, however, the Chief warned her that if the child was ever struck he would be returned instantly to his father up in the sky. Her family were overjoyed to see her again and she told them of her adventures and that she was pregnant. Soon she gave birth to a boy; he was just like all the other boys except he was smaller and had a habit of running out into the open during a storm and jumping up and down. All went well for some years until one day, when his grandmother (who worried whenever he ran out into storms) was looking after him. When the storm came, instead of letting him out she locked him in; he went berserk, throwing and smashing everything in the house. In an attempt to stop him hurting himself, the grandmother smacked him across the legs. At that moment came a blinding flash of lightning and the house filled with smoke. When it cleared the boy was nowhere to be seen. When his mother found out what had happened she explained that the boy had been taken back up to his father and they would never see him again. But because he was half-Indian, the Thunder People have remained friends with the Indians and will never harm them.

Avalanche pass

Once the thunder passed I continued, not with the sure-footed, speedy progress expected being so close to home, but slow and clumsy. The lugging of a 45-50lb sack in deep snow over three days was catching up with me and, thankfully, the way back was mostly downhill – though that was of little consequence to my aching muscles. Being tired (and having made the fatal mistake of stopping in the lean-to) meant I was to stop more often than normally. The only bonus was a few enjoyable encounters with wildlife, the first occurring just past Marcy Dam; I was able to study a squirrel's complex operation of obtaining food from a cone. Although only 1ft away, my presence didn't bother him. Next came a raven, regarded locally as one of the living symbols of the Adirondack Wilderness. I was as near to it as the squirrel and it looked huge and menacing, but very graceful, as it flew through the trees. The last breathless encounter was not with an animal but a scene; it came into view as I crossed the various channels of Macintyre Brook, now free of snow. It was nothing special and, being near to the trail's end, was seen by many but to someone who had seen nothing but white for days it was a sparkling treasure under a sun just emerging through cloud. The light reflecting off the water was too bright to take a picture, but I remember my legs feeling better for it!

Despite all my training and building up of strength for the trip, involving a daily routine of cycling/running, some squash sessions and in-line skating with the kids, I was surprised that the snow had tired me so much. For all that training was worth, in this environment, I might just as well have sat on my backside all day. I hadn't really accounted for the type and extent of snow cover I'd encountered. Mistake or not, this had nevertheless taught me a few things – mainly that the snow here is a lot more protected from the wind and it falls in greater volume than on the Scottish mountains, where I had spent some time before the trip. Even on relatively low mountain ranges, differing weather conditions should be anticipated and investigated, as much as – for instance – the local attractions and cuisine are when visiting new countries. Yet after saying all that, I did have a sound excuse for my fatigue and I stick to it – this being that the snow conditions would not have been as bad if it had not been for the freak snowstorm…. Sounds good enough for me!

But why was I whinging? Here I was, deep within one of the most glorious spots in New York State; and compared to obstacles that one local guy from Raquette Lake (William Wood) had to overcome, I had a mild headache. On a particularly bitter day in the 1850's he set out hunting but later developed severe frostbite in the lower legs. By that time he had been living in the area for roughly 20 years and, as well as being a close friend of an Indian Chief called Uncas (the Chief written about in 'The Last of the Mohicans' by James Fenimore Cooper), he was good friends with most of the local Indians too. They found him, then amputated his legs below the knee. The obstacle he had to overcome was to carry on living in the woods without legs, and it seems he did this quite well. The Indians made leather pads and snowshoes for his stumps and there are recorded instances of him covering distances of over 70 miles, carrying supplies and a canoe over portages, using his knees as substitute feet.

Fellow gatherer

The endurance and adaptability of humans, especially during hardship, and the stories that abound of people in this circumstances – whether involving long treks to freedom or climbing at high altitude – have always amazed me. Although I would dread confronting a similar situation, there's always the inner though – what if ? ....

Journey's end could not have felt sweeter as I walked the final distance through the natural arch of the last dense patch of ferns. What do I remember most after signing out in the Intentions Book?... First, the strange sensation of walking on solid ground; second, the happiest feelings on seeing the family again. The fuss they made of me was reassuring and the stories the kids told of their adventures were amazing. Especially one... While I'd been freezing all night they'd been scared out of their skins by a small chipmunk which had found its way into the cupboard under the sink and feasted on their crisps! That may not sound very scary but to a lone female and two young kids, in the middle of the night and surrounded by a forest.... Think about it!...

Mt. Jo - 877m - with the kids

+223m   3.3km

"Kids will be kids"... I know of no other sentence said by so many, often through grinding teeth whilst

Surveying a 'war zone' – i.e. what was previously a bedroom, back garden, precious painting, anything not firmly attached to the ground and/or is not made of reinforced concrete. People often comment on the purpose of silly little toys being provided with meals in various fast food outlets. Why is it done? Because the cost of the toys is far cheaper than repairs to damage created by hordes of children who cannot eat a meal without becoming bored. Toys distract destructive little fingers.

For the perfect family holiday find somewhere with similar distractions to keep the kids' attention for longer than a toy; this helps the parent's enjoyment *and* their overstretched nerves. So the amount of snow surrounding *us* provided that perfect place. We had occasional mishaps but our environment provoked no worries when they wandered off. In our first week we saw no one. Not until later, when the snow had melted, did we find occasional picnic benches scattered around the woods; these belonged to the area's 37 campsites. During our excursions around the wood, Heart Lake and to a small nearby skiing slope we found many lean-tos; the kids loved playing in them.

The weather stayed clear and sunny after my 3-day trip and often we'd find ourselves on Heart Lake, looking up at the low summit of the tempting, stunning Mt. Jo. After saying, countless times, how wonderful it would be to stand on the top, my eldest said he wanted to climb it. Before either of them could change their minds we made immediate plans for departure! This trip, in adult terms, wasn't far – approximately 1 to 2 hours. In kids' terms, an adventure, an impossible mission – to beat the dense, dark forest, overcome deep, hidden freezing cavities and become 'king of the hill'. Plus the added bonus of bombarding parents and each other with as many snowballs as possible. With these thoughts in mind – and their snowshoes in hand – I hoped it wouldn't result in me carrying them up the mountain!

View from Mt Jo

The first part of the walk to the foot of the hill was pleasant. Past the main lodge (Adirondack Loj, a spelling by Melville Dewey that stuck), out on to the deep snow past a small amphitheatre and natural museum (closed), along the Lake's circular track for a while to the summit trail junction. This took us an hour to walk, specially round the museum, where all the different trees bore name-tags/descriptions. I don't know whether they were really interested in knowing these details, or in seeing which of them could find the most! From the junction the trail curved gently up the slope and it was hilarious watching them make their way up through the wood, sometimes off the trail into deep snow during a fruitless game of hide and seek. Next game was their version of 'cowboys and Indians', with me as the cowboy. Naturally this involved many falls into snow but with the inclusion of two branches (bow and arrow). Always asking questions, my youngest asked 'where the Indians got their bows and arrows'. Usually I make it up but *this* time knew the Iroquois legend….

Long ago the only weapon the Indians had was a spear, tipped with flint, for hunting. This made hunting for black bears difficult and dangerous. Then a hunter, named Ohgweluhndoe, walked into a valley where many wild grapevines grew. It was the time of The Moon of Falling Leaves (October) and the grapes – a delicacy the bears loved – were coming into season. He quickly spotted a bear and began to creep towards it. As he was about to throw the spear the bear turned around and a chase ensued. The Indian managed to outrun the big bear for many miles but eventually began to tire and knew he must turn to face his enemy if he was ever to see his family again. As the bear approached he prepared to throw the spear but the end became caught on a twisted vine, the tip in an ash sapling. He tried desperately to free it but only succeeded in arching the sapling as he tried to pull it clear of the vine; eventually he let go of the spear, turned and ran. He soon realised that the bear was not following him and turned to see that his spear was in its neck. To figure out what happened he repeated his actions – and so the bow and arrow were invented. Since then this superb Indian weapon has rapidly developed, especially when compared to the small twigs my sons used. The Indians eventually used larger saplings for the bow and rawhide for the string; the spear was replaced with the smaller, lighter arrow – tipped with flint and feathers to aid flight.

Heart Lake

Not long after leaving the track going around the Lake we reached another junction, signifying the beginning of both long and short routes to the summit. Based on our rate of travel thus far, I will let you guess which one we chose. From here the going got tough, the terrain very steep; the boys did remarkably well, in some places better than we adults. But this was nothing new. Earlier in the holiday we went tubing down the landing slope of a ski jump (where Eddie the Eagle represented his country). Without fear or hesitation they flew down, whereas my wife and I had considerable reservations but dare not hesitate once our 4 and 7-year-olds had taken the jump! Back on mount Jo, I was surprised how steep the slopes were at one point; the mountain had looked gentler from below. But we enjoyed pushing each other up past a few small frozen waterfalls, which the kids found immensely interesting. Many were at different stages of thawing and the kids found it fascinating to feel and see many different crystals developing from thawing ice. It also kept their minds off me carrying them… I'd hoped we would see some early spring flowers, if not on the mountain then in the meadows and along the roadside, where most of the snow had gone. The kids would have liked that but there were none. Perhaps one day I'd visit a wilderness area in America just at the *right* time and not too late, as with Yosemite and not too early, like here.

The trail we were following took us up as far as bare rock face, then swung to the left following a gentler approach to the top of the rock face; it took us through some good short slides and exposed ledges, revealing our first clear view down to the Loj. After the two routes to the summit joined again the path flattened out for a while – just before the final push to the rocky summit. Free from trees, the views were fantastic. I could see why Henry Van Hoevenberg and his fiancée Josephine (for whom this mountain is named) bought this patch of land, back in 1877; he built the first tourist cabin here. From our very private viewing area our little 'kings of the hill' could see Lake Placid to the northeast, Mt. Whiteface to the north and most of the high peaks from east to west – including the mystical Indian Pass, a narrow avenue between two steep peaks. Its sharp edges looked out of place amongst the smooth lines of the mountains. And of course there was Heart Lake, whose bare white surface resembled an island in a sea of forests.

We were fortunate in that there was no wind so could comfortably stay on the summit for some time. The kids were enjoying themselves and there seemed little point in rushing down. The youngest was busy with a puddle, to which he was adding sticks, snow and mud – all essential ingredients for his 'soup of the day', which tasted surprisingly good! The eldest had collected birch bark on the way up and I helped him make a little fire, something he'd wanted to do ever since visiting relatives in Poland. One of them had told him how much they depended on it in the past, to make fires and baskets. Until the 1960s some were still using it in schools, for paper.

The legend explaining how the Iroquois found fire follows a similar line to my way of setting aside time in which to teach certain things to my kids. One day, when both are of age, I may even set them some sort of initiation test, to signify that they have passed from childhood to adulthood and would need to look after themselves instead of relying on adults. This tale involves the Bear Clan of the Mohawks and, in particular, a young Indian called Otjiera, son of a famous leader; he had come of age and was to face his initiation. Tradition decreed that once a boy reached the age of 14 winters (years) he must take the Dream Fast, a ceremony lasting up to 4 days. The boy was not allowed to eat, must drink only water and would succeed in passing into adulthood only if his Clan's spirit appeared to him during that time – revealing a plant, animal or bird which would forever after be the Indian's guardian. If this did not happen then the boy must return to his village – a failure.

Otjiera chose to spend his fast in the mountains on a large outcrop of rock, dressed only in his breechcloth and moccasins. He spent four nights there and began to worry that the bear spirit would not appear. Just as he was dreading the arrival of his father to take him back to the village as a failure, a severe thunderstorm approached his mountain and he prayed to the Great Thunder Man, Ra-it-we-ras, asking him to send his Clan's spirit.

Immediately after his prayer a bear appeared to him, telling the young Indian that he would receive a great gift that night; this gift would help all Ongwe-Oeh (Indians).

The bear disappeared as quickly as he had come and Otjiera awoke, still on the outcrop and surrounded by the force of the storm. Suddenly he saw a blinding flash, followed by the strangest noise. On investigation he found it came from two balsam trees that the strong wind had caused to rub against each other. As he watched, smoke began rising from the rubbing branches and the tree caught fire. The young boy was frightened but, after the storm had passed, he collected two dry balsam sticks and began rubbing them together, just as the wind had rubbed the trees. Nothing happened immediately but then smoke began rising and, with the aid of cedar bark and grass, he created fire. He had created the aid about which his spirit had spoken to him and so returned to his village an adult, with powerful medicine.

Eventually it was time for us to leave the summit. Sandwiches and drink had gone and soon tiny stomachs would be empty again. But if we adults imagined the return downhill would be quicker than the trip up, we were mistaken! The few short slides we had passed turned into a major amusement for the kids, especially after seeing Mum and Dad go head-over-backwards down one of them. In the end, though, if they wanted to climb the mountain more than once, up and down these slides repeatedly, then hopefully it meant bedtime would come earlier – a plus for all parents!

Bedtime is story time and, when in the woods surrounded by darkness, shadows and eerie sounds, they should sometimes be scary, horrifying tales. One sent shivers up my spine and, had I told it to the kids, would have kept them awake with nightmares. It is a Mohawk ghost story set in springtime and is centred around a lake – Rainbow Lake, near the present-day town of Onchiota and not very far from our small cabin.

Most Indians did not live within the wilder parts of the Adirondacks; they would only venture in to hunt or to harvest the many fruits there. One such family, the Kanienkehake, decided after a long day's march to rest overnight in a small bark hut they found by Rainbow Lake. While the rest of the family gathered wood and prepared the evening meal, father and son decided to check the loft, seeking evidence of the last occupants. All they found was an old bark container; inside was a skeleton. In respect for the deceased's bones they replaced the box lid and returned to their family. Soon, after their meal, everyone went to sleep around the fire.

Sometime during the night the father was awoken by an unusual gnawing sound. He relit the fire with more dry timber and was shocked to see the source of the sound. Opposite him sat his grandfather, obviously dead, with a skeleton eating his remains – feet first. As it turned to face him, the father – seeing the burning embers in the skeleton's eye sockets and fresh blood dripping from its jaw, realised that the rest of them were on his menu. So one by one, they made their excuses and left the hut. Each time one of them left the skeleton would stop eating the grandfather and watch them as they moved outside. The moment the father left the hut he too ran for his life. Just as the father reached his family the first light of the rising sun spread over the woods; they all carried on running until they heard an unearthly scream behind them, which increased in volume. From above them they saw the skeleton, its red eyes leaping towards them with inhuman strides. At the moment they felt it directly behind them it stopped, looked up at the rising sun, turned and fled back to the hut.

The family returned to the hut later with other members of their tribe; they burnt the hut but whatever demon had possessed the skeleton escaped as a white rabbit. The Indians didn't see this rabbit again but the film crew and actors on a 'Monty Python' film apparently saw it, centuries later, when it wreaked equal havoc.

Hike to Algonquin Peak (1559m)

+894m 13.4km

Algonquin Peak is the second highest mountain in the region, and was constantly in my line of sight from the porch of our cabin. So it was inevitable that I would have to climb it. For days I tried to ignore the mountain, concentrate on family activities but, eventually, I got up before the kids one morning and started along the same track I'd taken to Marcy Dam.

Algonquin is part of the Macintyre Mountain Range; its peaks stretch from S/W to N/E, exposing kilometres of unobstructed views for hardy hikers, those most likely to venture along it in September when the Alpine Zone flowers can be more appreciated. I saw none, neither did I really notice when the predominantly birch and fern woods changed to balsam and spruce at about 1219m and then, at the start of the Alpine Zone, into a maze of dwarf balsam, spruce and mountain ash shrubs (called the 'Krummholz Zone' - crooked wood). I was more interested in the clear view from the top, where I could be my own 'king of the hill' and, if the wind was not too strong, stand in awe of my surroundings.

The early morning air was sharp and crisp like the snow; the sun was bright and there was a distinctive hint of spring in the air. If the sky remained clear I felt sure the hike would be perfect. It felt especially good to be out and about that morning, walking among these mountains. I had the usual snow problems to deal with but, with a lighter pack, they didn't bother me, and *this* time, the summit trail was well defined, compacted and – until about half way – very wide.

For adventurous skiers there are plenty of downhill ski runs here. The trail I followed was part of one of them and, from what I could see, a particularly difficult one. It starts from the first summit of the range, called Wright Peak (Algonquin is the second); it joined my present trail at halfway point. When I reached that point and saw the steep ski slope up to the summit I was convinced it would be madness to even contemplate putting skis on, let alone cruise down through the dense wood. I can safely say though that, despite the obvious advantage of skis and disadvantage of snowshoes, when it comes to the thrill factor my method of travel was the right one. It may take longer but it feels so good to arrive with both legs intact and a head on the right way round!

Algonquin Peak from the cabin

If an accident befell a skier – or me – help would be on hand here. There is a heliport, plus two warden stations and the Loj, all a few kilometres apart. Help never seems far away, unless the accident happens in dead of night or you develop an ailment which only an old local remedy will cure – like baldness. The old time remedy for this comes from an ancient doctor's book: take the sole of a worn out shoe, burn it to a crisp, pulverise and mix with lard.

Massage this into the scalp for ten nights, by which time the condition should have been cured. The Indians have a more appetising remedy for baldness and grey hairs: massage the scalp with sap from grape vines. It's so simple it might even work. When did *you* last see a bald Indian, or one with grey hair?....

Some of the more delightful aspects of this area are the amusing remedies and strange tales originated by the early settlers. Most of them spring from local gossip, others reflect a longing for times past – good and bad. The Iroquois have unique stories; these were told by The Storyteller, an important man who was both teacher and entertainer. He moved from village to village with his bag of tricks, or rather his bag of objects, which helped remind him of the stories. For the following story he may have carried dried herbs; it is a mythical tale that explains how the Iroquois discovered the uses of the surrounding plants and trees for medicinal purposes. It was told to the young, as a lesson in being kind to the old.

Many centuries ago an old man dressed in rags walked into an Iroquois village seeking food and shelter to help ease his tired, old bones. Many separate clans lived in the village, each having a different animal as their emblem (i.e. turtle, wolf, beaver and eagle); these animals were displayed above the clan's bark houses. The man visited each of these, and others, but was refused help – until he enter the Bear Clan's house. Here he was allowed to rest but then developed various illnesses in the following weeks; each was cured by an old woman, after being instructed by him as to which herb would heal and how to prepare it. One day while the old woman was busy outside she was horrified to see a young man emerge from her house, his face as bright as the sun. She was afraid the spirits had come for her but he assured her that he was the Creator, who had come down to his people to teach them the wonders of medicine. Because of her generosity all medicine men and women from that time onwards have always been of the Bear Clan, passing their medicinal secrets down from generation to generation.

Continuing on my way, I was beginning to miss the wide ski trail. What had once been a motorway was now a narrow dirt track but the views were still good and I soon passed a good camping spot, plus a beautiful waterfall; probably impressive in summer. Now it looked fantastic, the sun glistening on its icy coating.

After the waterfall the trail levelled out as it traversed the slopes off Wright Peak; then climbing began in earnest as I started up possibly the steepest part of the trail. At times I was sure the angle of the slope exceeded 40 degrees and, forgetting the surrounding woods, was reminded of grade 1 corrie climbs – where an axe would have been useful. Apart from having fun slipping and sliding up and down the trail, the views were gradually improving over to Street Mountain and beyond; and these *almost* made up for the lack of an axe....

Eventually I came off all fours as the trail lead me between the slope and a low knob. From there onwards I only needed two legs to reach the top, plus sufficient clothing to cope with adverse weather (as advised by a sign here warning hikers not to proceed unless they are suitably equipped). Good sounding advice but considering the summit was so close, I wondered if a hiker ignored common sense (and knowing Mother Nature has a sense of humour), would he turn back? For today it was perfect T –shirt weather, sunny and no wind; but as I neared the top I soon realised how appearances deceive as my day sack was rapidly emptied.

Not until I entered the Alpine (or Krummholz) Zone at 1,270m did I realise the extent of shelter from the elements the trees had given. The name 'Krummholz' (or at least its meaning) fitted in perfectly with the surrounding maze of shrubs and all the trouble they caused me; they offered no shelter from the increasingly strong, biting wind. Twenty minutes and less than 150 metres to go I was still quite warm in a T-shirt but, as I left the last mangled shrubs behind and approached ice-covered boulders, I was in full winter gear and trying hard not to be blown over!

Frozen river

Technically there should be a side of a mountain that offers shelter from the main force of the wind. Of course there are exceptions to the rule and at times the only sheltered spot is on the mountain's vertical side. Those times are horrible, especially when there is a view to admire and you can only stay to photograph it – or risk being frozen solid. Luck – or fate – was with me on this summit; I took a few photos on the summit, until my eyes watered and I couldn't see. Finding a sheltered ledge on the south side, I stayed for an hour looking towards Mt. Mercy, Wallface Mountain and miles beyond. I saw in great detail part of the route I'd taken from Lake Colden to Avalanche Pass and the ski slope off Mt. Colden – the one causing so much danger at the time. From my high vantage point it resembled a scale model but I knew it wasn't and was thankful to have had splendid views through my binoculars. Happy and contented, I set off back to the cabin.

Being so near to the extensive chain of the Appalachians, you might consider that the Adirondacks were created in a similar way. Not so. The immense forces of two great continents moving side by side formed the Appalachians, whereas the rounded dome shape of the Adirondacks was created purely by the immense heat deep under the earth's surface –*not* by tectonic forces. The collective name for the group or band of rocks of which the Adirondacks are part is Grenville Rocks; they stretch from Labrador to Mexico. The rocks forming the Adirondacks are said to be about 1.5 *billion* years old and have only been exposed to the air for about 10 to 20 million of those years. During their time deep under the earth the granitic gneisses, marble, quartzite's and metanorthosites that make up the present mountains were created from the sand and limestone of an old ocean, from which they originate. Immense forces and heat were applied to these rocks and sediments by many oceans and mountain ranges that came and went in the intervening years – all of which finally gave way. For some reason a hot spot in the magma occurred in the N.E. of New York State, causing the surrounding rock to rise like a swollen blister. Over many millions of years the blister rose as the remnants of past mountains above it eroded. Eventually it reached the surface where, as other and younger mountain ranges crumbled under the extreme forces of ice ages and erosion, this one continued to rise faster than wind or rain could bring it down. It is still rising – at roughly 3 millimetres per year.

There is a drawback with these mountains which centres around a few fault lines all bunched together for about 10 to 20 miles in length, around the Blue Mountain Lake area not far away. Up to 400 tremors per day have been recorded around the lake, including one particularly large one in 1984, which was felt over a major part of N.E. America. The reason for the tremor travelling so far was ascribed to the hard, old and cold rocks of the Adirondacks which, in effect, allowed a wider transmission of vibrations than was normal.

A few days before this summit hike I'd decided it was time to venture out on skis and had selected a fairly level trail from the cabin to Indian Pass. If I'd remembered sooner, I might have used the preceding information as a good excuse for why it took me about 5 hours to travel six miles – the vibrations were causing me to fall over! Better still, I could have blamed my lack of ability on the Rock Fall lean-to and its beautiful and peaceful setting; but that would have been a lie. Instead, I had to confess that my uselessness on skis was due to hidden branches under the snow – again. After several family sessions on the Olympic cross-country course I thought I might have been inspired enough to ski gracefully along with timing and balance; instead I reckon the birds and mammals along that trail learnt a new string of profanities – produced by my ineptitude! The best thing about the day was the perfect weather, although memories of it still produce laughs from the kids.

During the periods between my ventures into the snowy mountains, other momentous days were spent with the family – some I will never forget and some I would like to! When we asked the kids for their memories of this holiday we thought it might be the tubing, the skiing, the climb, the snowshoeing –even the fantastic community-built playground we found behind the junior school in Lake Placid… But no. Of all the wonderful things they had seen, smelled and ate, it was the *bowling* they remembered most. Not so surprising – it was the only activity in which, most of the time, they could beat Daddy!

People remember this part of America for different reasons. I cannot put my finger on the one thing *I* will remember. The wind in the trees is as memorable as maple syrup on hot pancakes in the morning; the wonderful sight of the mountains and trees under cover of snow is as vivid as seeing my kids having another fight over snowshoes. The worst memory was seeing the snow thaw – slowly – signifying the inevitable end of our holiday. I did wonder if we could get away with telling the airline we were still snowed in…

Six mountain hikes from around the world

AUSTRIA

Stubaier Alpen

Peaked to Perfection

The Alps: a name given to probably one of the best known and most frequently visited mountain regions in the world. Their high peaks straddle in a long arc along the base of Europe, their wonderful scenery a haven of wildlife. The Alps may overlap many national boundaries, but their allure and attractions have no limitations, their beauty often compared to other mountain ranges across the world including New Zealand and Japan. If you have no specific area in mind, it is difficult to decide on which part to visit but, fortunately, I did. During youthful jaunts around Bavaria I heard of the Tyrol with its snow-capped peaks and quaint alpine villages – a 'must' for anyone who had appreciated the German Alps. Choices of locations were difficult to make but finally, after a short bus ride from Innsbruck, I arrived at my No.1 choice – the small town of Nedar. Here I would begin a 7-day walk involving heights of between 2000m-2900m, up and down the ridges/slopes of the valleys and mountains surrounding the beautiful Stubai valley, whose peaks of perfection can be achieved with ease. Staying at fully serviced Huts every night. To those not used to Alpine Huts, this means that there are not only sumptuous meals cooked at the huts to look forward to after a long days walking, but soft mattresses, the occasional hot shower, and more importantly – a lighter load to carry!!

Back in Innsbruck (the nearest city through which access is easily gained to the valley), waiting for the bus, I realized this trip would be one of my most memorable, not just because the weather was perfect and the area reminded me of Bavaria, but because the walk would involve much steep walking/scrambling. Even though

Innsbruck is situated in the wide, flat valley of the Inn River, I could still see and feel the presence of the 3000m mountains lining the valley above the six-storey buildings around me, hanging over the town like motionless tidal waves. Very different to the narrow, deep valleys towered over by sharp, craggy mountains similar to those leading off from the Inn valley and, more vividly, as I entered the Stubaital Valley. There I saw the absolute definition of an alpine valley – lush green meadows dotted all over with the first summer flowers, an occasional wooden barn, small towns full of houses with the characteristic and very attractive low-angled roofs extending over long balconies displaying colourful arrays of flowers. In the Tyrol the flowers might include a rose, said to protect the house against lightning. Above the towns the massive mountains dominated the view and tree-covered slopes. Further up lay Snowfields Glaciers and the Peaks – all indications of perfection to come.

Six mountain hikes from around the world

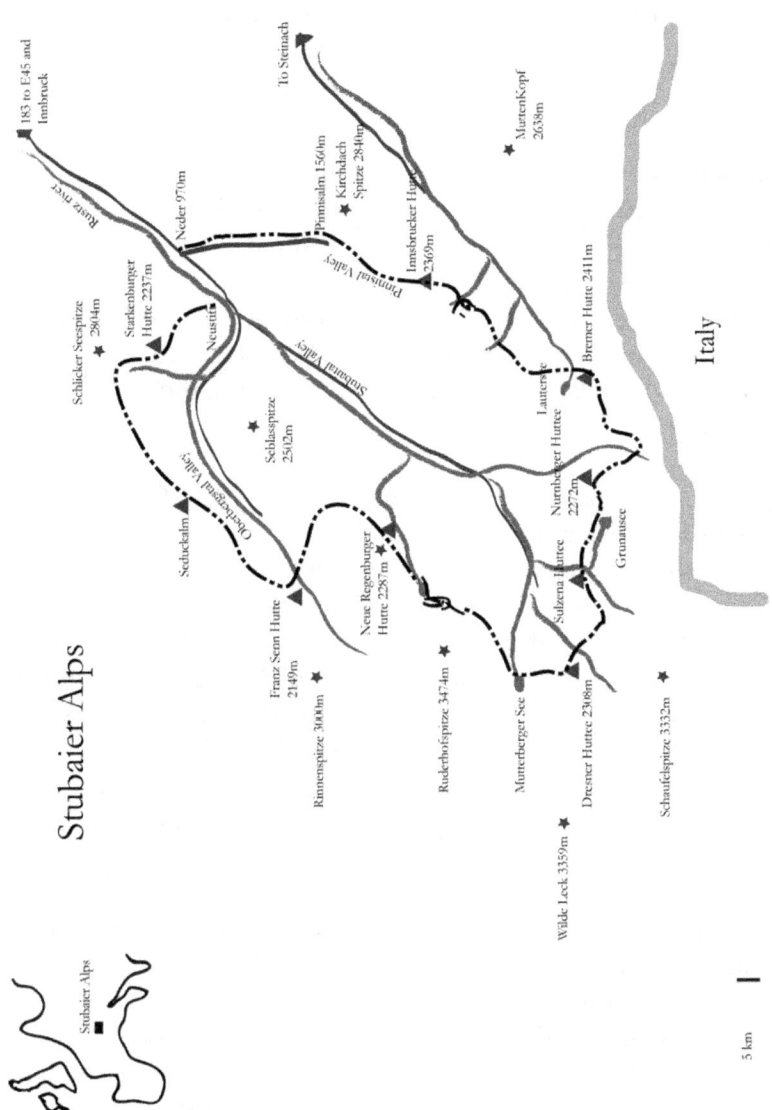

Day 1   Neder – Innsbrucker Hutte

+1405m   10km

The first hut of the route, aptly named Innsbrucker Hutte, was 10km from me up through the deep valley of Pinnistal. Situated at 2369m, it is 1405m above Neder. From Neder the jeep service could have taken me up the first 300m and I planned this due to the lateness of the day but my impatience to get into the mountains (coupled with hunger pangs) swiftly made my mind up to start hiking. On reflection, I think it was the thought of missing dinner that did it!

After a gentle ascent up through the town, the road became dramatically steeper above its boundaries, continuing for some way into the woods above. My route is described in the guidebook as a good introduction to the Stubaital Alps and its floral area, to which I can testify, although it soon became evident that this would be achieved only by hard work. If only I had tried the old traveller's remedy – a St. John's Wort leaf in my boots! This plant apparently prevents fatigue so, had I tried it, my first initial and very steep walk may not have seemed so taxing on the legs. So when a driver stopped and offered me a lift up to Issenangeralm Hutte, I didn't refuse!

The trees on the left of the valley gradually thinned enough to reveal meadows and the chalk cliffs of the Kirchdach Spitze range. Their greyish eroded pillars towered high above scree-covered slopes into the swirling, windswept clouds – giving the peaks a haunting feel. These cliffs, apart from offering a challenging climb, added variety to the scenery. If the wood on my right had also thinned, I'd have seen the contrasting, darker metamorphic gneiss rocks, leading to the Elferspitze summit; gneiss, along with slate, is found in abundance in most of this valley's areas. Varying amounts of metals and minerals (quartz, feldspar and biotit) are mixed with these two, giving the rock varying appearances all along the route. In the Fotzchertal Valley the mica slate in the rocks turns it a reddish colour. Apart from the chalk cliffs along which I was now walking, only one other chalk area – the Kalkkogel range I would see on my final day – would prove even more spectacular, set against a highly visible and ragged jungle of gneiss.

Innsbrucker Hutte

Many different rocks constitute the Alps as a whole, i.e. the limestone of the Jura Mountains and the granite of the Mont Blanc massifs. Like the gneiss, these were formed after many millions of years of heat and pressure forced on to the rocks deep within the earth as they were folded and pushed by the advancement of Africa into Europe. Erosion followed, wearing away the softer, over-laying rocks to sculpture the scenery seen today. Then early Man discovered metal here, allowing him to proceed up the next step on the evolution ladder. He may have even discovered what was found, by accident, in 1908, in the Karwendal Mountains north of Innsbruck. During a storm a pioneer sheltered in a hut. Within it a fire kept him and others warm but, frustrated when the timber ran out, he threw a rock on the fire. Everyone – including the pioneer – was amazed when it began burning like coal; all (except the pioneer) ran for their lives, thinking it an act of the devil. He remained, wondering what the strange rock was. It was oil shale, now used in treatments for rheumatism, phlebitis and frostbite.

After thanking my driver, the valley opened up considerably and the gradient became more leg-friendly. Colour filled the view as the sun penetrated the high cloud, capturing Nature's radiance; and the amount of passing people increased. After countless 'gruss gott' greetings my smile faded somewhat! A few asked where I was heading and their varying replies of "oh, it's not far now" and "it's only a little hill" did, briefly, spur me on but I soon realized most of them weren't tourists, but maybe locals, who walk up/down these mountains on most Sunday afternoons. Not the best people to listen to!

After passing Pinnisalm Hutte and the old grey jeep parked outside, the gradient steepened. Inside the hut the evening jubilations had begun whilst, outside, I still had 800m to walk up. I'd seen no other walkers for a while, the clouds had descended below the high ridges above and, once out of earshot of the hut, I felt I'd left the last post and was entering into the unknown again. I remember wondering how there could possibly be a fully serviced hut amongst the jagged ridges above me….

Just before the last major walk up to the ridges, I passed the last small hut along this valley. The trees finally dispersed and the meadows spread out before me, allowing a bird's eye view of the unique difference between the dark gneiss slopes of Elferspitze and the chalk cliffs opposite – a sight I still remember vividly today. Above I could see my destination, along the valley ridge top where the snow began – another mere 500m to go.

Apart from the short rest during the car ride I hadn't stopped, being pushed on by my increasingly complaining stomach; so I stopped, for a breather and intake of calories. Unfortunately the place I chose wasn't ideal: an ordinary field I thought occupied only by a couple of ordinary horses – until I took out my flask. For some reason this caused the horses to suddenly lift their heads, gallop over to me at full speed and, inexplicably, try to get at my flask! I'd had a similar experience on a campsite in Glenridding in the Lake District and, ever since, have doubted their intentions. I swiftly packed my sack and moved on.

Once on the scree slopes above the field I found some peace, and the start of what I call the 'shrub and heather zone' – my favourite. I also found an abundance of many more flowers not previously seen on the way up; they overgrew the narrow trail and it was difficult not to step on them. I saw, amongst others, the bellflowers that resemble bluebells, the yellow birdsfoot trefoil and some leaves that might have belonged to the rare (and protected) alpine columbine. All were within an arm's length when I rested near a small shrine. There were many shrines along the whole route, as well as crosses; one, 500m above me, marked my destination. There were a few plaques along the route too, placed in remembrance of the few walkers who had died here; these were good indications of the danger areas I was approaching and one of them was immediately obvious – the weather. In Neder it had been hot but now, as I climbed higher, it was much colder – not helped by a freezing wind. As I concentrated on going higher I didn't notice the boulders I was climbing over, nor the start of snow or even entering the cloud – except when I stopped briefly to look back down the valley; but then the wind chill rapidly moved me on.

Ever since I had left Neder earlier I hadn't thought I would make it in time for dinner but, 3 hours later, I found myself only 100m below the hut – a welcoming site. On reaching the ridge I was elated to be in time. Apart from the cross there was a seat, from which I could take in the view once more but it was now cloudy – and the seat had a layer of snow on it. Walking through the gap I was taken aback by the amazing transformation in the scenery between the two valleys. The snow on the Neder side had been quite thin and dispersed but here it was thick and plentiful. Thick cloud obscured almost everything, including the vertical cliff immediately below me and it wasn't until the swirling cloud parted briefly that I saw the hut. However did they build a hut on such narrow, steep slopes? But there it was, believable or not, on a small outcrop; in the fading light, under its covering of snow, it was beautiful.

The housefrau greeted me, her friendly personality and the warmth of the hut made me at ease and rested immediately. I was to sleep in one of the cheapest rooms (the matizzimmer) and even though it was cold in the sleeping room, the dining room was warm. I managed a chat in German with the housefrau; this impressed her and amazed me – considering I hadn't spoken the language for more than six years! She told me some worrying news about the snow I'd seen outside and that no one had yet been able to walk to Bremer Hutte, my destination next morning. I hadn't expected this problem in July but, as I learned later, quite a number of people had to change their plans because of it, so would have to wait and see if it also applied to me. For the moment I was only interested in the best meal I had seen in years being laid before me; I tried to savour it but it disappeared all too soon, along with the German beer – the best beer in the world.

Day 2 Innsbrucker Hutte – Bremer Hutte

+810m   -800m   9 km

Waking up in a cosy 'hut' on a mountainside may seem strange to fellow hikers more used to roughing it in tents. In these mountains, however, huts are not only easier to find than good pitching areas, but they do not take long to get used to – especially the soft mattresses and hot showers. Then there is the variety of food available – no horrible dehydrated foods, just inexpensive simple food like my continental breakfast and the tastiest coffee I had ever had in the mountains.

Sharing my table were two fellow Brits, Ben and Scott, indulging in a celebratory 'pat on the back' interail trip around Europe after finishing at university. Our conversation centred on the trip to Bremer Hutte and its ups and downs over three main corries and ridges, across boulders and slippery slabs – not helped by snow still lying over most ridges. This, I was told, was the reason for most people spending the previous day sitting around the hut; thick snow prevented them from traversing the ridges just above the hut. I had come to walk, however, not sit around in huts so even though the view from the window was a mixture of swirling snow and cloud, I had to discover if the snow had melted enough to allow access to the next hut. After having my flask made up, packing my bag and paying my bill, I ventured out – and very nearly went in again. I'd stepped from a sauna into a freezer! The weather down in the valleys might be that of a July morning but where I was it was very cold, the surrounding snow still thick enough to make a good sized snowman.

Just past the hut was its supply cable car and the first track marker of the route – the usual two red lines separated by a white one (basically the Austrian flag). As I was passing this point, I was aware something was coming up the cable. The noise of the motor behind me was eerie; I was surrounded by fluffy grey cloud, preventing me from seeing further than 10m but, as a large dark box emerged out of the cloud from the deep abyss below, it seemed even more out of place than the motor.

Towards Hohes Tor

Not far up the track I came to a lake, whose smooth flat, icy surface allowed relief from the boulders and gave me a chance to look around; there was little to see. The only advantage of the wind was when it intermittently parted the cloud, allowing glimpses of Mt. Habich above and the valley behind me. The climb to the first ridge was steep, made more exhilarating by the hard and soft snow hiding the trail; so the boulders were extra slippery. Thankfully it wasn't raining and my axe was driving home, giving me some grip; if I hadn't had that then I would have been all over the place. I wondered if all the other ridges to come had similar snow cover. Climbing up and down 200m at a time would be exhausting.

Eventually I reached the top and met Ben and Scott. This was the furthest they had achieved the previous day and were now deciding if progress was possible. The slope down the other side of the ridge looked severe, especially with snow cover; one slip and God knows what would happen to any of us. After this short descent, however, it appeared that level ground could be reached, past the outcrop of rock beside us. Actually getting there was the tricky bit. I'd have loved to christen the virgin snow and be the 'first over' of the season but they were as intent on reaching Bremer as I was and very carefully made their way down. I stood on the ridge for a while, not only making sure they reached level ground but also surveying the cloud and hoping to see more of the surrounding mountains. I did, briefly, including the wonderful sight of the hut below set against the chalk cliffs behind. Through thinner cloud I saw the mountains on the other side of the valley, the Tribulaun Peaks – a chain of about five peaks whose scree-covered slopes descended endlessly down into the unseen Gschnitzal Valley below. It was interesting to learn that the Brenner Pass is further along that chain, the only pass in this area open all year round – a fact obvious for hundreds of years to the many invaders and traders. One, Attila the Hun, probably used it during his assault on Italy in 452 AD, as did the Child Crusaders in 1212 who followed in the footsteps of their predecessors to capture Jerusalem. Apart from invasions of course it was useful as a trade route and, after the Romans built the first road over it, its accessibility increased its use. Today that first cobbled Roman road is buried under the huge E45.

After the ridge it did level out and I caught up with the Brits, having great fun trying to keep to the trail. It was difficult to follow its course through deep snow but, fortunately, there were a few places where deer had left their prints and channels; these were welcome as deep snow combined with walking at about 2500m was tiring me unusually quickly. Along the wider couloir I saw many animal tracks, one in particular that from a distance caused a joke, due to its similarity to kangaroo prints! The T-shape fitted the two feet and a tail of a kangaroo but close up, were those of a hare as its hind legs fall one behind the other. I also saw sheep and alpine ibex tracks, luckily we saw the ibex close up as we began another steep climb up to the Pramarnspitze; not quite as thrilling as the climbing of the first ridge but just as hair-raising.

Now my feet were wet with snow and we were all relieved to see that on the other side of the ridge there was considerably less snow – and less cloud. The Tribulaun Peaks revealed more and more to wonder at, including many new blooms flowering for the first time. What had been a black-and-white day was now full of colour – we saw rock jasmine and the versatile mountain Valerian (one of the truly indigenous species of this region that survived the last glaciers); it was used as a pain-killer and anaesthetic during past wars when conventional medicines were difficult to obtain.

I grew up in a world full of medicines fully analysed before being given to me, so it is fascinating now to see and learn about plants that, probably, even my grandfather was using to relieve various complaints such as headaches. Now it seems that the old legacy of local remedies is making a comeback; herbal medicines and the knowledge of how and which plants to use is gaining in popularity. I am sure herbalists today prefer to be referred to as 'practitioners' instead of, as previously, dubbed witch doctors or medicine men and women. They were once feared for the magical powers it was believed they possessed, and their abilities to cast spells. One such spell was put on a certain pear tree near Salzburg and it was said that it would only blossom whilst the Holy Roman or German Empire flourished. From between 1806 to 1871, when the Confederation of the Rhine was in power, it appeared to have died – until the renewal of the German Empire, when it blossomed again. Strange, but maybe true.

Like that tree, the corrie I was now in appeared as if it had magically sprung into life when the snow disappeared; after the thrills and spills of the walk thus far, it offered refreshing opportunities for a dinner break. We all stopped at various places along the trail, including an Austrian who said he was going all the way to the Nurnberger Hutte (another 4km and 350m ascent on from Bremer Hutte). I wished him good luck. I was looking forward hopefully to good views of the valley down from Bremer Hutte at sunset, said to be delightful. I still couldn't see any peaks clearly but the swirling and folding clouds played such glorious tricks with the sun's rays and shadows over the craggy peaks that I was content to marvel in their grandeur.

Sitting on the slopes of the valley, in what I considered the 'best seats in the house'. I noticed how quiet and peaceful it was and almost forgot the savageness of these mountains – only to be quickly reminded by a few plaques on rock faces along the trail.... They started me considering the possible dangers en route; the rivers I'd seen offered no real dangers, as they were low and nearly always covered with large stepping-stones. On the ridges and ascents to their cols was where the dangers lay. The next one was a good example, and particularly exhilarating considering that its 45 degree angled slope was still covered in thick snow. The snow offered some good footholds, unlike the large, flat slippery slabs above me that did not; one of the Brits was hanging on to one desperately as I was traversing the snow below. For a few seconds, after he had informed the whole valley that he was slipping, the air seemed full of tense expectation that an accident was about to happen. Thankfully we spent that night laughing about it – and not at the bottom of the valley under six feet of rubble!

The route down on the other side was just as steep. Fixed ropes helped a great deal but being 'cack-handed', I always seem to get tangled up in them. Now only one lower ridge remained – different from the others as it could be climbed in two different directions, both clearly signposted at their junction. I could go via the Lautersee and across to the hut – or the way I decided on after the Austrian told me of a dangerous climb that the latter involved. Approaching the last climb I wondered what the Austrian's definition of 'danger' really was. Unlike the other ridges, no cloud hid the top of this one and – before I knew it – I was standing under a massive, near-vertical slab of black rock, with the hut's supply cable standing almost 200m above me. Did I say that this ridge was low!

Even though the scramble up to the foot of the ridge involved an even steeper slope than before, the rock face slowly revealed a relatively easy zigzag climb up to its face. Occasional fixed ropes do help but, mostly, weren't needed. Initially the hut's flag informed me I was near the end and then the hut itself soon came into view bringing with it relief – and a tinge of disappointment that one of the most exciting day's walks I had in ages was over.

Bremer Hutte is smaller than Innsbrucker Hutte, but just as friendly and warm. Outside was a lake, which, I imagined, would encourage wonderful bathing in the coming weeks as the air became warmer. A large boulder outside the front door made me wonder which came first - the hut or the boulder! This dilemma was forgotten when the all-too-familiar smell of schnitzel wafted under my nose, along with gluhwein!

When I arrived the houseman asked if I knew of any others coming and I found it very reassuring when, about an hour later, he ventured outside to look for a couple who had said they would be walking this way today. They arrived as I was admiring the sunset, whose brilliant oranges radiated under the cloud that had risen drastically to reveal a stunning view down the valley. The rigours of my eventful day suddenly seemed all the more worthwhile – I was among the first few lucky hikers of the season to witness this splendour. Perfect.

Day 3 Bremer hutte- Sulzenau hutte

+690m   -930m   9km

What a grand day! Sunshine and cool, crisp air filled the room. I awoke feeling fresh – not heavy-headed as I half expected after all the gluhwein of the night before. I knew today's hike promised to be spectacular and varied so I felt I could run up the highest mountain and sing; but after breakfast I thought better of it! I needed all my energy for the hike, which involved two climbs over passes into small but awesome valleys. One of these, due to the weather, was vastly better than the other (view-wise) with a lunch stop at Nurnberger Hutte. Ben, Scott and I joined forces today and at first it did not look promising. We crossed the last remnants of a snowfield just outside the hut under a blanket of cloud; the sun and clear skies of earlier had disappeared. Afterwards we agreed it was basically hard, but rewarding.

The walk was quite easy at the start, rising only slightly through an area of boulders, grass, wild flowers and occasional patches of snow. With little to look at I adopted my bad habit of 'head down, follow the leader', not taking in my surroundings. We almost walked past a group of marmots; about the same size as a large rat, they resemble rabbits. Marmots were reputedly responsible for the bubonic plague after being brought here in the 14th century by the Mongols. You'd expect them to be used to humans, living near a well-used trail, but before I could grab my camera they had vanished into their holes. My fault for not watching where I was going; annoying, it was the first and last time I saw any. As the camera was out I photographed the roof of the Bremer Hutte, behind me, sitting in a huge sea of rock and cloud, looking small and fragile compared to the high mountains above and below.

Path to Nurnburger Hutte

Grunausee

When serious climbing began it became interesting, involving narrow ledges along cliff edges and up steep gradients of debris, all still quite waterlogged and slippery. I was thankful it wasn't raining and the cloud had given us a break for a while. While concentrating on my footing the cloud returned; suddenly, 'follow the leader' became 'find the leader'. Boulders gave way to large, flat slippery slabs as we climbed higher and, without the wire ropes, the going would have been harder. The final ascent up to the Slmmingjochl ridge made the blood flow and, on a clear day, can be classed as a great achievement. Unfortunately everything was blocked out by cloud, but we were relieved to reach the Zoll Hutte (or Police Hutte), up on top – which was used when the Italian-Austrian border was at this point. Now it is a 500m climb away. If it had been clear it might have been worth the climb just to have one foot in each country – or even be at a similar height to where the famous 5,000-year-old Glacier Man was found on Mt. Finail, perfectly preserved in his very own ice tomb. After a few minutes on the ridge we felt we might meet the same fate if we stayed much longer; my plans of a little breather were dashed by the icy wind.

Luckily the descent on the other side of the pass was not as steep, with thick snow still covering most of the rock; there was little to help distinguish between cloud and slope. Regardless of that problem our fun was not spoilt, as slow, deep and tiring steps became longhops down the slope – until we reached the large, shiny and slippery slabs.

Then it got serious – following the markers leading us along the slope into a large cirque, whose large, steep and snow-covered field of scree fell down and down into a void of cloud. The trail led us over the top of this semi-permanent snow sheet – just below bare, vertical and dark rock where once again the ice axe proved its worth; the wire rope was buried under snow. During the crossing I felt tempted to do an 'Eddie the Eagle' and take the fast route down the slope…. If I'd known what lay at the bottom I may just have tried but since the cloud still obscured everything, we carried on using good old leg-power.

When we reached the bottom of the void the cloud had finally lifted and, at last, we saw the size of this tight but deep corrie surrounded by tall cliffs. We realised that, if we had taken the easy way down, we would have enjoyed a great rush down the slope – coming to a timely and safe stop as it levelled out beside a little pond. This was surrounded, like most stretches of water up here, by grassy meadows and wild flowers; the small patch of serenity and calm seemed out of place, almost an oasis, amongst the tons of dark, savage rock. A group of the friendliest sheep I have ever encountered insisted on being in the frame of every photo and I wondered if all the animals in this area were friendly because they saw so many people. Or maybe there was something odd in the local water? Whatever the reason, they also had an affinity with my flask!

We decided to rest near the pond, where the corrie gave way to the Langental Valley; its immense size provided magnificent panoramic views from the grand glaciers above us, right down to where this valley joins the main Stubaital valley. Even though the valley sides looked relatively close together, their size and volume gave it an impression of space. This in turn made us believe that the dot of the Nurnberger Hutte, which we could see across the valley, was about 1.5 miles away as the crow flies; but in fact it is more likely only .5m away. The trail we followed to it took more of a curved line to the hut and then went round, following the gradient of the slopes via some very narrow, slippery trails.

With this new and hopefully permanently clear weather, the walk round to the hut was a pleasure – with occasional heart – stopping moments on the narrow parts. The increasing heat of the sun put extra life in our steps – and also dried out my boots, leaving them covered in silver particles prolific on the rocks and boulders. They glittered in the sun and looked more like an old pair of 70's disco shoes than hiking boots! Shoes that my brothers and sisters would remember – not me!

Nurnberger Hutte – one of the oldest huts along this route (all constructed between 1874 and 1976) – had the elegance of an elderly lady. The look, feel and smell of its interior took me back through her long years and the many climbers and walkers she must have protected from the elements outside. Today these elements had, in a short time, changed to sunshine and clear skies so we had no need of her solid walls, just the benches outside. We took great pleasure in stretching out on them whilst drinking cold Coke and admiring our surroundings.

The next climb, up to the last Pass – Nierderl – could possibly be described as the worst, mainly because of the slope leading up to it. The perfectly angled slope up to the ridge made it possible to see the top of the Pass – and every boulder. Not until we began climbing did we discover that most of the boulders could easily be missed by using the stepping stones provided, many of which, marked with the usual red, white and blue. The white paint stood out and, at one point, all resembled the centre line of a road, going up the slope. Even more amusing was the park bench on the top; similar to the type used in England by many an OAP while out walking the dog. We didn't expect to see any here but, just after we arrived (puffing) at the top, a group of them was happily coming up the other side! They had obviously come this way before and seen the views – at least I decided that was the only reason anyone would take the trouble to climb to this excellent viewing point and not marvel at the high tops before moving on, as they did. Especially this view; it was literally out of this world – Wilder Freiger at 3418m is one of the highest mountains along this route. From this Pass we could see its full glory, crystal clear, including a few climbers just approaching the summit. But the glaciers on her slopes were the most striking feature – a mass of solid snow and ice descending to its wrinkled and tarnished terminus just above the Grunausee, whose blue/green surface looked stunning against the rock. Below in the far distance we could easily make out the characteristic sloping roof of the Sulzenau Hutte, nestling in a

valley full of colour – our home for the night. Many others had also come to see it, judging by the numbers of people about. Until arriving at the last hut I had seen maybe 10 people en route; here they swarmed like ants, all taking advantage of the clear weather.

Nurnburger Hutte

We walked down into the valley quite slowly, partly because the trails were still quite soggy but mostly so that we could thoroughly absorb the views. We had covered the distance from Bremer Hutte faster than anticipated and didn't want to arrive too early, though I soon realised that sitting outside the hut talking and drinking with other walkers is just as much part of the alpine experience as walking in the mountains. The coming night brought our true introduction into the hut-to-hut experience as all the other walkers staying here returned later in the day and filled the dining hall – singing and talking as the beer flowed and hearty food appeared as if on an endless conveyor belt! What I didn't expect though was the curfew – at 22.00 hours.

Outside it was serene and quiet. On one venture into the steadily freezing night air there was just enough light to see the intertwining of the mountain slopes as the valley descended towards the main Stubaital valley. In the very far distance the only visible light was that of Starkenburger Hutte, just below the summit of Hoher Burgstall – the last hut on this route. It added new meaning to the saying 'the end is in sight' though, in this instance, the end was still four days away.

Day 4   Sulzenau Hutte – Dresdner Hutte

+480m   -360m   4km

Time was not something I had taken account of so far, having no strict agenda, especially today. With just a 2-hour walk over the Beijoch Pass to the Dresdner Hutte I considered it a rest day and intended taking my time rising and preparing for the hike – a fine art I have mastered over the years. Breakfast in the huts was normally served until 09.00 but, unfortunately, the times here weren't as flexible as in other huts (probably due to the larger amount of people they were catering for at the time). By the time I got up all the other walkers (and their heaps of equipment which had filled the hall the previous night) had gone. Even Ben and Scott had finished packing, ready to be on their way and continue Interailing.

The empty, dead dining room where I drank my coffee alone was very quiet after the jubilations of the previous night. I'd planned to stay until later in the morning but the place being deserted, decided not to hang around getting in the way of staff cleaning. And the mountains were beckoning. There was almost no snow on them now, except on the high ridges and, of course, on the intricate folds and cracks of the glaciers coming off Sulzenau Ferner – which became ever more impressive and vivid as I left the hut and gained height.

Sulzenau Hutte

Above the hut, on a brief flat of debris left by the glaciers, flowers, grasses and mosses flourished; the colours made an interesting change from the white/black of the mountains. The plant mountain houseleek, when placed on roofs, is said to give protection against lightning and fire. There was an abundance of daisies and spiniest thistle; it's said that if children or young animals step on the latter they will grow up stunted. Nothing for *me* to worry about, except whether insects would be attracted to them. My body doesn't react kindly to stings these days.

The best view of the day began as I climbed the nearest moraine to the glacier. The natural beauty of Wilde Pfaff, with its size, shape and the wide glacier flowing down its sides, astounded me and I realised that cloud could have obscured stunning views during the first few days. After a short, steep climb at the edge of the moraine I reached the Peiljoch Pass; its surface was littered with stone slabs, which other walkers had piled into high cairns all over the Pass's flattish top. Standing among them they could, in my imagination, be frozen people, or foundation stones, even straddle stones of old buildings. In any form they seemed eerie, especially against the glaciers; it wasn't a place to stay long. Had I remained I might have seen one of the strange creatures reputedly lurking in the Austrian Alps – the Tatzel worm (or Stollenwurm), a reptilian creature approximately 1.3m long with a snake's body and head/forelegs of a cat. There was a reported sighting in Hochfilzen, South Austria, by a herdsman and a poacher; they fired and missed it, whereupon it apparently jumped on them! A few have been reported killed but – so far – no bodies have been produced....

The Pass carries on from the cairns down a gentle slope to a rock outcrop; there, apart from a brief but steep awkward descent, the excitement of the walk returned, with a perfect view of the head of the Fernautal Valley. A good place to rest before the final unpleasant descent down scree to the oldest, and probably most visited, hut – Dresdner Hutte. The views of the head of the Stubaital Valley were superb and it was amazing how many cable cars and lifts were going up to the Daunkogel, Schaufel and Fernau Glaciers – and they didn't spoil the view. Apart from the shifting panoramic views of the mountain ridges above the valley, the line of the trail I would be following next day on the other side could be clearly seen. It didn't look too difficult, at first sight.

Dresdner Hutte, situated next to the cable car station, has everything a hiker like myself counts as luxuries – telephone, hot relaxing showers and a cafeteria that would put a motorway café to shame. A small museum contains ancient mountain equipment and the Austrian Alpine Club's Yearbooks. Unfortunately my knowledge of aural German was rustier then my oral. My arrival coincided with that of quite a few day-trippers coming up the cable car from the valley below and I'd planned to join them on a short ride up to the next hut under Stubaier Wildspitze, but my lunch was prolonged due to my love of Austrian food!

Sulzenau Ferner

After I showered I decided to enjoy the good weather and sunbathe, not something I normally have time for when hiking. But then this wasn't a normal hike – not being mentally or physically demanding. I hadn't expected it to be, with a backpack weighing less than 10lbs and sleeping on a mattress every night! It just proved that I don't have to push myself to the limit and/or get saturated to see wonderful views. And then there were the nightly parties.... It seemed time to sit back and appreciate Nature's own beautiful canvas.

The meadows outside the hut were covered in soft fluffy cotton grass, mingled with many flowers I'd seen along the route over the last few days. These included a surprise plant, one I didn't expect to see in the Alps, the versatile nettle. I couldn't get away from them. Their ability to survive in most places probably reflects the many uses Man puts it to. In the Tyrol it is thrown on fires to stop thunderstorms and collected at sunrise to protect cattle from evil spirits. Its medical uses are numerous and strange; the Roman soldiers beat themselves with the leaves to help bring blood to the surface of the skin; this reputedly kept them warm. Reflecting on the amount of times I've fallen into them I think the pain of being cold is preferable to their sting!

Gradually the day visitors left; the chair lift stopped and, suddenly, the bustling hut was quiet compared to the previous night's hut – and deserted. Whilst nursing a little sunburn I shared the hut with five others and dined alone in a dining-hall large enough for 100, reflecting that this is one hike from which I would return weighing more than when I set out. It was only 6 hours since my arrival but I couldn't stand the boredom so went to bed ridiculously early, more tired from loafing about than walking.

Day 5   Dresdner hutte – Neue Regensburger hutte

+860m   -890m   11km

Outside the hut past a Police Hut a vehicle track climbs up between surrounding rock and doesn't appear too steep. Further up the track the trail bears off, leading to an excellent view into the delightfully tranquil Wilde Grub – just 150m climb, going by the map, unlikely to cause much hardship. About an hour after leaving the hut, however, my opinion changed and became unprintable. I was breathless, my heartbeat had increased and my legs turned to jelly. Was it due to lack of oxygen or my failure to 'warm up' before the climb, or that the hot sun had been beating down on me all the way up? I had tired very quickly but on reaching the viewpoint soon regained the composure of the proficient hiker I was *supposed* to be. The magnificent scenery restored me to normality. Far below me, I could see many sheep milling about, near where two rivers collided, trying to reach the meadows below the few remaining patches of snow, a vehicle track wound its way up the valley and I could see a rubbish truck climbing up slowly. Apart from the truck slightly marring the view, the only other disappointment was the 200m descent to the valley bottom – and the thought of losing the 150m ascent I had sweated for.

Dresner Hutte

Today was the hottest day, and would be the longest, involving a long, steady climb to the highest ridge along the route of 2880m, with height gain of over 700m. By the time I reached it, it would feel more like 7000m, due more to time and distance it took to achieve it. This fact concerned me as the sun rose ever higher and I left the green colourful depths of Wilde Grub and began climbing.

As I slowly gained height the superb view down the Stubaital Valley diminished, as did grass and flowers; they were replaced not only by boulders but also clear views of the peaks and their glaciers. From the shores of the small, but fresh, Mutterbergersee, the peaks of the Austrian-Italian border (and those overlooking the valley far below) seemed magical, perfectly reflected in the smooth surface of the lake. Even the sheep looked interested in the sight – or maybe it was just my flask that excited them!

Thousands of people before me had experienced the peacefulness of the scene but now I had it all to myself. Sitting in the shade of a small rocky outcrop I felt on top of the world. It was a rare moment, in a place I was not eager to leave, but clear water and beautiful peaks would not nourish me so I had to move on. Centuries ago Man and Beast roamed these mountains – moose, brown bear and wolves – all fighting each other for survival. Unfortunately the only place I saw a wild beast bigger than a marmot was in Innsbruck Zoo! The lynx, surprisingly, is said to be harmless to Man; they still live in the wild, in certain Alpine areas, thanks to a programme begun in the 70s. Golden eagles may be seen gliding gracefully across the sky, on the lookout for their favourite food. Brown trout and Arctic char may be spotted in the high lakes, introduced by the Emperor Maximilian. So maybe it wasn't only annoying insects, spiders and sheep passing the time of day with me by the lake – maybe other living things were there, ones I couldn't see.

Back in the days where there was enough game to go round, there were – besides farmers in the valleys – a few people who decided that a place like this was ideal for them; they were, you might say, the first escapees from the rush of modern life – the locals call them 'hermits' or 'mood brothers'. One in particular lived in the

Enns Valley in Styria and he had a particularly bad time after being visited by the Devil. The devil in this story loved playing games with vulnerable people and, when the hermit asked him what he considered the greatest sin, the devil replied 'drunkenness'; but the hermit disagreed and a challenge was set to test both their theories.

View from Mutterberger see

After a few too many jugs in the local pub, the hermit left to return home – adamant he would do nothing wrong en route. Soon he met the most beautiful girl he had ever seen (but considering he was a hermit she didn't have to be *that* good-looking!); unable to control himself, he indecently assaulted and killed her. He tried to hide the body but unfortunately for the hermit, the girl turned out to be the Devil himself. For his three terrible sins – drunkenness, assault and murder – the hermit was sent to see the Pope in Rome. The Pope condemned him to a cell and he was forbidden to speak until he was redeemed.

The story did not end there. Many years later, by which time he smelled and looked like a hairy monster, a kindly Count and his dogs found him. Deciding he must be an unusual beast, the hermit was trained; he continued to amuse the Count for many years – until an Apparition of Forgiveness revealed the hermit's true identity. He then returned to his home and lived a more saintly life.

Back by the Mutterbergersee, I decided it was time to leave and return to the trail, before I became part of the rock I was sitting on – and met the first person of the day, on his way to Dresdner. Suddenly, for no apparent reason, the sheep began following me up the slope; at first I took little notice, concentrating on the magnificent mountain views that would accompany me all the way up to the Grabagrubennieder ridge. Then I saw something to put a damper on things – just over a low outcrop of rocks....

A dead sheep. From its appearance, not long dead. There were no flies, no smell but its eyes and woolly coat had an empty look. As I watched, the sheep following me approached it, studied first it and then me – as though it were my fault it had died. They circled it, smelled it, as if paying their last respects to an old friend before the earth took him.

Very soon the scree and boulders and some stepping-stones mingled with the grass; and my following of sheep increased! I wondered why, but soon had my answer. A barrel was perched on the edge of a small, flat area – presumably it held their dinner. After finally losing them I concentrated on the hike and approaching high col. There was a breath-taking panoramic view from the pinnacle, with the Niederl ridge clear above Nurnberger Hutte and the line of mountains leading up to Habicht, above Innsbrucker Hutte, all the way round to Stubaier Wildspitze. Countless other peaks lay behind. On the second col of the route I expected to have equally good views, but they didn't have the same magic as these. Little did I know, then, that I was only 180m below the finest views of the day, from the high col of Grabagrubbennieder; there I would have a bird's eye view down into the next valley – Falbesontal – and see the Regensburger

Hutte in the far distance. This hut I would find just as quaint and welcoming as the others

Grabagrubernieder

The final approach to Grabagrubennieder was gentle and snow-covered; mighty glaciers rose above it, intersected by the shark's fin shape of the Grabawand. This massive line of dark, jagged rock appeared to thrust itself up from the earth. After my gentle approach to the ridge I didn't know what to expect on the other side, so was surprised to see the vertical drop near to the cross on top. In all, it descended about 20m, on to a large area of steep snow dropping down to the grey of broken rocks and boulders far below. The valley opened, further along, then levelled out slightly to reveal high meadows and a mass of flora. It leads right up to the brilliant white walls of the hut and disappeared as the valley floor dived into the Stubaital Valley.

In bad weather this ridge would be badly exposed but today the weather was perfect and, after roughly 4 hours of continuous climbing, I was pleased it was so. There was little wind over the ridge, just enough to be pleasant and not cold. After about 10 minutes I curled up and slept!

During my doze a couple came up from the vertical side and offered some advice. Apparently the jagged vertical side was not as severe as it looked from above, even the wire ropes that on past slopes had been a necessity were not needed in places here. Once on the snow, they said, it was best to slide down. Not wanting a frozen backside, however, I decided to use my axe and the couple's foot holes in the snow. But – eventually – the thought of sliding on the snow appealed to the child in me so I took the easiest (and unquestionably more thrilling) way down!

From there on the trail went past the small lake of Falbesonersee and down through the Hohesmoos – the flat green area I'd seen from above and which now looked even more colourful. A small stream added to the tranquillity and I even saw a red admiral butterfly, the first for many years.

Low grassy mounds marked the end of the meadow just before the hut, then the valley dipped again. On the mounds many were enjoying the weather - reading, sunbathing and relaxing; a perfect day for it. Considering the height here, there can be few occasions when the ridge and glaciers are so exposed to hot sun. I decided to settle into the hut before venturing on to the mounds but it wasn't a wise decision; I should have stopped. Just over 2 hours later it turned cold and clouds built up, covering the valley; then the rain came which, according to the weather fax at the hut, would remain for several days. It meant no more views and also that the particular fly deterrent used at this hut wouldn't be needed. Not the usual light to burn approaching insects this time but two plastic bags full of water, placed above the front door.

There were no flies in the hut so it obviously worked and it added a personal touch to the character and comfort of the building!

looking back to ridge

Day 6   Neue Regensburger Hutte – Fanz Senn Hutte

+430m   -560m   6.5km

Well what can I say? The outlook today was windy and wet; dull grey clouds obscured everything further than 10m away – the complete opposite to yesterday. Yet it might make the day more thrilling... Potential dangers wouldn't be easy to spot; dark shadows and silhouettes would distort the appearance and distance of objects. My movie-dominated imagination could run riot!

About 20 minutes from the hut the guidebook detailed my trail, to begin the ascent to the Schrimmennieder Col, en route to Franz Senn Hutte; there was no information, however, about the signpost at the start of the trail. As I could see precisely nothing, to miss the junction would be both annoying and time-consuming.

Due to continuous overnight rain the trails, perfect yesterday, were muddy and slippery. Once found, the trail was particularly bad – worsened by its angle and the bare rocks; but it added to the experience. As the cloud descended I wondered if I'd forgotten to pay for something in the hut and this was my punishment! I took a few wrong turns up the zigzag trail, but not too worrying; far more disconcerting were the dark objects coming into view above me, accompanied by a strange scratching sound. Was it yet another weird creature reputed to exist in Austria – the Lindworm, a snake-come-dragon depicted on a fountain statue in Klagenfurt?

This creature has given rise to many tales. One tells of the beautiful queen from long ago who for many years longed to have a child. Deciding that if anyone could help her it would be the Soothsayer, she searched for and eventually found him. He gave her some hope, presenting her with two onions, which, he said, would be able to give her two handsome sons. On arrival home she ate the onions in such a hurry she forgot to remove the skin from one.

The Soothsayer was proven right. Nine months later everyone was summoned to witness the births; the first son was perfect. The second was less so – it was the Lindworm. Shocked and distressed, the Queen ordered her guards to throw the Lindworm into the forest.

Many years past and in time rumours reached the first son of a large beast roaming the forest, killing local people's livestock. This perfect son, who was kind and strong, had become a trained warrior, the pride of the land and its people. When the people begged him to rid them of this menace, he set out in true warrior style to meet the forest creature. He positioned himself at the edge of the trees, hoping to meet the beast as it went to feed. Very soon a large, slippery body appeared but, before the warrior could move, the creature spoke, revealing its real identity as the Lindworm – and the warrior's true brother.

Neue Regansburger Hutte

Apart from whatever long-lost brothers say to each other, the Lindworm told the warrior that he would never be able to marry – not until he had also found a bride for the Lindworm. Now the warrior realised why, despite being eminently suitable, no woman had ever wanted him for a husband. So he set out to find his brother a bride, which proved extremely difficult. Who would want to marry such an ugly creature? Then, in true fairy tale style, one of the potential brides met the same Soothsayer whom the queen had met many years before. It was easy to break the curse and live happily ever after, the Soothsayer told her. He explained that the only reason why one brother was born a monster was because the queen had forgotten to remove one onion skin. Therefore, if the girl persuaded the Lindworm to remove as many layers as he could, and then held him close to her, all would be well. It sounded and looked repulsive but the brave girl closed her eyes and concentrated on the promised happiness. Of course she obeyed! And, as soon as she held the Lindworm a blue haze surrounded the creature and from it walked the most handsome man she had ever seen...

There may or may not be other Lindworms hiding in the mountains and, luckily, the shadows above me didn't conceal one. I could see the dark rocks of the approaching ridge and hear sheep feeding on the sparse grass of the slopes. On the pass I saw the first (and only) snow of the day, lying between the steep ridges. I'd planned to climb one, to Besslerjoch, only another 200m from the pass, but in this weather not a safe option; if the extra height had taken me above the cloud it would have been worth it, if only to see the fantastic sight of surrounding mountains appearing to be a short walk away across the clouds. But the drizzling rain was obviously going to last all day; even my tea tasted flat.

The way down into the Oberbergtal Valley was gentle. I was becoming accustomed to the slippery gravel and broken rock, features of these mountains. Shortly I met a large group of Austrians, stretched out for some distance, who were coming from Franz Senn Hutte. Some – those looking wet and tired – asked what it was like higher up. I *did* intend to tell the truth but, due to my broken German and their obvious displeasure, I told them what they wanted to hear – that it was sunny and clear. They immediately perked up and walked on but I wonder what they thought of me later, no doubt regretting the smiles and thanks they had given me!

The way down was over rocks, streams and patches of meadow; one had an unusual profusion of flowers in just a small area – spiniest thistles, louseworts, scabious, a single orchid and others I'd seen before. Thereafter most of the meadows were daisy-dominated, specially where the trail flattened out on the final approach to the hut. Here I was walking amongst dwarf pines just above the tree line; I could just see their tops rising from the cloud-obscured valley, and the trail on the other side I would be following tomorrow. In one way the situation was boring but in others not so – the anticipation of what lay beyond the hut wasn't marred, as it had been on previous occasions.

Now I concentrated on the many hidden holes between the grassy boulders; a twisted ankle at this stage would be unwelcome. After what seemed hours on the flat trail I began thinking I'd missed the hut and was en route for Switzerland! I couldn't see far and, in reality, wondered if I'd covered more ground than I actually had. I began to hurry, needlessly; it wouldn't matter if I sat down and stayed all day. If the weather had been better I might have done but instead, rested briefly then continued. It was still raining but it felt warmer on this side of the valley. If I'd known then how close I was to the hut, I could have rested, as very soon it loomed out of the cloud ahead of me, like a ship emerging from the fog – a surprise and a godsend.

Franz Senn Hutte, named after the founder, of the Austrian Alpine Club, is large. It needs to be, to accommodate the hordes that attend various courses/seminars held here; several were taking place when I arrived. Full of sweaty, geared-up climbers/walkers it was the busiest hut I'd stayed in so far. After 6 days of relative calm and peace I'd hoped that the majority inside would be day-trippers, but the night produced just as many. Then, like a colourful needle in a haystack, I spotted a group of fellow Brits – distinguishable from the rest by the amount of beer glasses on the table! They were RN guys following the same route as myself and, during the following session of Forces' humour and many trips to the bar, they invited me to join them the following morning. As the night wore on, however, I wondered if I would be able to get up at all....

Day 7 Franz Senn Hutte – Starkenburger Hutte

+420m   -340m   12km

Next morning the sun shone on the hut and the Alpeiner Ferner Glacier above, it's early brightness glaring off the ice and snow. Misty clouds hugged the lower slopes, whilst higher up they hovered and weaved around outcrops of rocks until eventually evaporating. Those who were to blame for my glazed eyes and lethargy were already outside, with almost everyone else. We had all managed some breakfast but the cool, crisp morning air was the best cure for my own misty cloud.

The general enthusiasm was overwhelming, everyone keen to get up into the hills – specially the lucky ones going 'summit bagging'; on such a day it would be madness not to scale one of the surrounding peaks. But it was my last day above 2000m and any excuse to extend my stay was tempting. Unfortunately, my pocket not matching my appetite for these mountains, I began wondering how I could become one of those who spend most of the year up here – maintaining the trails, walking the highways/byways.... I saw one on the trail to Starkenburger Hutte, working contentedly amongst the deer – a million miles away from any stress. As I passed him I felt guilty to be adding to his reasons for being there but, if he was as happy in his work as he sounded, I had no need to be.

An hour after the RN bunch left I finally dragged myself away from the hut, through rain and thick fluffy cloud. I still couldn't see much of the day's route as the cloud parted only briefly to reveal an occasional tantalising view down the Oberbergtal Valley, the best being those of the valley floor far below. During these glimpses I could tell the sun was shining somewhere beyond the cloud hugging the slopes and I had to wait until the end of the walk until they disappeared; only then was I rewarded with the final stunning views.

Franz Senn Hutte

There were no walkers on the trail I set out on, despite the numbers I'd seen earlier, only a couple of deer emerging from the cloud and carrying on down the steep slopes. The first part of the trail traversed slowly across the type of slope I refer to as 'one slip and you're gone'; it didn't become easier until reaching the Seduckalm Hutte, halfway. There I caught up with the RN bunch.

Seduckalm is a small, old hunters' hut, about the size of an average house, built in the traditional style with a charming motto on the outside; 'My kingdom is a flock of white sheep and my little hut is my castle'. I don't think the hut was there for accommodation, more as somewhere to obtain coffee/breakfast. Due to my stomach still feeling empty from the previous evening, I had a double helping. Not only did I have a meal, but also a chat with the houseman, who was keen to talk. I don't think I've spoken so much German in one go in the last 6 years as I did to him; it just flowed and, for a while, it was good to exchange yarns with this old character before rushing off to join the RN bunch. I was enjoying something more than mountain views – learning about life in the mountains. I was able, albeit briefly, to see further into them than perhaps a casual observer would.

Some ten minutes' climb above the hut the trail began across steep slopes more towards the col of Sendersjochl. I finally had views out of the valleys surrounding Stubaier into the adjoining valleys of Senderstal and Fotcher; there was, to my amazement, no cloud and I could see right down into the wide valley of Innsbruck. These unobstructed views made my eyes jump for joy and my head dizzy with the sudden colour. From that moment the day steadily improved, especially walking on up to the Steinkogel. The chalk mountains of Kalkkogel slowly came into view, until they dominated most of the horizon. Their white chalkstone looked even more impressive set against the dark rock along the Steinkogel ridge. It took another 45 minutes before I stood beneath them at the Seejochl Pass. That time was taken up walking around a large, deep basin whose sides were littered with debris from the Chalk Mountains and Gamsogel above me, covered at the bottom by a small lake. The expanse was huge, exaggerated by Schlicker Seespitze which, at 2804m, towered 300m vertically above Seejochl – from where there were superb views down towards Innsbruck.

Looking back from Schlicker Seespitze

The walk from the Pass, under the Chalk Mountains on their loose scree, looked extremely hazardous. This fact was emphasised by the two plaques I saw en route, dedicated to two who did not make it across. One slip here would have resulted in a fall over broken stone for some way down. The rain of the preceding days didn't help and, as I reached the end, I decided it wasn't a challenge I would want to repeat; but, for the views, was worth it. The cloud had lifted somewhat and rested just below the summits, allowing a perfect line of sight right up to Franz Senn Hutte and the valley I'd just walked down. There wasn't a lot of detail due to distance but the one aspect of the valley I could see clearly was the change in it from the valley floor, over 1km below me, right up past the tree line over the rocks to the glaciers. It was as good a sight as I'd hoped to see.

Further along this magnificent vantage point the last hut came into view – Starkenburger Hutte. This sight along with the perfect panoramas of most of the mountains I'd walked during the last 7 days emphasised the fact that journey's end was near – and this gave me a feeling of great achievement. I know countless others have walked these mountains before me but I hoped the extra time I'd taken to study the environment had enabled me to see more than just mountains and valleys. The fence-like structure I saw in the Oberbergtal valley, for instance, coming down the slopes of the peak behind me. *Now* I could see that it wasn't a fence – but large, angled shields, designed to stop loose rocks and snow from falling on to the towns below. How they placed them there was an engineering miracle. Later, sitting outside the hut enjoying a cold Coke, I joked with the RN bunch that they resembled something from 'Thunderbirds' and, any moment, I expected one of their vehicles to roll out from the side of the mountain!

I've noticed one particular thing on all final approaches to the huts – they all have a slight incline just before each one is reached. Not really a major consideration perhaps, except that each incline seems to require great effort to scale it. The approach to Starkenburger was no exception. I'd already climbed over 450m today, with ease, but this 10m ascent completely finished me. If other hikers I'd met hadn't noticed it, then I would have decided it was simply me, but most commented on it. It's as if the body starts to 'close down' when the hut is sighted – and not when actually reached. But it wasn't a problem – two large bowls of soup and a couple of Cokes restored my energy!

I think I chose the better of the two directions this route can take. I can't say it was the easier, but the view from this final hut of most of the route I'd covered allowed me not only to see the mother of all views – now the cloud had gone – but also take time to reflect on all I'd seen and experienced. This might have been difficult from the Innsbrucker Hutte, although that could depend on personal preference. The directional plate just above the hut was the best place to reflect on the moment, as warm currents of air below allowed birds to glide in and out of the corries; and the cooler wind above soothed my aching bones.

I must admit that, considering this entire walk was technically around one valley, I had thought that seeing the same views – of the same mountains – would not appeal, but I was wrong. Each new angle and elevation along the circular route revealed the Stubaital abundance of rare sights that would have been missed had the route only been partly taken.

I've had my share of bad hiking trips, but this was definitely one of the best. As the sun sank low, light and shadow flowed over the peaks and valleys for the last time, creating their magic on a panoramic view that has, and always will be, the natural phenomenon that attracts all visitors to the Alps. It was also a perfect ending to a wonderful trip.

Day 8 Starkenburger Hutte – Neustift

-1250m   3.5km

The mountain hiking might be over, but the trip wasn't finished yet. Neustift, the official end of it, had still to be reached – an amazing 1.3km below through upper mountain meadows and pine woods right down to the lower mountain meadows. And it was as equally special and enjoyable as the high walking.

The clear evening skies of yesterday remained. It was going to be hot, a day bright with the colours of flowers – including the yellow pansies and buttercups in the meadow below, visible from the hut. They seemed to be the outstanding blooms, until the pines overtook them and the taller flowers proliferated – thistles, foxgloves, bellflowers and some of the unbellifer family. These could mostly be seen in the occasional clearing, particularly further down in the mixed wood. One patch of flowers not only shone with colour but also seemed to contain all the wood's insects, including bees and crickets, whose orchestrated sounds mixed with the many flowers and butterflies. It was a pleasant, if noisy, change from the silence of the high rocks of the preceding 7 days.

The walk down didn't take long but, compared to the hike up to the first hut, was naturally more pleasant considering it took little effort going down, but it was also due to the lovely fragrances of the alpine woods and meadows I'd been starved of in the mountains. There were also some superb views through the trees – everyone magnificent, every photograph a masterpiece and equal to (or better than?) those in the tourist brochures! The bright sunshine was a bonus, resulting in as good a day as any to bring a trip to an end – but especially one as enjoyable as this.

No blisters! Maybe I've found the perfect boot at last. I hope so; it's been a long and expensive search. There have been many laughs along the way, plus a few good challenges.

So it's over – and I've been really spoilt and pampered these past few days, living in 5-star luxury, but why not? I deserved it!

Six mountain hikes from around the world

Starkenburger Hutte

Six mountain hikes from around the world

NEW ZEALAND

Lake Sumner and Arthur's pass National Parks

Into natures untouched kingdom

Roughly 1,000 years ago, during a time when Europeans (or Pakeha, as the Maori call us) still thought the earth was flat, Polynesians sailed the Pacific in large, double-hulled canoes – in search of new homes. It was also around this time that a group of these canoes sighted land and what *they* saw, then, was much the same as *I* was to see from the air. 'Aotearoa' – the wonderful natural 'Long White Cloud', from which the Maori name for New Zealand originates. It can still appear over the Southern Alps, even if the Tasman Sea and Canterbury Plain on the East Coast have clear skies. This is due to the maritime climate of this narrow island. It must be seen to be believed. From above it resembled a soft white mattress, resting on top of its peaks. From below, in the valleys, its romance vanished when it emptied its contents on me during the hike!

For some time I had been excited as about this trip as a child anticipating Christmas. Seeing the cloud was like receiving an extended welcome; it sent my excitement into overdrive as I approached a country where 'adventure' is an expected part of life. Adding to the excitement is its striking beauty, which has evolved over thousands of years – aided by its isolation from other land masses. The result is a variety of flora and fauna that exist nowhere else in the world. Nowadays strict Customs Laws help preserve these delicate ecosystems whose presence today must surely be credited to the Maori who, from the outset, treated their new home in the same way as they had done for eons – by using their Tapus to guide them. Tapus, like the laws in Europe, are a whole series of prohibitions; rulings on how they should lead their daily lives, their religious lives and how to respect the earth and all it provides for them. These laws are still used today and, along with a low population, prevent this green land from being spoiled. Maori legends and stories passed down through the years provide a wonderful insight into how the early Polynesians viewed their world.

The Maori believe that life began in utter darkness and nothingness – until the first gods emerged from it. The first were 'Ranginui' (who made the sky) and 'Papa-tu-a-nuku' (the earth). These two were united in the darkness until they bore six children who in themselves represented the earth, sky, flora and fauna. At first Rangi and Papa did not separate; their love for each other was so strong, this prevented anything from living so, after eons of time, the children decided to try separating them. Unfortunately most of them – and the elements they represented – were not strong enough. Eventually it was left to Tane Mahuta who, being the Father of Day (the male element), the Forest and all living things in it, managed to separate his parents. Once separated all was well and the world slowly became the environment we see today. It began with the creation of the New Zealand islands, which contrary to popular belief, did not originate as part of the ancient Gondwanaland and travel to their present position via 'plate tectonics'. They were actually brought about during a fishing trip by a demi-god named 'Maui' (Maker of Mayhem and Mischief), and his brother. One day, whilst fishing, they caught something by using a magic hook and both began pulling in what seemed to be something huge. After some hours' struggling, an enormous fish emerged, which resembled a stretch of green land; its smooth surface was soon carved into the valleys and mountains by the brothers' weapons as they contested ownership. After the fight all that remained was the fish (which today is North Island), the canoe (now South Island) and, lastly, the anchor (Steward Island).

On a bright sunny day over Canterbury Plain I flew into Christchurch on South Island; from there, out of hundreds of hikes available nearby, I had chosen the trail over Harper's Pass – covering, roughly, a distance of 50-60 miles through Lake Sumner and Arthur's Pass Parks. Compared to the 'Great Walks' further south, near the epicentre of all things dangerous and adventurous – Queenstown – it was not a well-known route. But it had isolation, those all-important mountains, non-service huts to stay in and, more important, abundant bush from which I hoped to catch glimpses of the diverse flora and fauna. On completion I'd also see Mt. Cook, used by many climbers as a prelude and practice for climbing Mt. Everest.

There were many other things I would have loved to see and experience during my visit but unlike most other travellers I met, I had only 3 weeks to their 3 to 6 months. One easily envied them; New Zealand offers so much and is not so expensive. But my adventure was a hiker's perfect dream; sometimes easy, sometimes hard, occasionally downright dangerous – but never disappointing.

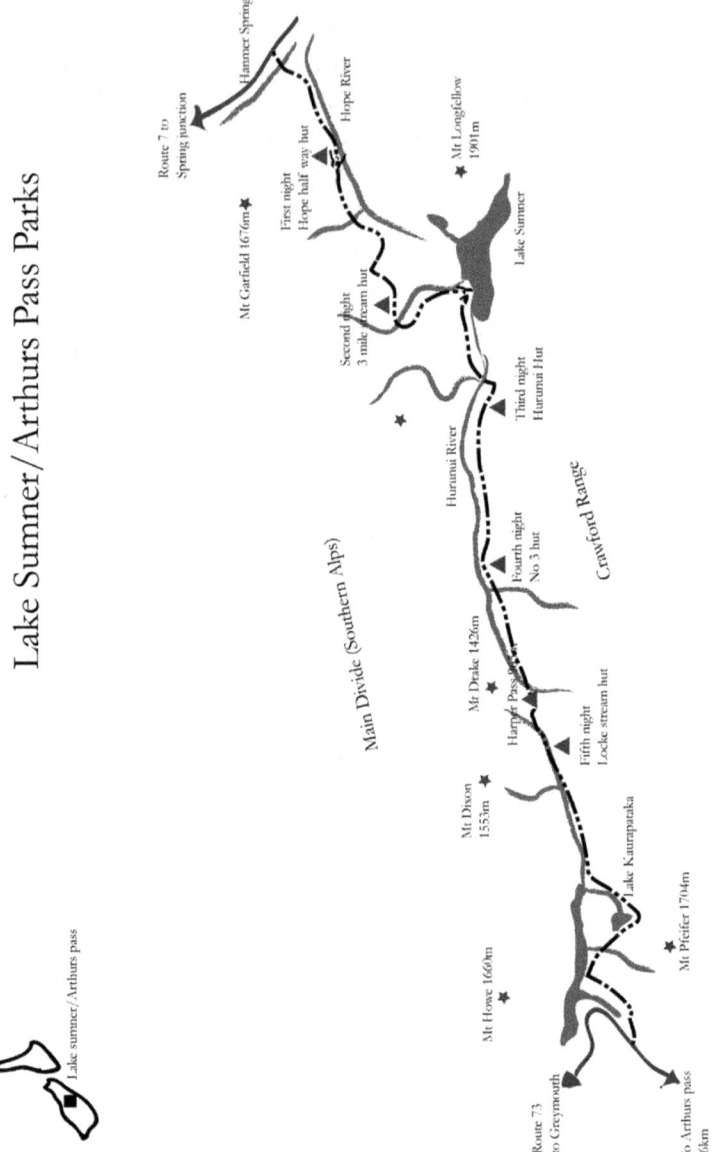

Day 1 Highway 7 [Lewis pass] – Hope Halfway Hut

+100m   7.5km

In Christchurch the sky was clear, the air warm and cool, sweet breeze blew gently on my face, not, however, in the Alps on Highway 7 – where I was dropped off at the beginning of the Harper's Pass hike. On the way over Canterbury Plain it had looked though it might stay clear but, as the road began its climb into the mountains, the lower hills gave way to the peaks of the Alps – and that Long White Cloud appeared. Except that, now, it was blacker than white and the cool breeze turned into a strong, cold wind. That did not stop me, however, from taking my first long look around at the unknown mountains in which I'd be spending the next six unhurried days – alone. My first impression was that the mountains did not appear as high as I thought they would, considering that Garnet Peak (behind me) and Mt. Garfield (in front) were both over 1,000 metres higher than I was. The valley floor was a lot wider than I had expected too, dwarfing the peaks somewhat. Even so, the sight was still all I'd hoped for; mountains, glorious mountains above two wide rivers meeting just below me – the Boyle and the Hope rivers, the latter being the one I would be following up to the first hut. Between the mountains and rivers there was an abundance of green; not surprising considering that the average rainfall in this area is 1,000mm P/A. As I set out I wished that about 999mm of it had already fallen!

Soon much of the surrounding bush was invisible, due to lowering cloud. Suddenly it looked about to teem with rain but being the experienced, fearless and increasingly optimistic hiker, I didn't think it would amount to much and carried on over the undulating trail, past the remotest school building I have ever seen and down towards Boyle River. I remembered to put my name/plans into the 'Intentions Book', positioned at the beginning/end of trails, and in huts. This excellent idea was instigated by the DOC

(Department of Conservation) who also, via the inexpensive annual Hut Passes, maintain the huts, trails and markers. Without these I might have lost my way on certain parts of the route. The last entry before mine, 2 days earlier, was by a group of about 30 Army cadets; somehow I doubted I'd meet them.

Bridge over Boyle river

The Boyle at this point is quite narrow and fast as it cuts its way through a narrow gorge of rock, a very noisy experience after the tranquillity of the valley. Using a swing bridge to cross this part of the river proved exciting as the bridge lived up to its name, tending to swing from side to side. I could also see the river below, surging past rock banks.

Once across I began gaining a little height and my rucksack dug in, finding its position. I was following a dirt trail, cut through the lowland bushes and tussocks bordering its edges. One bush is called Matagouri which, one friendly Kiwi warned me, should not be grabbed – at least until I could see what I was doing. Now seeing it close up I could understand why. The branches looked innocent enough but the needle-sharp spikes on them would be painful if I got any in my hands. Seeing the Matagouri served as a reminder – that I was venturing into a wood similar to those at home but which contained plants unknown to me. Apart from that one warning the Kiwi also told me of two other specific plants to approach with care and respect. The young flax plant, which when fully grown resembles a yucca plant, has very sharp needle-like leaves when young – not very bum-friendly if sat on! The second was a tree-like version of the stinging nettle, whose sting is not as visible but twice as powerful.

Looking towards woods

Most of the plants and trees I was to encounter in the bush had a distinct sub-Antarctic origin, originating from other land masses when they were joined to New Zealand via land bridges millions of years ago. After New Zealand broke away, glacial and geological events caused new species of plants to flourish in the isolation, resulting in the showcase of 'found nowhere else' wonders I was going to see in their own real environment – not in a temperature-controlled room. In England, this was the only way to see some of them.

One of the better-known and unique trees here is the Cabbage tree. The Maori have used it since their arrival for a source of starch and sugar, obtained from its trunk and roots. In a land, which was colder than the warm islands from which they had sailed, they needed cloths – and made them from its leaves. Both Maori and Europeans ate the succulent vegetable from inside the leaves, from which the tree gained its name, but it took the resourcefulness of the missionaries to discover a way of making beer from its roots! Sometimes it seems that if it had not been for the Holy Men, beer would not have been discovered anywhere quite as early as it was. At one time the tree was quite common but, after the Europeans introduced ready-made sugar and took over much of the land for grazing, its numbers soon dwindled. If it had not been for the spiritual significance that the Maori saw in the Cabbage tree, it may have vanished completely. I saw a couple on the way up into the mountains; they looked wonderful, but unfortunately they were not in flower. As well as being told they were beautiful, I learned that if they flower it signals a long, hot summer.

Once I reached the flat it was possible to see the bush (another meaning for Forest) ahead of me; although there was still a light drizzle, the clouds dispersed to reveal the snow-capped summits above and around me. If isolation was my goal then I was going to achieve it – despite constant rain – and it already felt good to be free from the daily hassle of life and demands of others. I don't know why, but I began to feel better hiking alone. As I approached the bush I imagined that the signs of the modern age (the trail, route markers and signposts between huts) didn't exist; that I was the first person to explore the area, similar to the first Maori, who came here to gather food… Or, more recently, a man named Leonard Harper who, in 1857, was the first European to cross the Pass. In a way I was also entering an unexplored area, an area I knew little about and one that had, until now, been a blank spot in my own worldly knowledge.

Cabbage tree

At the edge of the bush a little sign informed me that the Hope Halfway Hut was only 3½ hours away. It being Day 1, I didn't take too much notice of these timings – preferring my own, taken from the map; but I was soon to discover my mistake. Walking in the bush is not as straightforward as it may appear; in fact this first day was full of ups and downs, ins and outs, negotiation of soggy ground and thick, entangled tree roots. I quickly realized that walking in the bush meant a zigzag-style route to the destination, this becoming more apparent in the days ahead. Now I could see little of the trail; spring had been good to the low-growing bushes and they had overgrown it. Their bright green, almost fluorescent leaves resembled millions of tiny upside-down umbrellas – all acting as miniature reservoirs and soaking me the second I touched them. Towering above the bushes were red beech trees, their trunks black from moss, providing an interesting contrast to the low green bushes.

For the majority of this trip I would be travelling through bush like this, through silver and red beeches, cedars and several exotic trees such as Totara – which the Maori used to build their canoes. Also there was the unforgettable Kahikatea, which according to legend, comes from the feathers of a huge bird called 'Tawhaitari'; a chief called 'Pon-ranga-hua' plucked them from it. All these turned what could easily have been just a walk into both an adventure and an unforgettable experience. Some plants were good, some bad; those umbrella plants (as I called them) were one of the most unforgettable. After a while, as I walked further into the bush, they began fading away and the only real difficulty was avoiding the many roots and, at the same time, stay close to the markers. There were hardly any bushes between trees as I progressed and on several occasions I found myself straying from the trail as I listened to the sweet bird songs and tried to catch glimpses of the creatures. Ideally I would have had a better chance had I sat still for a while, but I planned to do so at the hut.

Sometimes I'd be walking near the edge of the bush and catch sight of the Hope River and the snow-covered ridges of Neschacker Hill. It was pleasant to see beyond the bush now and then, not only to confirm that I was going in the right direction but also to see some of the mountains under which I was walking. I'd been in the bush for a while now and felt tired. The wet socks, trousers and jacket I'd acquired from the bushes began to take the edge off the wonder of the place and I began walking faster, keen to get to the hut and, hopefully, warmth. Then I sensed movement ahead of me and, as I moved closer, heard voices. Initially I thought it might be hunters coming out of the bush, not expecting anyone else to be around in this weather. The combination of not really expecting anyone to be around and my being alone in a strange environment, put me on my guard – especially after having read a story about the New Zealand Gold Rush and the men who sometimes used this route to gain access to the Gold Fields further north. The story concerned one of the most notorious gangs – the Burgess-Kelly Gang, well known for their last crime – for which they died. They ambushed four gold miners in the bush, strangling one and shooting the others. They managed to live the high life with their loot for a while, but were eventually caught and hung for what became known as 'The Maungatapu Murders'. The spot where it occurred is now called Murderers' Rock and is between Wakamarina and Nelson, not far from this area as the crow flies. The good point of the story is that it all happened about 100 years ago so I had nothing to worry about now.... The voices came from a group of soldier cadets, in the process of putting up bivvies. From their visible stress levels it was evident it was not going to plan so, after a short greeting, I continued on my way and left them to it!

Hope Halfway Hut

According to the map the trail would emerge from the bush only a short distance from the hut, this pleased me as I neared open ground. But no sooner had I entered the Matagouri bushes again than it quickly became evident that the rain, which hadn't bothered me in the bush, had returned with a vengeance. I returned to the bush and decided to proceed around its edge until I saw the hut. No point in getting another soaking!

Ten minutes later I found Hope Halfway Hut, a one-roomed hut – the lowest grade and simplest hut I would stay in during the trip but, nevertheless, a penthouse suite to me at that moment. Inside it was simply furnished with wooden benches, bunk beds and a small metal sheet on the floor, which from the ash and burnt wood in evidence, was clearly the fireplace. At first it occurred to me that choking smoke might develop from a fire, due to little ventilation, but after considering my wet clothes (dripping on one of the bunks), I changed my mind. But, first, some relaxation time before starting the chores....

Outside the window the view wasn't perfect; clouds down again. But it was peaceful and would have been reasonably quiet but for the pitter-patter of rain on the roof and the cows near the hut chewing the cud. It was disappointing to think that if the rain continued there would be little chance of seeing the stars of the Southern Hemisphere when darkness fell – nor any shooting stars or meteors. Meteors are reported to be quite common in this area; at Dunganville, not far away, one of the heaviest meteors fell. I hoped a similar one wouldn't fall on me – at least not until I'd had my dinner!

Apart from the land I'd been walking on, it seemed there was something else I had to thank the demi-god Maui for – the power to create fire. Long ago the gods were the only ones capable of making fire, until Maui decided this should change. 'Mahuika' (Maui's grandmother) was the Goddess of Fire and her nails held the power of fire; Maui planned to trick these away from her. He nearly succeeded but, just as he was about to take the last one, she saw what he was doing and used her last nail to set the earth alight. After the flames had subsided she realised she had lost all her powers with that one act but she managed to hide a few remaining embers within various trees; these I could now use to make a small fire. Luckily the room did not fill up with as much smoke as I expected and it warmed up the hut perfectly.

Day 2   Hope Half way hut – Three Mile Stream Hut

+230m   -120m   14km

Cold, wet and soggy clothes can't compete with a warm shower as a pleasant way to wake up. So no way was I putting them on, which will probably surprise those who thought mountain hikers laughed at discomfort. Not me! Instead I used my gas to warm my cloths up. My feet and rear end are far too sensitive to bear wet socks and at least they might stay dry for a while. The day looked brighter and drier and, from the varied bird song, word of my arrival was getting round; it was pleasant to watch them stretching their wings as I ate my breakfast.

From the hut the trail took me down to the narrow, swampy bank of the Hope River. It was high and flowing fast and, if it had not been for an earlier bank slide, I would have had to climb back up into the bush to get along it. Looking at the river, it was amazing to consider that in drier conditions it can drop low enough to walk across – but that's in January, not December (when most of that 1000mm annual rain fall arrives). From the river bank the trail went into the bush for a while, then out on to a wide, flat and grassy bank covered with Matagouri bushes. The bank was a welcome change from the exposed roots and puddles of the bush, with superb views of the mountains either side of the valley and also the birds, which until now, I'd heard but not seen.

Spooky bush

From here it didn't seem to take long to reach the hut where I planned to have dinner – across one wider river via an even higher bridge than before. Then into the bush and, lastly, over a few moraines which not only revealed the width of the valley bottom but also the Kiwi Hope Lodge and one more difficult river crossing before I reached what must be the supreme hut in this area. I would have loved to stay overnight but – surprise, surprise – the remainder of the cadets were camping there. Bivvies surrounded the hut's perimeter fence and, inside, it was even more crowded; equipment and clothes draped everywhere. It resembled a sauna, with moisture from the clothes hanging in the air. The heat was produced in this hut from an old iron wood stove which, I was told, would be the same in most of the other huts; also for the water, which comes from large tanks of collected rain water. That pleased me as last night I'd had to collect it from a stream and I might have contracted Giardia from it had I not sterilized it enough.

The Maori I met there were very friendly, cheerful and extremely curious about Europe (and me) in general – so much so that I never really got a chance to ask them anything. The hour I'd allowed for dinner passed so quickly and I had to leave my new friends for the second part of the hike; this would be entirely in the bush, except for a few small clearings. Navigation would be more difficult as I wouldn't be able to see the usual landmarks; this time it would all depend on the compass and, maybe, the triangle markers that had guided me thus far – although this trail is classed as 'unmarked'.

Until now the bush had resembled the woods or forests of England; an assortment of different trees with low-lying foliage, along with many bare roots on an extremely marshy forest floor (due mostly to the high rainfall). But as the trail I'd been walking up for an hour began to level out, all this changed, as did the availability of markers on it. The bush floor appeared swampier and the trail was almost a stream. Now mountain beeches joined red beeches, cedars, firs and a strange looking tree whose bark seemed to spiral upwards. If I hadn't known otherwise I might have thought it had grown that way because a god had twisted it occasionally as it grew. But you never know....

The clearings presented a chance to check my position, using the few mountains I could see, though they all looked alike after a while. Matagouri bushes covered the clearings but were now covered in some woolly-like material that – along with the silence – made the place slightly spooky. The grass in the clearings concealed a little surprise – more swamps – and if the bush around the clearing had not been so dense I would have detoured. A few planks, clumps of grass and branches helped to keep my feet somewhat dry, but by the time I'd got to the second clearing I walked straight across – my feet were soaked anyway.

At the end of the clearing I decided to have a short rest before tackling the river, which I could hear. I'd left some tea in my flask and it was good to sit in the surrounding silence bathed in a rare beam of sunlight. No bird song, animal sounds or annoying sand flies stirred in this oddly windless place. In moments like these, when people are completely alone and slightly tired, they tend to spot unusual – or even unbelievable – things. This could well include a lucky glimpse of the Patupaiarehe –tall, white-skinned fairies – but considering they cannot exist in sunlight, unlikely. A young Maori chef, Kahukura, once used this fact to his advantage. There came a time when food was scarce in his village; this troubled him deeply and he had a dream in which he was told to go to a distant beach, called Rangiaowhia. He had no idea what he would find there but couldn't forget the dream so, eventually, made the journey. After a long time he arrived at the beach and laid down to sleep. When he awoke it was night and he was lying near a group of fairies that were fishing in the sea. Usually the Maori used a spear to catch their fish but these fairies were using something that was catching many more fish. Kahukura didn't know what it was but realised he needed to get one; slowly he moved closer to them and waited for sunrise; on their departure he took one of the things they used to catch their fish. In daylight he learned how to use this new fish-catcher and called it a net – with which his people soon used to fill their empty stomachs.

The remaining few miles to the hut were the most annoying; I had to back-trail a few times as I tried finding the markers (there was now quite a large interval between them). Many fallen trees hid both them and the trail; there were endless river crossings, including a thrilling 20M walk along two single stretches of rope wire (one for the feet and one at waist level). More than once I ended up horizontal rather than vertical. I suspected the cadets would have loved it but, about halfway over after almost dunking in the water, my views of it were somewhat unprintable!

Eventually, after a few hours and diminishing patience, the markers and trail had virtually vanished. At first I felt like striking out on my own bearing, as I knew, roughly, where I was in the bush. I decided that might not be wise, however, and reconsidered. Then, luckily, I stumbled on a marker and found the trail down to the Three-Mile Stream – 4 hours after leaving Kiwi Hut. The relief was immeasurable and the views, clear of trees, amazing. At this point the bush on either side of the river bed was close but further up, opened to reveal a summit of the Nelson tops; these I saw intermittently as the cloud drifted.

I had to follow Three-Mile Stream for a while, until I found the hut – set back in the bush. It looked old, but in better condition than last night's and it had an iron stove. Before I could feel real warmth again, I must cross the Three-Mile Stream, which in drier climates may resemble a stream. But today it was as fast flowing and wide as most of the others I'd encountered. I began looking for good places to cross but the last four hours in the bush had made me tired and rather impatient so, forgetting all the warnings, I strolled straight across it near the hut. I got a soaking and was nearly dragged under but what the hell? Fifteen minutes later I was in dry cloths, sitting by a warm fire, sipping cool mountain water – and lying on the most comfortable mattress I'd ever seen!

I would sleep well, warm and comfortable. Only one thing might disturb me (apart from wild beasts which may live, undiscovered, in the bush) – an earthquake; I was told they occur quite frequently in the area. I had to hope I'd not annoyed the god 'Ruaumoko' who, being the youngest of the six children of Papa, was still on her breast when she was torn from her husband. In order to stop the parents from joining up again, the other five children turned Papa over on to her front, thus trapping Ruaumoko underneath her, deep within the ground. It is his movements that now cause earthquakes and volcanoes to erupt.

Normally I wouldn't pay any attention to earthquakes. When you're having a good time you tend not to think of unpleasant things; but this time I really had to consider the possibility. I was only 20 miles away from the Alpine Fault in the east; this consists of two continental plates (the Indian and the Pacific), which move against each other in a sideswiping movement. This action is known to produce local rapid mountain building of between 6-10m per year. So far, apparently, 18 Km of uplift has occurred. Mother Nature's acts of erosion have certainly been over-active here to keep the mountains low plus, in the process, she has helped to create Canterbury Plain (which consists mainly of mountain debris). The last earthquakes to occur in Arthur's Pass certainly helped Mother Nature a little. It occurred in 1929, recording 6.3 on the Richter scale and causing the aptly named Mt. Collapse to shed 90 million tons of debris down into the Otehake River. That was something I didn't want Mt. MacKnob (positioned just behind me) to do, not now I'd found such a comfortable and warm spot on the mattress!

Day 3 Three Mile Hut – Hurunui Hut

+80m -250m 15km

What a grand, warm and sunny day greeted me! The birds were singing as sweetly as if part of a concerto, the insects busily went about their day and the majestic deer frolicked on the river bank! I'm sure if I hadn't been dreaming I would have woken up to a perfect day. In *reality* it was still raining… Slightly misty (said to be the sighs of Papa longing for her husband) and COLD. Soon the fire was alight and, slowly, I was again surrounded with warmth.

Long swing bridge over Huruni river

While drinking my tea I looked into the Intentions Book, hoping to learn something about the place. Not surprisingly many hunters had stayed in this hut – evident by the amount of empty whiskey bottles lying around it and the fact that there is a hunting area not far away. The mammals they hunt are, mostly, red deer, chamois and pigs. All these animals were first introduced on to the Islands by European settlers and were initially hunted to help reduce numbers. Nowadays they are hunted for sport, which doesn't always involve stalking and shooting as part of the act; helicopters may also be used, mounted with guns that eject nets to capture their prizes. One would think the noise of the rotors might make that very difficult but I suppose they wouldn't be used if it didn't work.

From the hut I could take two routes around MacKnob to the Hurunui Valley. The one to the left was shorter but meant I would not see Lake Sumner, which I wanted to see, and would if I took the longer route. The only disadvantage in taking the route to the right, apart from it being longer, was that it would involve another river crossing – an unavoidable obstacle in these mountains. The general direction of the longer route was easy to follow, along the edge of Three Mile Stream; I followed it until forced up into the bush by steep sides.

All along the riverbank I saw Flax plants, widely used by the Maori to make, among other things, clothes. They treated this plant with reverence, especially at harvest time. Mostly used were the plants' long, fibrous leaves, which after they were scraped and dried, could be woven into flexible, hard-wearing clothes. The skills required to do this are still practiced today and sometimes I wish I'd learnt similar skills when younger. Then perhaps, when venturing into a wood or forest like this one, I'd be able to see more than just exposed roots, trees and light green moss-covered boulders....

I hadn't found the entrance to the trail from the river bank and was now scrambling up over an excellent example of mossy boulders. My plan was to find the trail – which had to be somewhere – by climbing up MacKnob for a while and then walking along keeping to the gradient; there, technically, I should discover the trail. To my amazement it worked! If the entrance to it wasn't marked *then* it was now – amidst a floor of bright green moss that covered everything. I couldn't miss the dark brown of the trail winding slowly up the hill and from there on till Lake Sumner it was plain sailing – very useful in catching up on time lost trying to find the damned thing.

Coming from a country where the habit of summit bagging is the norm, I was constantly tempted to do that here. I suspected that if there had been little cloud then the gallant ridge-walker would have seen some spectacular views – if, of course, he could make it up through the dense bush first. I can now safely say that it wouldn't be an easy task but, with all the different valleys in the area and multiplicity of routes over the passes, there are still many great hidden views – just like the one I encountered on the shore of Lake Sumner at Charley's Point. From there I had a full 180-degree panoramic view of its stormy waters and mountains, including Mt. Longfellow, which at 1901M topped the bill as the tallest. Its steep sides dived into the lake, as did the other lower mountains around it, giving the northern end of the lake a look similar to that found at Milford Sound – completely opposite to the low mountains and wide river bank going up the Hurunui Valley to the south. The whole place felt very peaceful even though rain still hit the surface of this glacier-born lake, but it did not bother the ducks and geese – nor diminish my delight at finally seeing the lake for which I had come so far.

A good romantic Maori story is set on a lake similar to this one. It concerns a forbidden love affair between a chief's son and the neighbouring chief's daughter. On special occasions the two tribes would meet and, during one of these gatherings, the two lovers ('Tutanekai' and 'Hinemoa') first saw each other and fell in love. Both would probably have stayed with each other from that moment but Hinemoa's father had other plans for his daughter; so they had to part.

In time their love for each other grew and, even though not allowed to meet, both knew their love was undiminished. Most nights Tutanekai demonstrated his love by playing his flute by the lake that separated the two tribes, hoping it's sweet notes were carried across the water to his love. Unknown to him, they affected Hinemoa so much that one cold night she decided to swim across the lake, knowing that if she swam towards the flute she would soon be in her lover's arms. She reached the shore but could neither see nor hear Tutanekai, so thought there was no hope and she slowly froze. But of course she was found and, when her father heard about the risk she had taken to be with Tutanekai, he blessed their union and they lived happily ever after. Just as all good love stories should end....

At the time a little romance complemented the views but those thoughts rapidly disappeared once I was back on the trail. Since Day 1 I'd quickly come to appreciate just how affected the ground was by the amount of rainfall in the area. Trails do not necessarily follow the route shown on the map nor, for that matter, do they actually exist anymore – due to erosion along the river bank. My first experience of this, along with another encounter with the cadets, happened on the flats of the Hurunui River, where flooding from the river had all but covered the trail. This forced me to make my way up through the dense bush, made more awkward by my sack catching on every stray branch. When I reached level ground the bush thinned out and I was left surrounded by tall red beech – a short lived pleasure as I encountered yet another obstacle. This became one of the more interesting obstacles on the trip and naturally involved a river crossing – except that *this* river was 30ft below me, with steep sides. At first I didn't even consider a tree trunk that spanned the void near me but, after a quick look up the river, it seemed the only way.

I'll always remember thinking, as I took the first few steps along the 20ft span of trunk, how glad I was to be insured to the hilt and that, if anything *did* happen, at least the cadets might find me quickly. Little comfort to my wife, however, who would kill me anyway if she knew what I was doing!

There were a few hairy unbalanced moments on the crossing but I made it. I continued down to the flats again, where the river had snaked over to the other side of the valley and left me an easy walk. Mountain views would have been impressive had dense clouds and rain continued to obscured them. My only consolation was being in the bush again shortly, after I'd crossed the river via the most impressive wire bridge I'd seen thus far. With a span of over 50ft it was a revelation, especially considering that the wide, fast river just below was in spate and eager to whisk me away if I lost concentration.

On the opposite bank were two trails I could follow. The left lead towards dirt tracks and the way out; the right to the pass and deeper into the wilderness. I was going right and, according to the sign, was only 30 minutes from the next hut (aptly named Hurunui Hut). I'd taken 8 hours to reach this point.

High to my left lay the Crawford range, a line of peaks between 1600-1700m; these I would follow right up to the pass. These sandstone peaks, like most on my route, have evolved over millions of years, resulting from many collisions of volcanic rock and sediment from the time when New Zealand was still part of Gondwanaland. Since this massive rock split from the ancient continent, a great rift – the Alpine fault to the west - has caused most of the changes; the rift's uplifting movement (most of which occurs on this side) continues to alter the appearance of the mountains and indeed New Zealand as a whole. Towards the end of my walk I would not be far from the fault, walking on the harder rocks of Hasst shist and granite created by the increased pressure (and subsequent metamorphisation) of existing rock near to the stress zone.

Rapid uplift has overtaken the speed of erosion since the last glaciers, changing the character of some valleys I would see later in the Otira Valley towards Arthur's Pass. This valley, not the normal U-shape, resembles a deep gorge with very steep sides, this being mostly due to the harder rock found there. In time the Hurunui Valley may look similar, due to a smaller fault line (Hope fault line) running along its bottom to the Alpine fault. Who knows, perhaps one day the mountains surrounding me would rise even above Mt Cook – in geological time scales anything can happen.

I reached the rather cold, open Hurunui Hut in 30 minutes. The fire had apparently been removed for repairs and I sat on a long bench, freezing in my dry clothes. Last night I'd stayed in a hut just right for one, but this one was meant for a crowd. I felt small and lonely in my isolation, even taking out family photos to cheer me up. Already weak from an exhausting three days, my feet were sore and wrinkled from constant soakings. If I'd known about New Zealand's one very poisonous spider (the Katipo) it might have made me feel even worse – and stopped me walking anywhere barefoot. As it was, I simply felt miserable. After some high-energy drinks I warmed up, felt better and, in the coming days, placed plastic bags over my feet to keep them drier. Soon after my arrival a welcome platoon of cadets took refuge from the raging storm and the cheerless hut was transformed by warmth and noise. Company for the night and their offer of a dinner of eggs, bacon and Coca Cola was a great uplift. Most of the cadets had nothing to do with the Armed Forces but were out in the field for a week (with a few full-time soldiers) on an exercise – part of a longer, back-to-work programme.

Day 4   Hurunui hut – Number 3 hut

+120m   -50m   9km

Woke at 8.30, an improvement on the 05.00 thus far. First thing I heard (apart from cadets, who had been up for hours) was a raging storm; only later did I fully realize its potential impact on my plans….

Unfortunately most of the walk involved river crossings, pleasant in fine weather; and despite a rather wet trip so far, the rain had presented no problems. Now torrential, it would make most river crossings impossible – but I remained hopeful. One soldier told me that if the rain subsided for a few hours then, technically, all the water should have run off the mountains – leaving the rivers low enough to cross. Normally I'd be anxious to get going but today the storm didn't bother me; I was warm and dry, with the Maori for company. For the moment, anyhow.

There is always a reason for most 'natural occurrences'; the storm was no exception. It could be the fault of the maritime climate – or Tawhiri-ma-tea, son of the god Papa. Tawhiri-ma-tea, the god of storms, has been hitting the earth with his force ever since his parents were split – attempting to defeat Tu-mata-uenga, the fierce spirit of man. It felt and sounded as though he was doing his utmost to defeat us; for a while I thought he had. Momentarily he had foiled my plans.

Eventually, not being keen on sitting around, I decided to defy the storm and go on. It had abated and the sky was brighter. Tawhiri-ma-tea had, for the present, run out of breath! It was hard to leave the new friends I'd been privileged to meet – here, rather than in a tourist spot. The encounter had been accidental, the fun spontaneous, with food and friendship readily shared. Now we must go our separate ways. We wouldn't meet again; they were going home, I further into the unknown. Although I had talked to these Maoris I felt I would never know this island and its beauty as they do. Wherever I go I am always just a visitor, yet long to be more.

The heavy rain had waterlogged all the trails but, as I left, the sun came out briefly and rising clouds revealed the mountains towards Lake Sumner. It didn't last and soon the drizzle returned, leaving me to walk through puddles that soaked my (no longer waterproof) boots, but I didn't have far to go. Due to the delay I wouldn't reach the planned hut, settling for one nearer – my original destination for dinner.

I reached Hut Number 3 in less than 3 hours, despite losing time navigating the wet, swampy areas covering the wide green flats of the valley floor – plus a few cows that took a shine to my bright red jacket! If the weather had been better this valley would have been ideal for resting and surveying the landscape. I had fine views into the bush, the valley and the mountains and might have spotted some unique native birds; these have flourished, due to the lack of 4-legged mammals. I'd really hoped to see the flightless kiwi, or the bigger and more colourful takahe, the latter thought to be extinct until a colony was found near Lake Te Anau. Another bird I'd hoped to see was the only true alpine parrot – the mischievous kea – reputedly colourful in looks and character.

There are many more birds I could have seen, some sadly close to extinction; New Zealanders are trying to prevent it. Unfortunately it is too late to rescue the moa; at 12ft tall it was the tallest bird known to Man. Sight of it must have really shocked the Maori! In addition to birds, there are lizards. Legends of giant lizards thrived amongst early Maori and Europeans, i.e. the lizard dragon (taniwha), said to have a giant head and large bat-like wings – not difficult to envisage, with a vivid imagination! Giant skinks and green gecko lizards existed until the recent introduction of predators. One lizard, however, survives – the tuatara; if they could talk, their stories would be amazing. Their ancestors predated the Tyrannosaurus Rex. Thankfully, however, it is wingless, does not breathe fire and is only 2ft long…

Apart from stops to study wild life, it would have been pleasant to use one of the hot springs along the fault lines. One is unique, situated on a slope, where the D.O.C. have kindly built a retaining wall nearby to collect water and the result is a little pool just big enough for two. It felt warm and good, like any hot bath in the middle of nowhere. Try it if the possibility of catching amoebic meningitis from the tiny amoebas reputedly present in the water of hot springs doesn't put you off.

Number 3 hut

Past the hot spring the trail continued, out of the bush and back to the flooded river bank; the only consolation for being wet was the sight of the many rabbits whose homes had been flooded though they were probably used to it. But I had a dry hut to look forward to. In most huts so far there had only been enough dry kindling to make a fire for a few hours but when I reached Number 3 Hut I saw shed-loads of it. If I'd brought fireworks I could have had a

Bonfire Night! This hut, older but similar in size to Hurunui, contained the iron stove and this gave it a more homely feeling than Hurunui; or maybe it was just the heat from the fire and the prospect of drying my clothes.

I was glad, somehow, to be delayed and not walking to the next hut, Cameron's Hut. A soldier had told me it looked more like an old shed than a hut. Tomorrow, along with the Pass and the exotic plants, I would see for myself. If the cloud lifted during my stay up there I'd be a happy man....

After all yesterdays company it felt strange to be alone again; so, as my body relaxed, I reflected on memories. I felt rather low, not helped by fears of having to turn back if it rained heavily all night. On this side of the Pass the trails and the wide river bank were sheltered but, in the next valley (Taramakau) the trail runs virtually alongside the Taramakau river. Its riverbanks are not as wide, therefore if flooded I'd either have to struggle through dense bush on steep slopes – or swim. Neither appealed, especially after hearing about a woman drowning in the river a week earlier. Deep down I knew I'd still go, despite the rain; I'd already had 4 days wet bush-walking in so didn't expect it to be much more different or difficult in the next valley. And, if all hell *did* break loose, I carried a certain little yellow device, which contacted a Rescue beacon using satellites to pinpoint any person's position within 1km. This was the first time I'd brought such a device, previously relying only on a whistle or flares but, mostly, a 'gut feeling' – which, in the past, had made me stop and retrace if conditions worsened. *This* time I had no such feelings.

Day 5 Number 3 hut – number 4 hut

+290m -460m 14km

My clothes had dried during the night, except the boots, but this didn't matter considering the number of rivers yet to cross. The preceding four days had taken their toll of me – my clothes and boots too. I knew I smelled and looked disgusting, unlike those annoyingly smart hikers who look as if they had stepped out of a show room. But there *is* an advantage to being a mess – you don't look out of place among the cow pats! As I set out the sun was up, with little cloud; I tuned my hearing to the bush and picked up birdsong – some new to me. I could now scan scenery looking vibrant after the rain, like a perfect spring day; last night's worries vanished.

From the hut the trail meandered along the riverbank, in and out of the bush. Being muddy and not swampy made staying near it easy. The first crossing I reached was low enough to stone-hop across but as someone had carefully built a wire bridge across, I took that. Soon I reached Cameron's Hut, situated in a large clearing; smaller than most single bedrooms and looking so old that one strong gust would surely blow it over. The soldier hadn't lied. It had an open fire inside; the last occupants had left wood and paper. But rain down the flue above had unfortunately turned all into mush. No chance of a fire there…

About two miles further on the clearings stopped as the valley narrowed and bush took over, so I began the climb to the Pass. The bush so far had consisted mostly of beech but, as I climbed, it changed. The low ferns were striking, with fronds mostly over 1m long. The Maori used these for bedding and their leaf pattern (along with the koru plant) as the basis for their tattoos of spirals and curves. Roots were used for food, the stalks for darts. This fern was the most widespread, along with the taller tree ferns beginning to tower above me at about 800m where the sub-alpine zone began. So I was finally walking amongst trees to the exotic plants I'd been waiting for.

The Hurunui river, which I'd once crossed on a 50ft wire bridge, was narrow enough now to jump over; it was banked on both sides by dense grass hiding many boulders, with intermittent rich bushes of foxglove, snow tussock, daisies and more ferns. Most of these plants exist elsewhere of course but their subtle differences set them apart. There were also some of the weirdest trees I've ever seen. One in particular reminded me of a certain Dr. Seuss story, with its long thin trunk topped off by small bunches of short spikes – the cabbage tree. Sadly I hadn't come during the flowering season, so was probably missing some of the area's most spectacular sights, but it still seemed like Nature had created a wonderfully varied and perfect garden.

Not far into the shrubs was the last place of refuge on this side of the Pass. Classed as a bivvy, it's about the same size as Cameron Hut and an ideal place to sit in and absorb my first real close-ups of the mountain scenery. The slopes now rose steeply on both sides and I was amazed to see the tall trees of the bush still standing on slopes angled between 45 to 50 degrees. There seemed little for them to cling to, standing precariously as if waiting for the next flood to wash them down.

On the last little climb beside the river, the trail and markers were very difficult to follow. Somewhere along the way I lost a marker and had to follow the river. I can say now that this is not advisable as it turns away from Pass and on to its source, banked by large moss-covered boulders with thick shrubs; it's also quite fast-flowing. It occurred to me to return and find the right trail but by then it was too late; I had to follow, or rather scramble, up a smaller stream joining the river from the direction of the Pass. Struggling up until I eventually found the trail again, I managed once more to see the weird and wonderful plants around me.

Near to Harper pass

Despite persistent cloud on the peaks the view at the head of the Pass, down the Taramakau Valley, was fantastic. I could see down its entire length to just before the Kiwi Hut about 12km away. Seeing the valley slowly widen as the river meandered down its course felt strange at the time as, being just below the clouds, I felt suspended under them looking at the earth 500m below.

The fact that this Pass and the route to it are scenic, with plenty to offer the adventurous, has little to do with why it has been marked – but more to do with history. The first people to use the Pass were the Maori, from the Ngai Tahu tribe; originating from the east, they used this valley for its abundance of food – needed during their search for the green stone or 'pounamu'. A semi-precious stone, they used it to make their most prized possessions – i.e. weapons, tools and ornaments. All held great religious significance and honour for the owner, as the green stone was regarded as offspring of one of the gods.

The first Europeans to reach the Pass were in a group led by George Edward Mason; he, after seeing signs of Maori occupation in the area, thought the Pass might provide a route over to the Westland's. He only managed to reach the headwaters of the Tamankau river, however, when bad weather forced them back. Some months later Leonard Harper (namesake of the Pass) and his group completed a trans-alpine crossing of the Pass. Another five years later a packhorse trail was constructed over the Pass and supply stores built. At first these were intended for the earlier pioneers and cattlemen using the Pass but, in 1865, gold was found in New Zealand; the fever that followed brought thousands of prospectors, who used Harper Pass as a route to the west coast gold fields – until the better route over Arthur's Pass was opened. It's said there is still some gold in these mountains and, if I'd had time, it wouldn't have taken much to persuade me to stay in one of the huts and 'pan' for a while – if only to get the price of the airline ticket home! If I'd thought I might find a nugget the same size as 'Honourable Roddy' (said to be worth £450 in 1909), then staying would seem attractive. But I decided to proceed before the idea became *too* attractive.

Many prospectors didn't come out of the gold fields alive, let alone rich. There is the sad tale of the man found by a fellow prospector named Rigney; he, not knowing the dead man's name, marked his gravestone with the words "Somebody's darling lies buried here". Later, when Rigney himself died, he was buried next to the stranger and *his* gravestone marked "Here lies William Rigney, the man who buried somebody's darling". Both stones can be seen 8km downstream of the Clutha Millers Flats.

View from pass south

From the Pass to Number 4 hut there's a 360m drop over 3 miles, which meant a steep walk or run down. For the first half mile the going was easy – only one small trickle of a stream, the beginning of Taramakeu river.

The views were still magnificent and I took many photos of scenery and exotic plants as the trail lead me through the rich flora of a moss-covered forest. There were scattered bands of tree fern, multiples of different shrubs and the tree sting nettles I'd been warned about; on parts of the trail I could grab it to avoid a fall. Eventually I left the sub-tropical zone and returned to the bush, where podocarp, i.e. the red pine (or rimu) and broad-leafed trees dominate the beech. This was a welcome change. What was *not* welcome was the steeply descending trail. Recent rains had turned stretches into pebble-covered streams and I couldn't avoid sliding down. In other places deep trenches had developed where the trail had been washed away and, just when I decided life couldn't get worse, I came to a deep, fast-flowing tributary of the Tarmakau river – and had to immerse myself up to my neck to cross it. So, another soaking – seems if the rain doesn't get you here then the rivers will! After another half hour rushing down in the bush I came to what I hoped was the bottom. The first thing I saw was the now wide-surging Taramakau – with thankfully a bridge to cross it. The trail did then flatten out and I rapidly made my way along it, feeling slightly chastened and very, very wet…

View from porch of Locke Stream Hut

Number 4 Hut, unlike all the others, is built in the bush with only a small clearing the size of an average garden fronting the river. When I thought I must be near, I didn't actually see it until bumping into it! But it was a pleasant hut in an attractive location. Inside was an old, stone-built open fire; when lit it created a pleasant warm atmosphere. It also had an emergency phone in one of the dormitories. What I enjoyed most was the outside verandah under which, even in the rain, I could sit and observe my surroundings – something I hadn't been able to do in the other huts.

Sitting out there reminded me of stories and pictures I'd seen of Victorian adventurers sitting on their verandahs sipping tea and admiring the African scenery. But I was in New Zealand and needed only the bush and mountains to help me unwind after a hard day. At the far end of the clearing the clear, cool water of the river surged quietly over unseen boulders, surrounded by lush bush buzzing with early evening birdsong. In the background the setting sun created colourful patterns on the slowly-moving cloud, revealing the peak of Mt. Dixon – an epilogue to an artist's dream.

Day 6 Number 4 hut – Highway 73[Arthur's pass] and Bealey

+90m   -390m   25km

My last day – and what was to be the longest and hardest day so far. Luckily there had been no rain overnight. I awoke to sunshine reflecting off the dew on the windows, said to be the tears of the pining Rangi for his wife. But even though lack of rain might mean low river levels, I would still have swampy ground left behind to cope with; and my main worry was the big Otehake river. I must cross it to reach the end on time and catch the last bus into Arthur's Pass town.

Initially, the trail was misleading. I walked through a serene forest of cedar and fuchsia, which should have continued for some distance, but, not far into it, the scene changed. I suddenly came face to face with an example of Nature's power – the whole of my side of the river was covered in boulders. They had obviously rolled down the mountain to the river, taking with them all signs of the bush. It was the largest landslide I was to meet; hardly the most dangerous but a good example of what to expect.

For the first few hours I met several more landslides until the valley bottom eventually widened; a few were so steep I had a few heart-stopping moments when the ground beneath me gave way and I almost dropped into the fast-flowing river. As soon as the valley widened I found some level ground to walk on, until the river occasionally swung over during its snaking route down the valley. Then I was forced on to high ground or into the swampy bush again which, compared to the previous day, now looked different from the Hurunui valley. This valley, classed as a rain forest, had ferns all the way whereas I had only discovered them near the Pass in Hurunui. The trees were different; liverworts dominated the grass on the narrower river bank and, if it wasn't for the matagouri bushes, I could have easily thought I was on a completely different island. I still had 16km to cover in less than 6 hours but was thankful for small mercies – the trail was *not* in the river (as the map showed) and it wasn't raining!

As the valley floor widened the walking improved; most previous obstacles could be avoided and I could see further back up the valley and across to the mountains on the opposite side. I was disappointed not to see the Pass but did glimpse a few red admiral and peacock butterflies – beauties I'd not seen since childhood. I began spotting deer trails. For most of the day's walking I hadn't seen any markers so made my own way, following the occasional deer trail I saw, as obviously they would take the easiest route, though I wasn't too hopeful of seeing one. As animal sightings went, I had to be satisfied with an abundance of rabbits, plus birds flying across the valley that I saw here. Perhaps all these were signs that the weather was improving – just my luck when I was about to leave…

One of the few markers I was using to track my time was the Kiwi Hut, on the opposite bank. I passed it right on time and proceeded at full speed to where the Otehake river joined the Taramakau. First thing I saw was the large, wide expanse of the river's mouth between the mountains. I couldn't actually see the river from the bank, only a jumble of rocks and stones on the river bed; my hopes rose that I could cross it. Initially I met several small channels – no problem. Then I saw the main channel and knew my plans were dashed. It was only about 10m wide but, after a few steps into it, the water was up to my waist; the current, along with loose stones underfoot, began dragging me, I looked up and down river for an easier crossing but finally realised I must opt for Plan B – a few more miles in the bush, missing the bus – *and* hoping I'd be able to hitch a lift.

Mt Howe

Plan B took me up river about 3km to a wire bridge. Fine – there was a bank to walk on. But going through the bush was much harder here, much denser along the steep slopes of Mt. Koeti. Just before I saw the bridge the river came out of a narrow gorge and, if I'd not seen the bridge, would probably have missed it and carried on walking, thinking I'd soon have to swing from tree to tree across a vertical cliff! The bridge was about 20m above the river; a distance I thought would keep it well above the water. All this time I'd been walking along the Otehake and thinking its present size/speed were typical of a bad spat, but storm damage on the bridge proved it could get a lot higher.

The trail on the other side of the bridge took me past a lake and around a mountain, then back into the Taramakau valley. There I would revert to my original plan. From there I had to walk over another clearing, again leading to the bush – or thick forest as it happened. Before I could enjoy all the pleasures that would bring, however, I first had to find the trail to the Lake.

Although I didn't want to go this way, I'd originally planned to spend a night in this area – mostly to see the Lake. According to the D.O.C Route Guide, Lake Kaurapataka is a delightful forest-encircled lake, ideal for swimming, lunch stop and/or a night's camping. Its Maori name means 'kau' – to swim, and 'kapkapa' – flapping. So to 'swim with much flapping' refers to the ducks in flight. The rain was torrential when I walked past it and, though I tried, I couldn't imagine relaxing by its shores now. It was impossible to lose sight of the swampy forest I was trying to walk in, surrounding a lake being bombarded by millions of bouncing raindrops. I never thought I'd ever see rain going upwards!

By the time I reached the banks of the Taramakau again (still raining) I'd been walking for about 8 hours; time was no longer an issue so I decided it was time for a rest. Removing the rucksack was a relief, I felt instantly lighter and sitting down was a struggle, but worth the effort. I was relaxed and calm – until a few thousand unwelcome visitors arrived: sandflies, small but very annoying. I knew they'd pay me a visit sometime during the trip and, until now, rain had kept them off but I could have done without them now. The Maori, unsurprisingly, have an old tale about these bloodsuckers, and those other pests, mosquitoes. The god Tu, despite being a god, was bitten by a sandfly. He punished the sandfly, after which they and the mosquitoes formed an alliance in order to inflict as much pain to humans as possible. Therefore sandflies attack in daytime, mosquitoes at night. I thought cigarettes would deter them, as does an open fire, but no – they just kept coming – hungrily sticking their miniature Frankenstein-like jaws into me. After ten minutes I'd had enough and moved on.

The trail, now marked and following the wide, flat banks of the river, was overrun with the spiky thorns of the Matagouri bushes; they not only limited visibility but also hid many grazing cows. During my brief time in the open the views of the surrounding mountains were wonderful; cloud had dispersed at the end of the valley and I had my first real alpine views – the snow-capped summits of Mt. Alexander and Mt. Howe. I hoped the good trail would continue for the last few kilometers to the bridge over the Otira river and the end of my trip; not to be. Instead I met a last-minute setback from the bush – a trek through it on the steep sides above the Otira involving countless ups and downs over fallen trunks, roots, streams and – worst of all – many small landslides. The last stretch took me 2 hours and seemed endless; I kept seeing and hearing cars and trains on the opposite bank and was so relieved to reach the bridge (less than 100m away was Highway 73); there – hopefully – a kind soul would stop and give a very wet, cold hiker a lift to warmth and real food. But, I had two things to do before that. First, take a final look at the bush – my home for the last 6 days. I was still annoyed by the rain and the hardships it caused but knew that the memories of my trip would remain with me forever. Even if Time and Mankind changed it, I had seen some of the wonders Mother Nature can produce in her isolated greenhouse – given the space. Secondly – mundane but important – I must sign the Intentions Book. To write that I was 'going for a pint' seemed apt, at the time. Three months later a

New Zealand friend told me that the summer I'd been there was one of the driest on record... Why did he have to tell me that!

Highway 73 began life, as an old Maori trail then, much later, became a quick route to the coast during the Gold Rush years. Today it's a stretch of black tarmac, picking its way through the narrow, steep sides of a beautiful gorge as it winds up towards Arthur's Pass; there the bends are sharper and higher, the drop a long way down. I was grateful to the driver who stopped and gave me a lift, enduring the resulting smell and wet seat – also for his expertise as he sped along the road (it was somewhat hair-raising!).

Much history surrounds Arthur's Pass and the trails in the surrounding mountains, i.e. Avalanche Peak and Punch Bowl Waterfall. I'd planned to stay in the little town but my driver suggested somewhere further on more suitable to my needs. So we left the town, which had reminded me of old mining towns in California, and reached the Bealey Hotel. He was right – a gorgeous steak, smooth beer, hot shower, soft bed and enjoyable company! After a gruelling 12-hour hike, just what the doctor ordered!

Christchurch

Seeing the mountains fade from view as I travelled back to the city was not as depressing as I'd thought it might be. The thought of seeing Mt. Cook in two day's time, with a couple of relaxing days in Christchurch in between, made up for it.

Christchurch felt like a very proper English town, with its cathedral, statues of famous people and a selection of pretty gardens – hence its name, 'The Garden City'. Punting on the river

Avon (running through the town) did, however, clearly make me regard this town as 'proper'. It occurred to me that it would be something to tell the folks back home about, if I'd punted on both river Avon's but that's where being alone spoils the fun. Those few attractions were, however, where the resemblance to English towns ended. A grid-like system of roads lined with buildings of many different designs reminded me more of towns seen in other parts of the world. It was amazing how much I learnt from the people of many different nationalities staying in my hostel, not only about their journeys around New Zealand but other places too. Everyone was really friendly, the pace of life slow and relaxing. After such an enjoyable walk the last thing I wanted was for my body to be instantly dragged back into the faster pace of life.

Christchurch, not central to the Alps like Queenstown, may not be the hiker's first choice to stay in but, being a city, it has much to offer – especially if time is needed to do some repairs between walks. I didn't but the lounging around in the Hotel's garden, chatting and drinking under the hot sun, was unbeatable. There is also the International Antarctic Centre here, next to the Italian and American Research Centres. The museum is very interesting as is the fact that there are at least 3 flights per week to the bottom of the world. If only I had the money…

New Zealanders have perfected the art of sport. Whilst most Europeans are too busy being 'stressed', Kiwis are too busy having fun. Where else could you do a bungee jump, paraglide off a mountain, have dinner on top of a glacier after a hard morning's skiing, then maybe spend the evening watching All Blacks v England rugby match? During my stay I was lucky enough to see such a match (on TV); the match was in England but it was good to be here on an occasion when England were beating the All Blacks at half-time with a score of 23-6. And this against a team I'd never thought we would have a chance against, a team that performs the dreaded 'haka' and who notched up an incredible 145-17 against the Japanese... (The game ended in a draw).

River Avon in Christchurch

Mt Cook 3754m

Mt. Cook is awesome, a place so great that it has a few names: 'Aorangi' (ao – cloud, rangi – sky: so, cloud in the sky) and 'Kirikiri-katata' (kirikiri – a mass of rock, katata – sharp points: so, a sharp-pointed mass of rocks). Driving up, as I did to the highest ranges of the Southern Alps during a clear, cloudless day one gets the full impact of the mountains even from as far away as 60 kilometers, where all the peaks look like stepping stones leading to the top of Mt. Cook. From Lake Tekapo, only 40km away from the divide, the size and clarity of the snow-capped mountains make a perfect picture as their reflection shimmers on the Lake's calm surface. From then on the mountains increasingly filled my view and made my coach trip a little late, stopping often as we did for photographs.

The Youth Hostel where I stayed was part of a small town situated just under Mt. Cook; from the back patio I had a perfect panoramic view of the surrounding ridges and mountains. Mt. Cook is 16.5km from, and 3000m higher than, the town but to my eyes looked much closer and lower; but if towering, snow-capped mountains have ever surrounded you then you'll understand my misjudgement of distance. I must have appeared stupid, gazing in awe and talking to myself about the clearest and best views I'd ever had of a 'tallest summit'. But sights, indeed moments, like this are rarely seen and felt; and I was determined to make the most of it.

Mt cook and its glacier

John Thomas, the first non-Maori to do so, explored this region in 1857. There was much interest in the area after his visit and soon many climbers arrived. It wasn't until 1882 that the first serious attempt was made on Mt. Cook, however – bad weather turned them back. Many more attempts followed until, on Christmas Day

1894, when 3 New Zealanders (Tom Fyfe, George Graham and Jack Clarke) reached the summit. In true mountaineering style, different routes to the top were then sought and climbed – the last and most hazardous was finally conquered by two Zealanders, Peter Gough and John Glasgow.

Many mountaineers still gather here. For some of them Mt. Cook is used as practice for an ascent of Mt. Everest as its terrain and height are similar. Height gain from base camp to summit of Mt. Cook is also 3000m. Sir Edmund Hillary, also a New Zealander, was the first to conquer Everest, in 1953 – along with Tensing Norgay – but only after he had reached the summit of Mt. Cook via the south ridge, in 1948.

I had no plans for climbing during my visit; lack of experience, and climbers, scotched that. I did, however, have inclinations to scramble up the slopes of Mt. Ollivier (1917m), the first summit that Sir Edmund Hillary climbed here. In such weather the views would have been superb but 'excuses, excuses' – my feet and boots were still recovering from the battering of the hike over Harper's Pass and, though I knew I'd regret the decision once back home, I opted for a relatively low-level walk to the terminal lake of the Hooker Glacier. Better, I decided, than all the other things I could have done – like skiing down the Tasman Glacier (on the other side of the Mt. Cook range) or taking a flight around the range. But, let's face it, you'd rather slog up the side of a hill, wouldn't you…

Mt. Cook town is quite small, compact and very comprehensive considering it operates within a National Park. It has a 'holiday camp' feel and there is even a school for employees' children; it has a large hotel, a few huts for visiting climbers and a pub; I was told there was a Macdonald's too and to look out for the 'Big Mac' – but this was a joke. 'Big Mac' is, in fact, the name of a peak north of Mt. Cook and *not* what I thought so, reluctantly, it was the pub for me. It was however, a good place to dine out and enjoy the highlights of the All Blacks v England rugby match, along with a few other Brits with similar ideas.

It was dark when I returned to the hostel and, for the first time, a cloudless night revealed an array (to me) of alien star formations; all shone very brightly due to very little artificial light. Compared to the Northern Hemisphere's stars, the sky seemed overcrowded but at least the full moon looked the same, adding brilliance to the stars. To the Maori, stars are the sparkling eyes of tiny invisible people and the moon is the god, Maram'a; Maram'a only began to give off his soft grey light when the god Tane asked him to light up the night a little. So when I look up at the moon I am looking for the so-called Man in the Moon. But the Maori look for the Woman in the moon – Rona. She used to live amongst her people until the day she swore at the moon god, calling him a 'Pokokohua' (or cooked head); for that crime the moon forever imprisoned her on the moon....

In the morning it was fine, the bright early sun sparkling off the snow peaks like crystal. I was looking forward to the walk, which would take me to within 9kms of Mt. Cook. The trail began at the top of the town by the hotel and continued through the only small patch of bush on the walk. This time there were no roots or fallen trunks to manoeuvre around; there was one really wide trail, with name markers by each plant. This time the bush was dry and looked much more pleasant. From here the trail continued in an almost straight line towards the first moraine, where a memorial stands to all those who have lost their lives in these mountains whilst pursuing their dreams.

The trail was well trodden all the way up so I spent more time looking around instead of watching my feet, something I constantly had to do during the hike. The snow on the mountain was more detailed now. Large, thick and irregular blankets of snow clung to the mountainsides and, like the trees near Harper's Pass, looked about to fall off at any moment – especially as it was hot down where I was. Further up the trail I heard a tremendous thundering noise to my left; frantically I scanned the blankets of snow above and, thankfully, nothing was racing towards me. I saw nothing move on my side of the range and presumed it came from the other side but, like the people I could see above and below me, stood still and looked around. It was odd how everything went very quiet immediately after the noise.

During my trips into the hills I normally take a few photographs; these usually serve as a record of the route I took. This time I was behaving like the many Japanese in the hostel, shooting from every angle of Mt. Cook! Once into the Alpine meadow I took more, changing position to ensure I included all the different plants – including the famous Mt. Cook lilies, daisies and Spanish Grass.

On reaching Glacier Lake it was still very warm so I decided to rest on a rubble-strewn bank. I felt pretty good – taking in the unobstructed views of Mt. Cook high above me, breathing in cool, sweet air and watching the mini icebergs (as I called them) floating away from the glacier to where the lake overflowed and ran down to the Hoover river. In the heat of the day they seemed out of place but their presence was a reminder of how bad conditions could get in this area. Not today, though; shorts were in order and picnic boxes covered the scree. A day to enjoy and I strongly suspected that the clear views I was enjoying were rare; I wondered just how many people had taken advantage of the weather today, had also taken a photo of the Mt. Cook lily with the summit in the background.

If, by chance, visitors had not come to this area to look at the Alps and their massive, ever-growing glaciers, then they must have come to catch a glimpse of the many birds here – especially that most intelligent, noisy and mischievous of all mountain parrots – the kea. Though I hadn't seen any on the way up, they are reputedly quite common; there is the aptly named Kea Point above Muueller Glacier. This isn't far from Glacier Lake, only 3kms further on from the memorial and, from what I heard, well worth a visit.

When I arrived there I discovered I wasn't actually on Kea Point; constant landslides had ruined that area but the trail ended near the cliff edge in a position where the birds are still said to fly around looking for handouts. It was colder on the exposed ridge, but a few people joined me in the hope of seeing a bird not seen back home. I wanted to take photographs of one but, with my camera, it would have needed to be very close and very still – an unlikely situation when surrounded by people. After 45 fruitless minutes my patience ran out and I returned to town, disappointed

The high Country

I wasn't totally disappointed however. Whilst sitting on the hostel rear patio writing my diary, a robin arrived; it didn't stay long but simply collected as many insects as the cool summer evening provided. I recalled how helpful these birds have been to Man in the past and how legends say they have been rewarded. Even though the European and New Zealand robins are not related, stories of how they obtained their colours are similar. In Europe their red chests came from the blood of Christ when one tried to help him by removing a thorn; in New Zealand they have a snow-white head, received from the demi-god Mau when he was in trouble and one gave him water.

Situated between Mt. Cook and Christchurch is Mackenzie country or 'the High Country'. It is a rich country of low, undulating pine-covered hills and fertile soil; the first recorded person to see all this was Jock Mackenzie, in about 1843. During my visit this wonderful area produced some of the most stunning photographs I have ever taken. When developed they resembled pieces of fine art. A memorable area indeed, in so many ways.

Today Mackenzie's name is legendary; he had the courage to bring 1,000 stolen sheep into this wilderness, accompanied by his dog Friday. Naturally he was caught and ordered to leave the country but after his visit here, it opened up land that had previously been regarded as too hostile to live in. What it must have been like to live in newly discovered areas? A dangerous, uncertain experience, following in the wake of New England colonials, finding new homes – or gold. From what I had seen I reckon that the settlers coming to New Zealand had the better deal – with so much open space to stretch their wings and begin a whole new and exciting life.

Man has not spoiled the South Island of New Zealand too much, as yet. If there is a place that feels like home but still captures the wonderful and exciting potential recognized by the first settlers, then it is here. There is so much more to this amazing country than bush, mountains and adventure sports.

The incredible and amazing sights I saw during my all-too-brief visit were more than enough to seize my imagination and made New Zealand, for me, no longer an unknown place on the other side of the world but a breath-takingly beautiful country – and only a short flight away.

NORWAY

Jotunheimen National Park

Where the giants still reign

Bergen – my gateway to the many mountain ranges of this country. A city whose mixture of medieval and modern buildings, narrow streets and busy harbour reminded me of the town I grew up in – Lyme Regis, in Dorset – except that the coastline and surrounding areas were higher and harsher. Before this trip the only photograph I had seen of Bergen was on a Jigsaw I had as a boy. Seeing it now, for real, I was struck by how much larger and more attractive it looked – especially on a sunny and dry day, rare in Bergen.

Bergen

The scenery matched perfectly the harsh and rugged landscape I associated with the Vikings (Scandinavian for 'people of the bay' or Anglo-Saxon for 'pirates' or 'sea raider'). They called this land home and sailed in their impressive warships across the harsh North Sea to explore the unknown, rather as I was now – except that my visit was not likely to mark its mark on history.

After a few hours in Bergen I too set sail from the harbour en route to a certain National Park within whose boundaries lie the highest mountains in Norway – Jotunheimen – better known as 'The Land of the Giants'. I did not know then that the highest of the high would certainly show me just how harsh they can be, even in July; the trip was one I would almost rather forget – but the lessons learned there will never be.

First, however, came the boat trip down one of the longest fjords – Sognadalfjord; a longer way round to Jotunheimen but scenically preferable and on a comfortable ferry. I had no idea what lay ahead except that tall, steep cliffs would line the channel of sea. Although I had come mainly to walk in the mountains, I also wanted to see the fjords and had formed images of this harsh yet mysterious country; soon, as we progressed down the fjord, my expectations became reality and I was not disappointed.

Leaving Bergen behind we navigated many rocky, costal islands and finally reached the open mouth of Sognadalfjord. At first the mountains didn't seem quite as vertical as I had imagined but this changed rapidly as we edged deeper into the flooded gorge. Wherever the mountains gave away to narrow and small openings near sea level there were towns, at some of which the ferry stopped. The ferry provides not only a passenger service but also delivers supplies and mail. Most of these towns were isolated as they were in the time of the Vikings, separated from one another by mountains and rivers. It was difficult to imagine living in some of them, especially in winter; even the trees growing on the sides of the fjord seemed to be struggling to retain their precarious positions.

Within the fjord

After about two hours the dark clouds, frequent here, moved in overhead and the once-bright fjord rapidly seemed to narrow as its steep sides were overwhelmed by shadows. The high, jagged masses – 1000m guardians – closed in around the deep, cold and unforgiving sea. The ferry felt even smaller as it made its way up the fjord, creeping further into an enticing ice-borne and mysterious trough.

As evening approached, the clouds – after a brief clear spell – closed in, once again blanketing and darkening the mountains and sea. The ferry, now out of the main fjord, was sailing down a narrower fjord en route to Sognadel, my stopover for the night. Halfway down I saw pylon lines crossing high over the fjord, suspended from the mountain tops. I imagined that if anyone used them as a sort of 'death slide', the experience would be thrilling – if not electrifying…

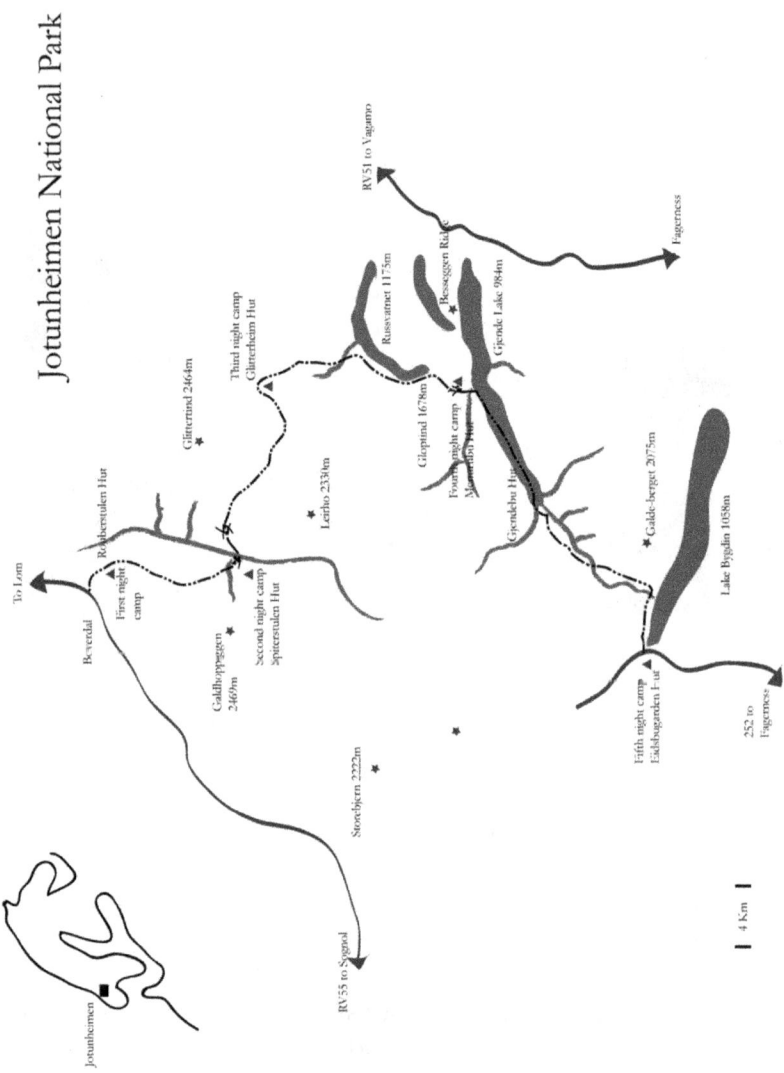

Overall I was pleased to see this place for myself. During the trip down the fjord most passengers had, sensibly, stayed inside. Not me – the little kid on a new adventure had stayed on deck! This was my only chance as I was returning to Bergen by bus and I was determined to see as much as possible, although I was cold and (due to the sea salt) sticky.

Talking of salt, there is a quaint little Norwegian folk tale which explains that burning question – why is there so much salt in the sea? It began long ago, with a small, very special grinding mill; this mill, when asked, would produce endless amounts of whatever a person wished for – until a few secret words stopped it. I can only imagine what people used it for, for you can never have enough of something until it kills you – which explains the mistake one particular man made. He was a sailor and, after an unsuccessful trip across the sea in search of salt, decided to ask the mill for the cargo of salt he needed. It complied and when the ship was nearly full he panicked, realizing he didn't know the magic word to stop the mill. The ship dipped lower and lower into the sea – and sank – taking everybody with it, including the mill, which continues to produce salt to this day. So now you know!

There are many tales of this kind, retold and spread amongst the many small villages in the mountain valleys – proving that, despite their fragile and challenging existence – the native people have a good sense of humour.

The myths and epic tales of the Viking gods appeal to me the most and three main characters stand out from the rest. Firstly Thor – probably the best known – defending the good and slaughtering the bad, aided by his hammer Mjollnir.

Second is Odin, Thor's father – the oldest and therefore the most revered god – who can see and hear everything from his magic chair, Hlidskialf.

Third comes Loki, friend of Thor and Odin, who is technically only half-god, half-human – which probably explains why he is known as The Trickster. Of the nine worlds of the gods, Jotunheimen was one – along with the Tree of Life, called

Yggdrasil – the ash tree (formed from Yggr, a surname of Odin and Drasil, a horse); it kept all the worlds (heaven, earth and hell) together. A 17th century writer called Snorri Sturluson, thankfully, kept all the tales and stories of their adventures alive.

There are many other gods, all of whom resemble the Vikings, strong and warrior-like. The Vikings are also portrayed as ruthless but, after experiencing this country for myself, I would say they needed to be – in order to survive. As in most civilizations, however, they were not only warriors but farmers, traders and craftsmen who all traded with merchants as far afield as Byzantium (later Constantinople, now Istanbul). There were also explorers who sailed the rough seas not only to escape from the overcrowded valleys but also – at one point in history – the rule of Harald Fairhair, Norway's first king. Naturally they also went in search of gold and riches of every kind.

By AD985 Erik the Red had discovered Greenland – so called to attract other settlers. When his son, Lief Eriksson, became a man he too took to the seas and discovered Newfoundland around AD1001, roughly 500 years before Columbus visited the same coastline in 1492 and just when the last colonies of Vikings were leaving Greenland.

After a comfortable night in Sognadel, I traveled on a coach along an ancient trade route between Sognadel and Lom, running along the western side of the park, taking me from alpine meadows onto high mountain glaciers. From sea level the road climbs to 1400m so quickly that it made my ears crack, as they do in an aircraft, but the panoramic views from the large windows were superb. I decided there couldn't be another road in Norway offering so much in its breath-taking ascent of the steep valley sides but I was wrong – the descent surpassed it. Part of my return trip would take me via Ovre Ardel. This small town is virtually surrounded by high cliffs and, as the bus began its descent, I felt I was being driven straight over the cliff into a deep abyss.

The road, following an ancient route, had its fair share of stories. One tells of six men, driven by famine, who set out in the depths of winter over the mountains, only to freeze to death near a stone called Fantesteinen – a common resting place for vagabonds and villains. There is also a hill called Oscarshaug (or Oscar's Hill) although I couldn't find it on my map. It is said that Oscar, brother of Prince Karl VI, had his first sight of the Hurrungane Mountains from this hill. I might have seen this great mountainous mass once the road reached its maximum height had the clouds (or snow) not descended to obliterate the view. In less than an hour I had come up from the colours of the fir trees and mountain meadows to the plateau where colours and views vanished. This was not only due to the cloud but also to snow, lying high above the sides of the road. I wasn't expecting such harsh conditions and, for the first time, wondered what lay ahead, particularly as I would be walking only just below my present height. If I hoped for savage landscape it seemed my hopes would be realised, with weather to match.

Twenty minutes later, the coach having descended into the Boverdalen Valley, I reached the small settlement of Boverdal. Surrounded by woods and meadows, it appeared to be geared up in readiness for the season's expected hordes of tourists. It seemed I was the first.

My final destination was 300m up a track into Jotunheimen, and the Raubergstulen Lodge. Before coming to this region I had anticipated a bus running up to the Lodge – but there was no bus today. The walk up to the Lodge wasn't too difficult; the sun came out as I set off. My pack, loaded with tent and supplies for several days, weighed more with every step. Positive aspects did however counterbalance this subtle introduction to these mountains. Namely the woodland the road winded through – the only woodland I was to see until the end of the trip. I was lucky enough to see a hare on the road, his long ears alert and eyes watching my every move – the first hare I had seen in years.

Eventually, as the road finally levelled, I spotted a cluster of buildings near a small lake. I should have been elated on reaching the start point of my hike but the road had done its usual damage to my feet in the form of two fat blisters. The clear bright views all around soon reminded me of my purpose in coming; painful blisters were forgotten. There was no snow where I stood, at 1000m, but it covered everything else – the steep valley sides, the broad plateau of the Boverdalen Valley behind and Visdalen ahead. Occasionally there was a clear view up the slopes of Glittertind.

The main Lodge was large, with the cosy feel of old-style timber lodge cabins. It was full of skiers using the Summer Ski Centre under Norway's highest summit, Galdhopiggen. Next day I would be trekking its slopes on my way to Spiterstulen in the Visdalen Valley. Several skiers advised me that the snowfall had stopped and a thaw was under way. At the time I was pleased; it meant the snow would melt and temperatures would rise, exposing green colourful meadows and the sounds of migratory birds. I really didn't believe these mountains cause me too much hardship but, unlike other mountain ranges, this one did not intend to reveal its true beauty until I had earned the right. On reflection I should have heeded the warnings and sensed, from my surroundings, that the next few days would be far from easy. But no adventure is exciting without a few unexpected thrills – is it?

Day 1   Raubergstulen – Spiterstulen

+880m   -840m   15km

Norway has a perfect law for those wishing to camp wild. Camping is allowed anywhere, providing you are 150m away from the nearest building and, had I been with a group, I would have taken full advantage of this law. Due to travelling alone I opted to stay near the Lodges, for the company I would meet and – most of all – their very useful kitchens and drying rooms.

My route on Day 1 would take 6 hours including a lunch stop halfway, in Juvasshytta Lodge near the Ski Centre; from there I hoped to see Norway's two highest mountains – Glittertind and Galdhopiggen; whose summits differ by a mere 5m. If the weather was good I planned to walk on up to the summit of Galdhopiggen, an ascent of over 1400m, but one I considered well worth the effort.

From Raubergstulen a road runs all the way up to the Ski Centre so, if the plan was to reach the summit, it might be advisable to follow it and drive up the first 800m – but that meant missing one of the best parts of this walk. It is well known that Jotunheimen is home to some of the highest-growing plants in Norway, plus other species of flora only found in one other country – Canada. Just ten minutes into the walk I reached an area which would have delighted any flora enthusiast, so it seemed only natural to drop my bag and look closer; such opportunities are rare.

Unfortunately there was little in flower as the snow had only recently melted, but great efforts were clearly being made to encourage growth by the collection of as much water as possible as it flowed down the mountain. To my left was the slope I intended to climb, covered in small dense scrubs of willow and dwarf birch; the Vikings used birch bark to write on. The ground was slightly flatter where I stood, damp in places from many streams congregating at this point, an environment ideally suited to heather and the small scrubs dominating the area – cloudberry and creeping azalea – plus isolated, stunted birch trees.

Between this spot and the tree line below was an area of mountain meadows where, according to the locals, the beautiful globe flower, mountain arnica, monkshood and wolfsbane grow. The latter two are poisonous and were used on arrowheads aimed at wolves – hence the name. Above the scrub I would reach the region of the hardiest plants – a mixture of European and Canadian alpine plants said to have survived here, on top of the highest mountains, since the Ice Age. Alpine rock cress and Alpine catchly, along with purple saxifrage, rocky campion and mountain aven (once known as the blessed herb for its magical powers) grow here. The highest flowering plant grows 100m below Glittertind – the glacier crowfoot. It is said to be especially beautiful on a clear day, with its mountainous backdrop and I kept a sharp lookout but, due to low cloud and lingering snow, there seemed little chance of seeing it.

One plant I was very keen to see was the cloudberry. Norway has many other berry scrubs but this one has a mythical background. A favourite with the trolls, they used it to make porridge. These ugly, misshapen creatures were artistic enough to have created Odin's spear and Thor's hammer yet cruel enough to steal children and women. They avoided humans, specially in daylight, when legend said the sun would turn them to stone. If unlucky enough to wander into their domain you might see one or three, as the case may be, as in the story of two boys who met three trolls on their way to Hedal in southern Jotunheimen. The trolls, despite being handicapped by having only one eye between them, succeeded in scaring the boys by shaking the earth beneath them as they approached. The boys, however, were not stupid and managed by a clever trick to secure the eye, thereby reversing the situation. The trolls were the losers for, instead of enjoying a tasty meal, had to give the boys a share of the gold that trolls reputedly hoard. I hoped I wouldn't bump into those trolls – they might still be looking for revenge.

Trolls were far from my mind, however, as I began climbing up through the scrub – a much harder climb than anticipated. I have learned from experience that even if a map indicates a good track, it doesn't necessarily mean it exists – and this one was an example.

The ground was quite mossy and soggy, with a maze of avenues through the scrub to choose from.

Catching sight of the occasional car on the road didn't help but, due to my preoccupation with the dense scrub, I hadn't realised the weather was closing in – a potential danger. Even when I reached level ground and scrub gave way to moss and lichens on bare rock I still failed to notice, because I had suddenly found a colourful sight amongst the grey of the mountains – a mountain aven plant. They were smaller than I expected, with an ingenious way of ensuring that a few insects venturing this high do visit them. They do so by reflecting and concentrating heat from the sun's rays between their petals, giving insects a small patch of warmth whilst helping to pollinate the plant. Warmth makes flowers – very clever!

The track meandered ahead between two small hills and at this point I finally reached the clouds and the snow line at 1450m. Visibility was reasonable, I could see the next cairn and the snow was initially sparse but firm. As I gained height the snow cover increases and icy rain tore at my waterproofs. The wind's increasing speed and strength didn't help and it was hard to believe that just 30 minutes earlier I had been admiring stunning views down the Boverdalen Valley in sunshine. Now everything was obscured, I was wet through and feeling cold despite walking. Then, for a second, I saw something that made me forget my problems – gold – and, being on Feldspar it *could* have been, considering the two are said to go together like coffee and cream. Unfortunately it was just another lichen but its radiant colour amid the black and white was welcome.

At about 1800m I saw the sign for the Lodge and knew I was close. Visibility had deteriorated and I was saturated; the gentle slope offered little shelter but at least the snow was firm. It was still quite deep, occasionally I fell into it up to my thighs but the snow cover increased as I climbed and I progressed towards the

Lodge more quickly. Shortly after reaching 1835m I saw the Lodge looming out of the blizzard – a golden palace of salvation. Inside, the warmth hit me first, like opening a hot oven. To those cosily settled inside I probably resembled a sorry poodle after a walk in the rain – and felt like one!

Of all my planned walks in Jotunheimen this was the only one with a Lodge halfway; for the rest I must rely on good weather or my own shelter. From the conditions experienced thus far and the state of the ground covered, I would probably use the latter. I hoped the mountains might take pity on me as the first–aid applied to my blisters hadn't worked and even my waterproofs were soaked. I *wanted* to shout at the mountains that enough was enough and from then on I expected warmer temperatures similar to those found in an oven, not a freezer but doubted shouting would have achieved anything....

Raubergstulen

My Lodge companions began preparations for a trek to the summit of Galdhopiggen. I thought they were mad, in such weather – what would they achieve? If there was no snow they might see boulders and lichens, but little else. At roughly 600m higher the weather would be much worse and I wondered whether the fellow wearing jeans realised that. *His* trip would not easily be forgotten – similar to that which Thor and Loki took with their servants to visit the King of the Giants, Utgard-Loki.

On arrival, instead of being honoured, they were asked to show respect to the King before being allowed to stay. This 'respect' took the form of various challenges, which enraged Thor and Loki. Loki lost the first challenge, an eating contest. Next, Thor's servant lost a race against a giant called Logi. Thor's turn came and, reputedly undefeated, he expected to win his challenges – but he lost a drinking contest. This angered him but he became further enraged by losing the next contest, against an old woman who defeated him in a test of strength. By this time Thor and Loki, stunned and ashamed, left the King's domain. Later the King met them on their way home, explained he had played tricks on them as revenge for a bad deed they had done him, and they felt better. It transpired that the giants they were matched against were not all they seemed. Loki had been competing against fire, whose hunger never ceases; the servant had raced against Thought itself, whilst Thor had drunk from a horn connected to the sea, which could never be emptied. The old woman was Old Age itself which of course even Norse gods could not defeat. After learning against whom they had been matched, Thor and Loki returned home, feeling they had done very well against such impossible odds. But they had learned their lesson – and neither forgot the experience nor mistreated the giants again.

Just after leaving the Lodge I realized I would not forget this day either and wondered if someone was trying to teach *me* a lesson. I was between two well-used Lodges in a virtual white-out, with everything blocked just 2m ahead of me. Every step in the soft snow drained my energy and the rain added to my discomfort. Lack of visibility prevented any sight of cairns and I resorted to the compass. Later I learned that this can be risky in Jotunheimen, due to a mineral in the surrounding gneiss which affects and distorts compass readings. Not knowing this at the time, I was unaware how lucky I was to reach my destination. The flat ground began to dip down into the Visdalen Valley and there I not only found the track again but, thankfully, gained shelter from the wind and rain.

After a few more metres' descent out of the cloud I finally made it to shelter, with soggy feet and frozen trousers. Now I could see the mountains towering above the valley floor far below, which should have cheered me, but I was too overwhelmed with relief at reaching safety. The distance from the Lodge had been short but the weather atrocious. Sometimes, it's said, a dose of horrendous weather is good for the character. I tried to regard this weather as good for the soul but simply couldn't agree with McCarthy, one of Shackleton's crew. During their journey back to safety he described such conditions as 'a grand day'.

I soon found the main track and followed it across the face of the valley's wall, over large boulders and a river roaring down in full spate from the Styggebreen Glacier. I crossed it using the snow bridges, still quite firm in places. Not until the track became steeper did I appreciate the depth of the valley floor. I could see the tiny collection of buildings making up Spiterstulen, seemingly surrounded by vertical mountains. To the left of Spiterstulen was the entrance to a hanging valley, the first place I had seen once out of the clouds and my destination for the following day. On first sight I thought it was the top of the mountains but then, without the obscuring cloud, could see higher summits on either side of the valley's entrance towering above me; their immense size adding to the depth and volume of the valley. Behind Spiterstulen, 1000m higher than the Lodges, rose Mt. Skautho, its summit still in cloud and this added to the illusion of walking down into a huge cavern. The glaciers of the past had done wonders for this valley, some of them could still be seen further up. Here I kept my eyes on the steep vertical sides and the magnificent waterfall from Mt. Skautho; it brought life to the river Visa along the valley floor and to its plant life. The panorama was vast, its atmosphere wild and untamed.

Spiterstulen

The walk down to Spiterstulen should be taken cautiously, especially when wet. The combination of mud/scree proved very slippery, I was sliding even when standing still. Near the bottom of the slope I came upon thickets of small birch and willow, where I would camp overnight. I found a sheltered position near a small cabin with stoves – for cooking and warmth – but before I unpacked I paid a quick visit to the main Lodge.

Like most Lodges in the park, this one could best be described as a haven in the wilderness – with the services of both hotel and café in one. It had a large log fire and comfortable chairs perfect to relax in, sip a beer and discuss the day's adventures. I was *almost* tempted to book in and enjoy a comfortable bed, but resisted. The Lodge also had a good 3-D model of the Park, very useful, as was the drying room. The latter must become more than a little 'high' when the Lodge is full!

After collecting my semi-dry clothes and boots I returned to my less attractive accommodation for the night. It was still raining and I felt the rigours of the day overtaking me. Still overwhelmed by the day's sights and appalling weather, I was having difficulty imagining how both could improve in the days ahead, but remained hopeful. Alone in the cabin, still damp and listening to the rain, I felt that if the weather didn't improve I could easily resort to sulking, crying or even stamping my feet. Such measures of relief had always worked in the past but, failing them, I could use 'The Look'; but if Mother Nature was like other women then her answering 'Look' would be infinitely worse than anything *I* could produce!…

Day 2   Spiterstulen – Glitterheim

+680m   -300m   20km

I awoke to birds singing, a gentle breeze and no rain – my spirits lifted immediately! Not quite so reassuring, was the cloud – lots of it, obscuring the best views. But the day was young, it might clear up; I was hopeful.

New arrivals had appeared around the kitchen building during the night; tents dotted about gave the vicinity the appearance of an international anthill convention. Some had arrived the preceding day by heated coach, heading for the welcoming comforts of the Lodge; its luxurious conditions were an ironic contrast to the stark emptiness of the surrounding wilderness.

Before the mid-19th century the Lodge was a 'seter', or farm; agriculture and hunting were the main occupations, as they had been for the preceding 5,000 years. Around 1836 tourists discovered this area, coming to enjoy walking and the beautiful landscape – *and* they were willing to pay for the privilege. The owners of the seter naturally decided to take advantage of this and promptly built accommodation. Now the descendants of those astute farmers own one of the largest Lodges in Jotunheimen. It is well located, just below the two highest peaks in Norway and close to some early settlement sites. One site is in the high valley I had seen the previous day, on the route to the next Lodge – Glitterheim, situated under Glittertind. According to the guide this was only 5 hours away, involving a mere 650m ascent, so I hoped for an easier day. Surely it couldn't be any harder? Oh me of little faith!...

The day began with a steep but relatively easy climb up to the hanging valley. Stepping-stones helped and these, along with fine views up and down the Visdalen Valley made the climb not too much of an early morning shock to the system. At the top I looked for the primitive reindeer traps I'd been told could be found but didn't see any; no point in searching for deep, wide pits when there was such wonderful scenery to admire as I progressed up the valley, improving with every step. The length and width of the valley gave the impression of a huge space, emphasized by the cloud cover resting on the peaks. It meant I could not see Glittertind but the illusion of vastness was overwhelming.

The track was clearly marked by cairns or boulders, with the typical red 'T' mark found on all the tracks in this region. Soon the track split in two; one lead up to Glittertind and I took the other. With hindsight I wished I'd taken the Glittertind track – not to climb the mountain but to take advantage of the easier river crossing on that route. On *my* chosen track I would cross the river Skauta much further up, where it was in full spate from melting snow. I don't know why I hadn't expected that but, after a few attempts at crossing the torrent, made another ill-fated decision.

Instead of back-tracking to where the river was narrower, I decided to follow it to the lake above (from whence it came) and walk around it; it didn't seem far. But the higher I climbed the deeper the snow became and, up by the lake – as I made my way round it – the snow completely blanketed the ground so that I fell into smaller rivers and streams hidden beneath the surface.

Struggling, I made exhausted progress through the soft, thick snow near to the lake, adding two hours to my day; but at the least the cloud stayed summit-high. If it had come down by even 50m I might have lost sight of my goal, a narrow pass between the present valley and the Veodalen Valley – and the lodge. I could have used the compass, as well as pacing, to help me find my way around the lake and on to the Pass but it matters had become that serious I would probably have back-tracked rapidly.

Veopallen from Glitterheim

Considering the present conditions I wondered what the earliest settlers here lived on or hunted. This area has deer in abundance, with trout and red char in the rivers. With rations on my back and a Lodge nearly every 8 miles, I could not compare my hardships to theirs. They might have hiked for miles searching for food, whereas I was hiking for pleasure along well-defined tracks. It was easy to imagine those early settlers following these tracks en route to the seter, or the river to fish.

A story about the Viking Gods Odin, his brother Hoenir and Loki begins with them travelling along a river like this, on their way to the Land of the Dwarfs (Nidalellir). On crossing the river they saw an otter and killed it for their lunch. Unfortunately this otter was no ordinary animal, but one of the Dwarf King's sons who had changed his shape to that of an otter. The gods didn't know this of course, but the King soon appeared and demanded their lives – or gold – for their misdeed. Gold was the obvious choice and the easiest to give; soon the gods were on their way

That wasn't the end of the story. Amongst the gold Loki had acquired through his usual trickery was a ring, with a curse on it. The holder of the ring would be filled with intense jealousy. The dwarfs, the only ones to touch this ring, were instantly overcome by the desire to have the King's gold for themselves. Soon afterwards another of the King's sons killed his father for the gold, after which his other two brothers planned to avenge their father's death. The new holder of the ring foresaw this and turned himself into a huge dragon, to protect the gold. A fresh plan was then made and the youngest son, Sigurd, was given a magic sword with which to kill the dragon. With the aid of this sword and a clever hiding place he managed to stab the dragon and, after an afternoon's fierce fighting, killed it. During the fight Sigurd was covered in the dragon's blood, giving him the power to understand animals. Soon he overheard some gossiping birds talking about his brother who, at the moment, was approaching Sigurd's hiding place to kill him. After he had dealt with his brother Sigurd was alone – and the ring fulfilled its curse. The moral of this story is to leave all things as you see them, for you do not know if they are what they seem – especially in this region.

Once back on track I met my first two hikers of the trip, who said they were heading for the Glittertind summit. Rather them than me, in this weather, was my opinion. Then I met a Scot, who confirmed that the hikers were heading towards an extremely challenging area. On the previous day, 100m below the summit, he had encountered snow waist deep. I had no wish to be caught out in such conditions, specially in an unfamiliar place.

If tackling Glittertind you might be advised to take a Geiger-counter. Apparently there is radioactivity up there, originating from the mineral biotite in the rock. Considering that the Jotunheimen rocks are predominantly the same – namely gabbro and gneiss gabbro – this could produce a large area of radioactivity. This doesn't mean that the geology of this area is simple; in fact – like the plant life – the rocky substance I was walking on was just as complex. The many different colours visible on a geological map of the area clearly and beautifully illustrated this.

So, if cursing the many boulders you trip over or cut yourself on, look closer at the rocks and *not* just the colour of your blood. You will see many minerals within the multi-coloured speckled and banded rocks, such as olivine and serpentinite; both are mined in the Visdalen Valley. Look out for magnetite too, it causes compasses to go haywire; then there is the old favourite Feldspar, found here in large blocks.

Among the theories as to how the mountains here came to be, the favourite is that 900 million years ago this area was part of a thrust sheet of pre-Cambrian crystalline rocks, situated next to the main Baltic Shield. Tectonic action over millions of years moved the sheet – along with an underlying base of Caledonian rocks – up and along the Baltic Shield. During this process it was subjected to severe stress, heat and pressure as it was folded and thrust upwards. After this the remnants of the pluton surfaced, whereupon cooling – then erosion – occurred. During this process, when the rock was very brittle, a final pressure point created a fault line, the Laerdal—Gjennde fault, named from the two points at each end. The rocks on the eastern side of the fault, where I stood, have proved very resistant to erosion; this is partly the reason why the highest peaks in Norway are to be found here.

Towards Glitterhind

The western side of the fault has been less fortunate. Here the pre-Cambrian rocks were eroded to reveal mainly chalk and slate rocks. Scenically this meant that the mountains I did see on the eastern side looked much craggier than those on the western side. More fascinating was the layer of consolidating debris that had built up along the fault. This is partly revealed above Gjenda Lake. As I sailed underneath its steep, high side some days later it was strange to see this thin layer of darker rock glistening from rain and sun, after the pale colour of the gabbro seen on previous days.

Back in the valley I was nearing the Pass and although it hadn't rained, I was soaked from the deep snow of various detours; I was looking forward to that well-earned rest break and some food. Drained of energy, my dinner ration didn't compare to the longed-for hot food and cool beer. Beer may not be a good idea after a hard morning but it didn't stop me thinking about it. In reality I was having a cereal bar and tea! A meagre meal perhaps, but all I can usually take during a hike, particularly as my senses become enhanced after a few days in the hills – and food stored in plastic bags begins to smell! I just hoped it wouldn't kill me, unlike an unlucky troll....

The story tells of the troll who died from food eaten after capturing a rather clever boy, the Ash Lad. When the Ash Lad arrived at the troll's den he remarked how hungry he was and asked the troll to participate in an eating contest. The troll was sure he could easily win against a small human so accepted the challenge and both sat down to eat. While the troll was busy gobbling spoonfuls of porridge, the Ash Lad was pouring his into a bag hanging from his waist. When the troll was full and said he could eat no more, the boy said he was full too and then proceeded to cut open the bag – allowing the porridge to pour out. The troll stupidly concluded that the bag was the Ash Lad's stomach and asked if it hurt? When the Lad said "no" the troll tried the same trick – and died. The Ash Lad then took all the troll's gold and returned home a hero. After my own dinner I gained but a few ounces from a now-empty flask – and the edge of the Pass!

At first the track descended steeply into the Veodalen Valley. Cloud still obscured the surrounding peaks and my attention was drawn to the Veodalen Glacier to the right and the river Veo flowing from it, widening and swelling further along the valley as many smaller streams joined it. The way down was easy; with much less snow and it helped being able to see the boulders and gravel. I was more relaxed than earlier and, after about 30 minutes the track curved round the valley and the Lodge came into view, though it looked small in this broad valley. The sheer size of these valleys and mountains was deceiving to the eye, making rivers or lodges seem smaller or nearer than they actually were. After 15 minutes after first sighting the Lodge I seemed no nearer to it, but seeing it was comforting.

Between the Lodge and myself were several rivers, but only one proved difficult to cross. This was just before reaching the Lodge, coming down from the high lakes on the Glittertind massif and presenting the mountain's last test for the hiker before refuge is reached. The waterfall could be heard and seen much sooner than the river, in fact the river (or channels of streams, which it more resembled) was so well hidden by scrub that just when I thought I had crossed it, another channel appeared – annoying but not a problem. Markers indicated the right way through the maze of scrub, where wooden planks cross some of the channels, but these could easily be missed. After a few wrong turns I gave up looking for the correct way and just waded through the remaining channels. I was now so close to the Lodge that another soaking didn't matter; Glitterheim Lodge had an excellent drying room.

The area around Glitterheim has been inhabited for about 2,000 years. Evidence of human habitation can be seen in deer pits and hunters' small, improvised caves. There is no kitchen here for the campers but, like the Scottish hiker I met earlier, I decided to bin some of my rations and enjoy good hot meals at the Lodges. If I had known the extent of the Lodges' services in advance I wouldn't have bothered bringing my own. Meals were large, filling and cheap and – apart from being a good morale booster – resulted in lighter baggage.

After meeting so many people at the last Lodge I was surprised to find but a few at this one, but those I met were very friendly. The innkeeper spoke excellent English and towards evening, as I sat in my tent, I saw the reindeer he had spoken of, coming down from the high lakes to drink from the river. Two, in playful mood, chased each other down a patch of snow, sliding and skiing to the obvious amusement of the rest of the herd. Farmers own these reindeer and, even though they are still hunted, they appear free and wild in an environment that suits them perfectly. They could frolic in peace without a fence in sight.

At twilight the sound of the river increased, the cloud cleared to reveal a few stars. All the night needed to complete a perfect moment was the Northern Lights or the Aurora Borealis – but I was too far south for either.

According to Viking mythology, the Northern Lights represent the magical beauty of Gerda, a Frost Giantess, who is forever joined to Frey, the God of Summer. A very unlikely combination, but no more so than the way in which they met – or at least the way in which Frey first saw Gerda...

One day he found himself – alone – in Odin's throne room. He decided to sit on the magical throne, Hlidskialf, an honour permitted only to Odin and his wife, Friigga. From Hlidskialf he was able to see all that was happening in the nine worlds. Immediately he sat on it a vision appeared of Gerda; her grace and beauty attracted him instantly, so much so that he felt he could not live if he did not meet her in person. He did so, though initially she was not very welcoming and refused to see him. But after a touch of magic and the slight threat of a curse she agreed – and they have been together ever since. I didn't see any signs of the Northern Lights, just the mountains and the stars, and as I drifted into peaceful sleep wished for good weather the following day.

Day 3   Glitterheim – Memurubu

+430m   -805m   21km

Some say the best mountain range views are from summits on a clear day, but I disagree. I have seen few summit views to beat sunrise in the valleys; these, when combined with early morning mist and the shadows and shifting colours of the sun, give life and meaning to any scene.

I awoke to a clear, dry and hot morning; out came the sun-cream and glasses, waterproofs were packed away. Apart from a few stubborn clouds clinging to the highest peaks, most of the other mountains and lower peaks were visible. Patches of snow still resisted the heat of the sun, making a chequered-shape effect all along the valley floor and slopes, glaciers in the background merging with the persisting clouds on the high peaks. After two days of bad weather this near-calm and silence of the giants inspired me with a new sense of purpose. I intended to enjoy this day!

It was a short walk from the Lodge to the wooden bridge over the River Veo. From habit I still had my map out but should have realised it wasn't needed – unless I planned to get lost. Signposts and markers made my direction obvious so little navigation was required to find the track up to the Pass beneath Vestre Hestlaegerho; From there I would head for the Russvatnet Lake and on to Memurubu.

The track involved the familiar boulder-hopping, but now grasses, mosses and flowers carpeted the ground and intermittent snow-covered slopes. I saw a lovely spring pasque whose white petals were only half-open, as if it was just testing the air and not totally convinced of good weather. Slowly the flora changed as I gained height; multi-coloured lichen replaced grasses, heathers and moss.

Snow began covering most of it, though there was a distinct lack of lying snow compared to the previous day. Higher up the slope the river I was following had cut a deep mini-gorge into the rock and the thick sheet of snow built up above it was beginning to melt and fall apart. This revealed not only how far down the river was, but also the giant arched caves made by the remaining snow. How many of these snow bridges had I wandered over, without knowing it?...

According to the inn-keeper the previous evening, the amount of snow was unusual for this time of year because, by now, it has usually gone. But last year was what the locals referred to as 'the one hot summer' – which occurs only once every 100 years; just my luck to have missed it by such a small margin! Jotunheimen is also one of the few places where the glaciers, like the one I could see near the Pass coming down from Glittertind, are *advancing* – due to more snow falling than can actually melt.

I was told that if I wished to see flowers I was two weeks too early. By then, hordes of other enthusiasts would be here and their numbers may have prevented me from seeing more of the wild life I hoped to see now – i.e. reindeer (like the previous evening). Other mammals live in this area – the wolverine (a large bear-like carnivore), lynx, Arctic fox and even wild otters. Just to see one of these graceful otters outside a confining enclosure would be a dream come true. I have heard they were once plentiful on the banks of the Thames but now, like most wild creatures, are difficult to find.

The weather over the preceding two days had not provided perfect opportunities to sit around watching for wildlife, but perhaps today I might see something. As I neared the Pass it seemed my luck was in when I saw, only 40m ahead, the herd of reindeer from the previous night – but much closer. Unfortunately we saw each other at the same moment and they began moving around the Vestre slopes. I felt like a gunslinger as I zapped out my camera, aimed and shot. Many years ago that shot would have produced a bullet – not only aimed at the deer but at the larger mammals once roaming these mountains, namely the brown bear and the wolf; both are now found only in North Norway.

The Vikings must have considered the wolf a very dangerous creature and, like many other civilizations, they embodied this fear in the creation of a mythological animal suiting its reputation. This took the form of the Great Wolf, Fenris, a truly fearsome creature born of the union of Loki and an ugly giantess.

Apart from Fenris they had two other children, if 'children' is the right word, for they too were hideous. The second was an ugly giant who, being half-life and half-death, was called Hel; the third, a very long and giant snake named Jormungard, was reputedly so large that his outstretched body completely encircled the mythical middle worlds. Fenris, however, was the creature that caused the most trouble…

Like most newborn, he began life as a small, cuddly animal – but grew to become a real threat to the gods. Eventually they were forced to resort to trickery to capture and chain up this unruly creature. A god called Tyr, however, was not afraid of Fenris, having been with the wolf since his birth. When Fenris agreed to be tied up and one of the gods had to put a hand in his mouth to do it, Tyr accepted the task. Unfortunately he lost his hand when Fenris realised their plan, but the gods *had* managed to capture the creature and it was said that he will only ever know freedom again when the last battle of Ragnarok takes place….

I reached the top of the Pass to be greeted with the best clear views so far. A large basin spread out beneath me, its surface pitted with scree and snow; the clear, crisp atmosphere beyond revealed peaks and ridges in the far distant mountains encircling Lakes Russvatnet and Gjende. To my left the slopes leading to the summit of Surtningssua (said to have the finest views in

Jotunheimen) still retained large cornices of snow and, further up, glaciers had carved out a wild paradise.

Gloptind

Until that moment I hadn't noticed the wind – or lack of it – but suddenly realised that everything was still. No sound. Just reindeer hoof-prints as evidence of life in this desolate place. Its wild, harsh appearance was for me the perfect back yard – with space to breathe and freedom to live. At that moment, overlooking the silent giants, I experienced an inner feeling impossible to describe – and almost equally impossible to walk away from. Two men, who became friends during their periods of residence here, probably had similar feelings. One was General Blackwell, an Englishman who rented Lake Russvatnet for a time to hunt and fish from the small Lodge he built on the lakeside – where I planned to have lunch. The other, Jo Gjende, is described as a hermit and hunter who reputedly shot approximately 500 buck reindeer. With the sun's warmth on my back and perfect views all around, it was easy to romanticize about their exploits and adventures, to imagine life here then.. Deep down, however, I am too addicted to the conveniences of modern life and wouldn't endure it for long. But anyone can dream....

The slope down into the basin was steep initially and covered with thick snow. I walked carefully, then yielded to temptation and slid down the remainder. Unfortunately this caper didn't last long as I soon had to cross the many streams coming from the melting snow and return to the track.

At the lowest point of the basin were two small lakes. The river from these I would eventually have to cross and the map indicated there was a bridge over the river, but only in summer. I hoped that, despite the snow and time of year, it was still there; to my relief it was. A wire bridge in fact, which I didn't spot until I reached the point in the basin where it descended to Lake Russvatnet. The section of the river spanned by the bridge appeared to be at the wildest, narrowest and strongest point – just before it shot over the vertical sides. The delta it created into the lake below was quite wide, its surface smooth due to the lack of wind. It revealed perfect reflections of the surrounding mountains, especially at the far end with the cone shape of Mount Gloptind.

The heat of the day made the area buzz with activity as I recommenced my descent through the heather and shrubs. These were literally heaving with insects, especially mosquitoes, all eager for a share of my blood. The scene was completely different – and much more welcoming – than that of the preceding two days. It is remarkable what a few hundred metres up or down, and a few degrees' difference in temperature, can do. Although constantly harassed by insects during dinner, it was preferable to the conditions I had endured previously.

I had lunch by the lake, just under General Blackwell's Lodge. Looking at the clear water and steep mountains surrounding this end of the lake, I could understand why he had chosen this spot.

Further down the lake the mountains are lower and more open, but here their closeness seemed more friendly, welcoming and – safer. On my way along the lake to this point is an outcrop of rock above the lake; there I met a group of campers and gathered from them that they shared my feelings about the homeliness of the area.

I learned the reason why Scandinavians enjoy the reputation of going nude. It is apparently due to the lack of sunshine here so, when the sun *does* shine, they strip off and make the most of it. As I left the lake to begin the last leg of the day's trek up the valley of Nedre Russglopet, I was delighted to meet three women striding along with their day sacks – wearing only bikinis. A common sight on beaches but seldom in mountains!

The slopes marking the end of the valley were steep. As I approached them the clearer the route I must follow became. Once on it didn't seem as vertical as it had appeared from the base of it. There were two main slopes to climb, with a level area to rest on; the first slope was simple but at the top of the second I could only see cornices of heavy snow hanging over the edge. I thought I saw footprints over part of these so made for them.

As I climbed higher I saw people coming down from the line of mountains edging the lake where I had had lunch, and Gjende Lake, following a track from Gjendesheim. This is probably one of the best-known trails in Jotunheimen, and not only because of the spectacular near-vertical ridges at Besseggen. It is famous because of the story by Henrik Ibsen of Peer Gynt and his adventures – including the tale of how he jumped off the Besseggen Ridge on a donkey. As he was in Jotunheimen it would have been simpler to use a reindeer!

Once I had carefully crawled over the cornice (the 'footprints' were actually stones), I tried to locate the vertical drop under Besseggen, if only from a distance. To do this I left the top of the track and moved to the edge of the mountain, overlooking Gjende Lake – hoping the slight curve of the mountains along the lake would allow sight of the ridge. I went as far as I could (without standing on fresh air) and still couldn't see it, though I was certainly aware of the near-vertical sides of the mountains adjoining it. I was roughly 500m above the lake; at Besseggen I would have been 400-600m above it, with sheer drops on both sides. At that point vertigo would be a possibility for some. No time to admire the views – watch your feet and convince yourself you are having a good time!

Although I didn't see the Besseggen, the surrounding views were excellent – not only of the 2,330m Mt. Tjornholstind across the lake from me but also those down towards either end of the lake. The high mountains, hugging and guarding the lakesides and giving way at the ends to low valleys, looked eerie – standing in darkness from the silhouette of the mountains against the shadowing clouds and their reflection on the water.

In the time taken to climb up from the Russglopet Valley the clouds and wind had built up; it was time to descend to tonight's destination. The track down to Menurdu involved a very steep descent. If, like me, you prefer ascending to descending, this part will not appeal to you; it took most of *my* energy to stop sliding down on the loose rocks and gravel. The lower slopes gave way to silver birch, with easier walking to the Lodge. Below it the ground evens out at lake level, where there are deciduous trees and a small field; just the place to camp overnight, in the company of cows.

Someone made a wise decision to allow cows in these fields, not only to keep the grass short (which campers appreciate) but because there are few other usable patches of grass around this lake. What I did object to about these particular cows, however, was their constant noise. It's strange, but I had always thought cows were quiet and slow. Not these! They nattered continuously, often thundering past my tent when I was trying to sleep. I dozed off wondering – would I wake up covered in hoof-prints?

Last day coming up, involving a short but luxurious ferry ride to Gjendsbu. This hiking trip may have been short and sweet but it had certainly also been varied. If the weather report at the Lodge was correct, my last day's walk to Fondsbu on the shores of Lake Bygdin would be as pleasant as today's – thus equating out the good and the bad.

Day 4   Menurdu – Fondsbu

+410m   -340m   17km

One of the great things about camping is that time is immaterial. No-one cares if you sleep late or simply decide to stay in bed until the sun outside is hot enough to cook your breakfast on a stone (it *is* possible in some places). Nothing *really* matters, so why – during hiking trips – does *my* body insist on waking up at the ghostly time of 6am? Then, when I *do* have a deadline to keep to, why do I wake up late? I awoke at 8, still in one piece, but immediately stressed as I had just ten minutes to assemble my belongings for the ferry ride. Twenty minutes later I was waving goodbye to the cows and Memurubu, with bits of equipment hanging off me everywhere! The smartly-dressed tourist who boarded the ferry at Gjendesheim probably decided I was a tramp, but I didn't care. At least I hadn't missed it!

The ferry was the size of a small yacht. The rain had stopped so it was pleasant to sit on deck and study the Lake. The mountains on the north side are by far the steepest, their dark appearance created by the rock formations mashed up by the fault line. The steep sides glistened in the morning sun as melt water cascaded down. On another day it was probably a good climb but, now, the idea of camping along the narrow, tree-lined bank below was more appealing, as it was to other hikers.

Gjende lake

At the end of the Lake is a large expanse of flat, marshy land stretching down from the surrounding valleys. It appeared lusher then anywhere I had yet seen and a possible place to camp although; unlike Gjendbu (friend of General Blackwell) I didn't plan to stay. After a stop at the Lodge for breakfast and money-changing, I was off. The flat areas just past the Lodge were dense with silver birch, shrubs, heather and an occasional stream – the perfect place to camp, with superb views down the Lake. Despite signs discouraging it, there were indications of people having camped there and, if I'd known of this area in advance I would have preferred to camp on the open flats rather than beneath the giants along the Lake.

I began the gentle climb up the Vesleadalen Valley leading to Bygdin Lake, a mere 400m ascent and providing some of the loveliest views of the week. Beyond the shrub and a few stubborn cows, just as the sun decided to come out and the clouds retreated to the summits, I came upon a small wood. This was delightful, with bright light penetrating the foliage. The trees and other flora here must have been a blessing to the first settlers, who would have used them for survival – with the possible exception of one plant, which caused the death of one of the Viking gods.

It began with the birth of Balder, Frigga's favourite son, the Holder of Goodness and Wisdom. Balder began having nightmares and fears concerning his death. Frigga, greatly distressed, decided to make all living things promise never to harm Balder. The task was huge, the journey long. On returning to Balder, she passed a mistletoe bush. Feeling tired, she looked at it and, considering it too small to be a threat to her son, continued on her way – *without* asking for its promise.

Time passed and other gods learned of Balder's invincibility. They organized games in which they threw things at him, including Thor's hammer, but everything bounced off him. Loki, meanwhile, was up to his usual trickery and decided there must be *something* to harm Balder; so he disguised himself as an old woman and visited Frigga. Having learned the secret from her, he formed a plan to test his new-found information. He made use of Balder's brother Hoder who, being blind wouldn't know what he was throwing and just consider it a game. Loki made a dart from the mistletoe bush, which Hoder threw at Balder – and killed him. In more recent times the writer/poet Robert Graves experimented with a mistletoe dart, to see if it could kill, it could.

High Plateau

The walk through the woods was brief and I returned to the moss, grass and lichen-covered rocks and boulders. This landscape continued for most of the way, until I crossed the river Vesleaa. From there I could see the two low summits, Geitho and Rundtom, a natural signpost guiding me to the track passing between them. From these summits the view of Lake Gjende begins to slip away and I took a last look at this magnificent sight. It looked beautiful from down amid the trees but, with height, was magical.
Just before these two summits a track split from the one I was following, heading towards Olaysbu, the one Lodge in the Park accessible only on foot.

Near the summits there was snow, higher than on previous days, but retaining a tight hold. Between the summits was a lake, still covered in snow and ice, a warning that although it was hot and the cloud had virtually disappeared, the weather could easily deteriorate in moments. After crossing a few low slopes I reached an area whose open expanse made me stop in amazement. After being in confined valleys for some time, this breathtaking vastness astounded me. In front and below lay a wide plateau encircled by high mountains. The dark blue sky overhead and the lighter blue along the summits added strange dimensions to the illusion. It was as though I had walked up through a tunnel into a stadium, except that this stadium's side was covered in rocks and wide streams. Just before my lunch stop I reached a stream too wide to jump over, so opted for the snow bridge; but the snow was too soft to take my weight and all hopes of staying dry evaporated along with the bridge. Such is life!

The track and the line of red markers, vivid against the snow, headed towards the river Hoystakka, where this wonderful plateau ends. From Gjende the fault line paralleled along the track I was following and one of the many exposed rock faces visible around the plateau was of a similar colour to the lakeside cliff. Whereas all the other rock faces and mountains here are a dull grey, the black of the fault line rock stands out magnificently, providing a lasting reminder of this area in the days to come.

After crossing the swing bridge over the river I was greeted by one of Norway's collection of geographical spectacles – a waterfall. Not particularly big or of huge volume, but powerful – evident by the deep corries it had carved out of the rock. I had hoped to see the Vettismorki waterfall, but it was at Olaysbu. With a free fall of 260m, it is the highest in Norway. But there are so many here; several rivers I had crossed had falls gushing down to the valleys below, their noise and size adding another exciting dimension to the unique attraction of these mountains.

Looking down on Lake Bygdin, its greater width over Gjende and the gentler slopes lends it a completely different appearance from Gjende – more open, spacious and, on that day, somewhat warmer. There was more colour along its banks and on the track descending to its shore. There were some flowers, their colours and scents attracting not only me but the blood-sucking insects I had, thus far, managed to avoid. I was almost tempted down to one of the small beaches, to dive into the lake to escape from them. Surely a fitting punishment for Loki and Hoder would be to endure constant harassment by insects for 100 miles? No, what they had in fact received for the killing of Balder was somewhat more dramatic…

Fondsbu

A warrior named Vali, specifically trained for the deed, threw a dart and killed Hoder. Loki, being Loki, managed to escape and hide for a time – until Odin and Thor found them. They tied him up in a cave, with the intestines of a wolf (which had been another of Loki's children). Finally a giantess brought a snake, placed it above the rock to which he was tied, and it constantly spat out painful venom on him. He was destined to remain there until the coming of Ragnarok, at which point his pain and suffering would end.

I was near my own end, of sorts, and not looking forward to it. I felt I'd made the right decision to shorten the trip because of my blisters, but now it was nearly over (and despite having another trip planned for the coming week) I did not want it to be. I hadn't seen, or done, all I had planned and was unhappy about that too. That's life! It's said that even well-organised train schedules fail to run perfectly. But I wasn't out of the mountains – yet.

Further along the Lake was the beginning of a road connecting all the private summer lodges dotted across the slopes above the Lodge. The preserved buildings of the first settlers are also here so, combined with the rustic but comfortable Fondsbu Lodge, the area resembled an old settlement. The ferry landing stage was not just a simple wooden platform like those on Lake Gjendsbu, but more of a small concrete harbour. A large sculpture of a face, that of the old poet Aasmund O Vinje was erected on it; he owned the old preserved grass-roofed buildings. He was also one of the founders of the DNT – an organization that had supplied me with much information and established the tracks I'd used. DNT takes responsibility generally for the care of all parks in Norway.

Later on I enjoyed dinner among more people at once than I had met in four whole days, most of them on a three-day summit-hiking trip. This surprised me as I was once told that Norwegians prefer walking the valleys. Their explanation made perfect sense: normally some would just hike between lodges (mostly in high season, when some summits might resemble a Saturday afternoon in Oxford Street). They were currently taking full advantage of the empty mountains. With this I could sympathise for I've often wondered just how many Company Board Meetings are held on certain summits in the Lake District. This is why I now prefer to walk along the valleys and glens, rather than concentrate on summit climbs. It is not only the solitude that draws me, but I feel closer to the hills, see much more wild life and meet fewer people.

Tired from the walk and slightly tipsy from Norwegian hospitality, I slept in a warm, cosy and not-too-expensive bed. Next morning I studied the map, wondering if I could – or should – continue with my plans, which, from here, would not prove difficult. But the trip wasn't *quite* over yet. Norway is full of mountains and I still had the outgoing coach drive to Bergen. This could prove equally as spectacular as the incoming boat trip.

From the coach I absorbed my last memorable views of Jotunheimen before descending the precarious road to Ovre Ardel, which lay snug under the 800m mountains.

From there back along the fjords, on narrow roads and through tunnels blasted from solid rock. A short ferry ride across the fjord, then the coach headed inland to the mountains I had not yet seen. We passed mixed forests, pastures and meadows now overflowing with colour, stopping occasionally at small communities. Finally, we reached Bergen.

My trip would not be over until the last craggy summit along the coastline had finally disappeared from sight. Out of sight, yes. But never, ever out of mind.

Six mountain hikes from around the world

SCOTLAND

Monadhliath and Cairngorm Mountains

Guardians of Speyside

The A82 from Glasgow to Fort William is said to be one of the most scenic roads in the Highlands. After traveling most of the Highlands' inner roads, it is hard to say which is best but the A82 is certainly one among superb routes. It didn't feel as isolated, nor as empty, as other roads but as an introduction – from urban sprawl to the Highlands – it's hard to beat. I appreciated this as we left Glasgow behind and the unique, spreading panorama of the Highlands opened up – peaceful under a clear, deep blue sky. After all the planning (and agonizing waiting) the adventure was under way, into an area of the Highlands I had rarely visited. Ever-changing scenery, coupled with the generosity and friendliness of the locals, had made previous trips memorable and I looked forward to similar experiences.

Loch Lomond soon came into view – dark, calm, very long; it took 45 minutes to drive from one end to the other, even at breakneck speed. Just past the Loch, one of its claims to fame (and partly the reason why it is to be designated Scotland's first National Park) came into view: somewhere in its depths lies the Highland Boundary Fault, where the Lowlands end and the Highlands begin. The mountain looming ahead more than proved the point – Ben Hope – with its mass and wildness, typical of the mystical mountains which brought me here. We had arrived.

The scenery and atmosphere of Rannoch Moor seemed completely out of character compared to that beyond Ben Hope. One minute I was deep in the glen looking up at the ridges of the Munros, then suddenly a wide expanse of heather and lochs appeared – eerie, quite and empty (except for the A82 and the small bridge over the River Ba). Such a dark, forbidding place was an ideal setting for tales of secrets, villains and heroes. I began to unwind as mountain and moor flashed past the window, aided by a beautiful waterfall half way up Glen Coe, its thin line of water cascading in the light down from the ridges of the Three Sisters. A mountain goat perched precariously on a ridge would have completed the picture. Glen Coe is famous for the massacre of the Macdonalds by the Campbell's in 1692, in the reign of William III and, more recently, for the discovery of gold in the river below.

Twelve hours earlier friend Mark and I had left London on a bus to the Highlands and, though stiff from sitting for hours, I would not have wanted to go by air. Seeing the ever-changing scenery – the low pasturelands of England changing to the high, rugged and wild mountain ranges of Scotland – whetted my appetite for more; my imagination moved into overdrive. Coming from an area in England where the pace of life was fast, my present surroundings (along with a few drams later on) helped to slow me down. Separately they have always greatly affected my body clock, particularly at Hogmanay and, if there ever *is* a right time to overdo the whiskey then Hogmanay is the one. But be warned! A 'dram' is a lot more than a 'shot' and there is probably more than one house to visit… yet it would be impolite to refuse, wouldn't it?…

This didn't happen on our first night, at the start of the walk in Roybridge but might have done; sampling local delicacies is an accepted part of any trip. Hangovers however, are not pleasant before a walk, though acceptable at the end – in our case in 5 days' time, in Aviemore. We planned an interesting/varied route along the edge of the Monadhliath Mountains (the 'grey mountains') to Kingussie; then into the wilds of the Cairngorms (the 'red' mountains), wild camping all the way. This is the best way – no schedule, no rush – and, as the morning mist rose slowly, our first day began in sunshine.

Six mountain hikes from around the world

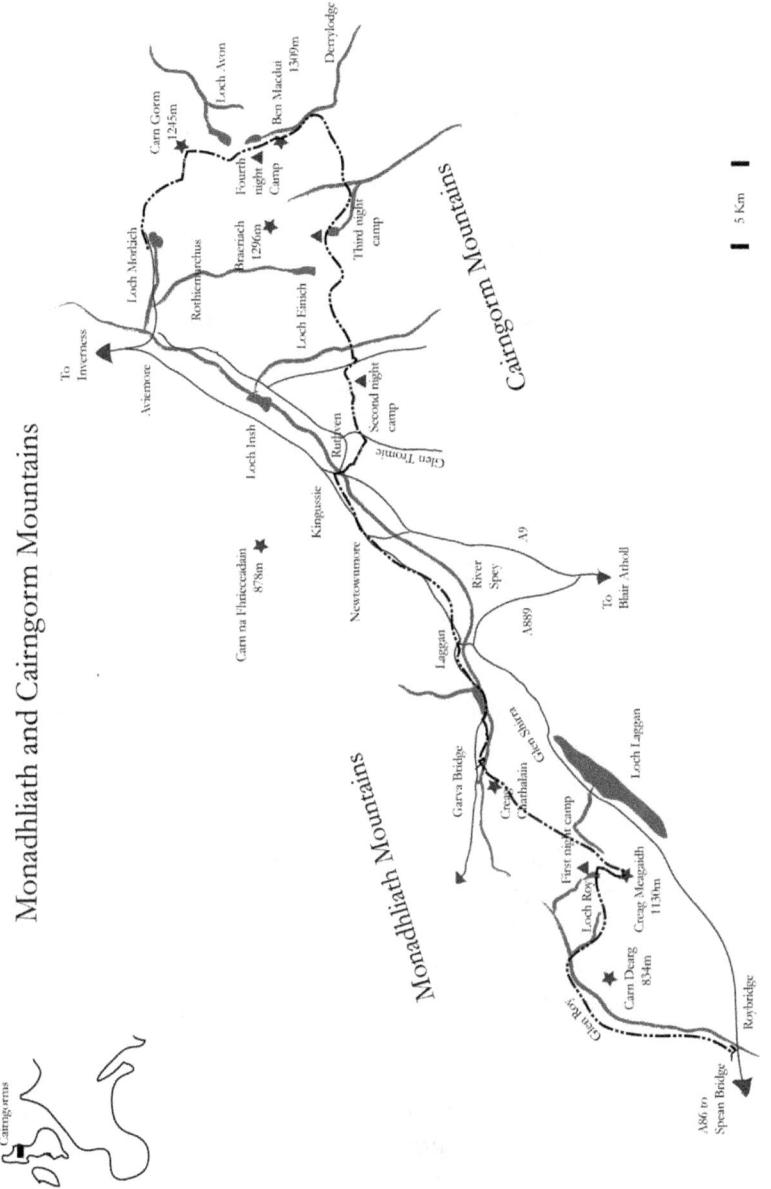

Monadhliath Mountains

Day 1 Roybridge – Loch Roy

+540m -50m 26km

Our route from Roybridge would follow, as closely as possible, the river Roy up to Loch Roy. Unfortunately, this meant the first 8 miles were on the road as far as Brearoy Lodge – unpleasant but unavoidable if we were to see the parallel roads in the nature reserve. From the lodge we would then strike up into the hills and make for the Loch.

Roybridge was very quiet, a refreshing contrast to London. Even this small town has a history of bloodshed – the Heppoch Murders. The cousin of two men murdered at a clan banquet avenged their death by killing the murderers – by cutting off their heads and displaying them to the local Laird. It sounds brutal today but in years past things were different. Bloodthirsty and gruesome tales are part of local history, giving the mountains their individuality – like the tale of Loch Ness in the Great Glen. Created by a giant fracture, the Great Glen is the longest in Scotland and contains the deepest lochs in the Glen's vast trough but, if legend is to be believed, Loch Ness was *not* created by glacier melt water. According to legend, many centuries ago – during the reign of the Pictish King Bridei – the Great Glen was a beautiful valley with just a small well and no lochs. The well was magic and commanded respect because, if the lid was not replaced after use, water would pour from it. One day the inevitable happened; a woman drawing water heard her ailing child cry in the village and ran to it, forgetting to replace the lid. The whole valley began to fill with water and the terrified villagers ran away shouting "the loch nis ann" ("there is a lake there now"); from that saying came the word 'ness'.

Meanwhile, back in Glen Roy, we emerged from the pine and birch wood; the bark was once used to make dry white wine, reputedly an aid to baldness. Slowly we gained height and Glen Roy came into view. Near this point, the parallel roads began, higher up from our present position and out of sight. I looked behind me – a backward glance sometimes reveals a better view than the one ahead. There, in perfect clarity, lay the ridges and tops leading up to Ben Nevis in the foreground – a very impressive sight even at this distance. I was walking into the Monadhliath Mountains, a range once described to me as featureless and containing only peat and bog. Behind me lay one of the highest, most rugged and corried ranges in Scotland, probably a more popular choice for hiking, but for that reason I chose these lower hills. Solitude was guaranteed, along with the excitement of exploring the wild and pathless slopes. If thirsty we could make moorland tea, using the heather flowers and the cool water of the River Ba (a favourite of Robert Burns). If Norsemen had not killed all the Picts on a certain island, we could have used an old heather recipe to make a particularly good heather beer.

Parallel roads within Glen roy

It is strange to consider that natural forces could be responsible for the creation of the parallel roads, clearly seen from the car park. There are three levels of what are now known to be shore lines; these are all so precise horizontally in relation to each other that you can imagine they were man-made. According to legend, this is true: they are the 'King's hunting roads', made by an ancient monarch. But in 1847 a Swiss glaciologist discovered that the parallel lines were old shore lines, made by a lake held in place by a glacier. As the glacier retreated so, the level of the lake dropped. Looking down the Glen to the point where it turns, I could see the lowest parallel roads on both sides of the Glen clearly, matching up precisely level; a strange sight in a rugged area. If the lake still existed, we would be 100m under it.

Looking back down the glen

This part of the Glen seemed more U-shaped, with the hills very close and high above it, but further on – we turned towards Brea-Roy Lodge – the valley floor widened considerably and the surrounding hills seemed to shrink back as we approached the Lodge. The valley floor flattened, causing the river flow to slow down; its snaking route creating deep, inviting pools on the bends. The temperature was rising, my feet were burning and occasionally I walked on the sand and smooth pebbles washed down from the parallel roads – which brought little relief.

Ahead lay a small pine wood, hiding the Lodge from view. Pines would look out of place anywhere else but, here in the middle of the Glen and surrounded by ancient hills, they added character – and provided welcoming shade. Once out of the wood the road ended, to our relief, and we crossed the river via a small wooden bridge and stopped for lunch (and a chance to soak my feet). After our fillet steak and Caesar salad (we wished!) had disappeared we followed the path into Brea-Roy forest, which like most places here with that name, had no trees – only petrified remains of old stumps in the peat.

From then on we were in the isolated wilds of the mountains. We'd seen few people and did not expect to see more, even though civilization was just a few miles away. In places like this you only have the thick, dense heather to keep you company – and insects, millions of them, drinking your blood and slowly driving you mad. Yet the sense of freedom and the challenge of an unknown environment has drawn me here repeatedly – *not* the continuous scratching of mosquito bites. Capturing the spirit of these hills is a wonderful reward.

Once we had left the path, past the beautiful Dog Falls of the Burn of Agie, we saw some of these 'spirits' – a large herd of deer, almost fifty of them. We tried to get closer for photographs but they sensed us and galloped off through the thick heather, gracefully and sure-footed, as if gliding. In contrast we were clumsy and heavy-footed, stepping from hidden holes into sides of rocks, but it was wonderful to stand and watch them move across the gentle slopes of Creag Meagaidh (Bogland Rock or The Crag at the Bog). The stag was magnificent; he stopped and, shadowed by his lieutenant, checked our position. Fortunately we all seemed to be going the same way, through a small pass below Carn Dearg – the sort of place Prince Charlie might have used on his way to Clunies Cage. There I finally took my photo as the stag stopped on the lip of the pass not more than 25m away. It was exciting to stare straight back at him – until Mark caught up and he disappeared.

Dog Falls

The second 'spirit' I saw came in the form of grouse, whom I had only previously seen on whiskey bottles! Today I heard them more than I saw them. Going round Carn Dearg towards Loch Roy – with the rolling hills of the Monadhliath in the background towards Corrieyairack Forest – a vast low area of bogland covered with streams and pools opened up. Nothing stirred, no noise, even the insects were quiet. Whilst taking my time through the heather and admiring the scenery ahead, twenty or more grouse suddenly erupted from the heather – swooping overhead and down into the Glen – the noise was deafening and the shock almost made me drop my camera. Over the coming week, this happened several times in the heather – where they nest, hide and feed. I never managed to photograph them but these brief, uplifting encounters with wildlife convinced me I had made the right choice to trek in a lesser-known area, rather than where hordes of hikers keep wildlife at bay. When we eventually reached the clear, cool and shallow waters of the Loch I felt the day had gone well, despite developing blisters from road walking – but that's part of the experience, like the lovely dinner we had to look forward to.

As the sun began to set, only a few high clouds remained; the stark light lit up the rugged sides of Creag An Lochain overlooking the Loch, making the pools and streams below sparkle like jewels. Above, the deer were still keeping watch and I hoped our presence had not distressed them too much. All combined to create a very special moment. When we hit the sack it was dark and I have no recollection of my head touching the silk pillow…

Day 2   Loch Roy – Glen Shirra

+350m   -700m   19km

At home I'm normally catapulted from sleep by my earth-shattering alarm but today I was woken slowly and peacefully by the same noise that had *sent* me to sleep – the cascading waterfall off Creag an Lochain, shining brilliantly under a clear, sunny sky. I felt like lying there all day but there was a grueling hike ahead and a breakfast not unlike yesterday's dinner to look forward to. I *had* to get up.

Today's walk would take us up to our first Munro (Scottish mountains over 3,000 ft) – Creag Meagaidh. From there we would be able to see the nature reserve below, and partially into

Glenshirra Forest – which we would cross before making our way down to Garva Bridge then, finally, into Glenshirra and another wild camp.

There is an excellent advantage to camping high apart from superb views – you never have to walk far to reach summits. Instead of walking up the usual 900m to reach a summit, it could be achieved in less than 500m – as it would be for us today. Being that the summit above is a Munro, there might be a chance of meeting someone up there who was also aiming to add to their list of achieved Munro summits. If I had the time I might try this myself, if only to tour the Highlands and experience their wonderful diversities – and get fitter in the process.

Eventually we finished packing and took a last look at our home for the night; I don't think I've ever stayed anywhere as pleasant, in such good weather, in Scotland, anyhow; if only the grass had been cut I would have given it 5-star rating!

Loch Roy

As we neared the top of Stob Poite Coire Ardair the grass was slowly replaced by broken rock – and the Monadhliath Mountains

came into view. None are over 900m, which made the extent of view quite large, highlighting their unique differences crystal clear. During the last Ice Age, these hills were transformed into the low, rolling hills of Mica-Schist, from where their grey colour originates. Then peat built up to give them their present distinctive appearance, a total contrast to the nature reserve below. The reserve covers 10,000 acres, surrounded by step corries and thinly-wooded slopes which, from the small loch below, descend in a V-shape down almost to the shores of Loch Laggan. The surrounding summits of this large loch were hidden by haze, but its island was just visible through binoculars. It is called Eilean An Righ (King Island) and on it are the remains of an old castle, believed to be the hunting lodge of King Fergus (c330 BC). The protected nature reserve below is used for a variety of reasons but mostly for the conservation and education of its wildlife; the steep cliffs and shallower slopes serve as areas for climbing training and skiing.

Glenshirra Forest

We enjoyed the luxury of walking along a well used path for a while, until heading towards Creag Chathalain. Once again we descended into a maze of thick grass and heather, criss-crossed intermittently by occasional streams (havens for insects, which Mark found particularly annoying). Having decided to wear shorts he was already regretting it – the insects found his legs irresistible! Further on, past the Creag, areas of woodland dotted the slopes from General Wade's Road – their symmetry resembling legions of Roman soldiers lined up for battle. Had the Romans settled in the Sprathspey after the Battle of Mons Graupius with the Picts (or 'painted men') – and not just ventured there afterwards on patrols from Inchtuthil – I might have seen ruins here similar to Hardknott in the Lake District.

Even so, many other historical treasures still exist in the Highlands, including one not a million miles away in the form of an old 'standing stone' near Melgarve. It has a sad, yet heroic, story connected to the naming of a hill just ahead – Creag Chathalain (Chathalain's Rock). It happened around 1532 when Cluny Macpherson was holding a wedding festival for his daughter, who was being given away to a great Irish chief. He brought a few warriors along, one of whom took a fancy to the bride's sister. His feelings were reciprocated – they fell in love and wanted to stay together but, because he was not a Chief, this was unlikely to be granted. So they decided to elope, using the Pass of Corrieairack for a quick escape to a waiting boat that would take them to Ireland. It was the height of winter, however, and the young girl found it hard going in the snow. Eventually they found a small cave on the slopes of a nearby hill (Creag a Chathalain) in which to shelter. Unfortunately this gave Cluny's men time to catch them up early next morning, further along the Pass. They cut out the warrior's heart, as Cluny had ordered, though he was unaware at the time of the warrior's high standing in Ulster. In his remorse Cluny decided to erect a statue in memory, where the warrior named Chathalain was buried. That same statue still stands near Melgarve.

The area we were walking through towards Garva Bridge was by the far most difficult and tiring of the whole week. Dense clumps of grass and thick, bushy heather made hard going, as did the many surprise holes, streams and hidden rocks. Relief came in small doses from deer tracks – a godsend which prevented us from further damaging the vegetation. But there was no relief from irritations caused by an assortment of flies, dragonflies, frogs and lizards. Eventually, due to the heat, we were forced to stop earlier than planned for lunch, eaten on the peat banks of one of the larger rivers on the moor. Just ahead lay our original goal, under Creag Liath, where I had seen trees that could provide shelter – but later we found a fence around them. By the amount of deer tracks around them it must have been erected to keep them out. Thankfully, as we approached it from higher ground, the fence did not spoil the lovely view of the trees lining a small river flowing down towards Garve Bridge.

Back on the moor we were enjoying ourselves, trying to eat flapjacks whilst (unsuccessfully) attempting to keep the flies away – not only from the flapjack but out of our mouths, noses and ears! One consolation was the peat not being as smelly as I thought it might. It's strange to realize you can use it as fuel and that the many oxygen-starved layers of sphagnum (a kind of botanical sponge) that thrive on it were not only used for the sterilization of wound-dressings during WW1, but also hold clues – through carbon processing – to the vegetation once covering these hills. Peat isn't something I'm particularly interested in, I'm more of an animal lover, but it is indeed a surprising substance. Peat is, in fact, an accumulation of dead mosses, sledges and heather; and it can survive the wet acidic conditions found here. This builds up over time into layers of impermeable nutrient peat – which explains why, when everything around it is dry, peat still springs under foot – especially on those areas bare of any heather, where we stepped over many stumps and branches of white, dead trees.

After lunch our progress improved. Firstly, the deer tracks were more numerous; secondly, we were off the slope and on to the flat of the moor; finally, for no apparent reason, my body decided to wake up! These factors combined to make the final part of our trek faster and therefore more enjoyable – a bonus considering all the time lost stumbling through thick heather.

It wasn't until we were down to the River Spey and Garve Bridge that we began to appreciate how hot it was. During the week, the temperature was in the 90's in this area, which apart from being pleasant, was very different from the more typical mountain weather I was used to. What was even more amazing was the fact that, for one day, Scotland was the hottest place in Europe! People refused to believe we had been in the mountains when they saw our tanned faces – thinking we had been sunbathing in the Med!

The River Spey (or Hawthorn Stream) could be described as a river that not so much chuckles along but grumbles and roars. This, in olden times, ensured people both respected and feared it. In turn it made them believe that the evil spirit of a White Horse (or, in Celtic, the Ant-each Ban) lived within its depths and claimed human victims on dark, stormy and windy nights – preventing the frantic splashing of victims from being heard as they were dragged under the surface. Luckily for us it was a bright day and the water was calm as we soaked our sore, hot and smelly feet. Looking up at the mountains skirting the Monadhliath range, I was regretful yet thankful we were leaving these quiet, isolated hills; sometimes it is pleasant to walk in uncrowded places, follow hidden paths, escape into the wilderness where the average hiker does not venture. Following well-worn paths is not enough for me – I prefer to explore the mysterious beauty of the unknown, sense its atmosphere; the lack of specific paths to ease the way can sometimes be useful. I regretted leaving the un-spoilt, mysterious Monadhliath but glad the popular Cairngorms lay ahead.

We reached our camp destination late. Millions of hungry midges were waiting, which spoilt an otherwise superb location next to a small outcrop of rock under a tree, by a river – hence the midges. The view encompassed a small plantation of what appeared to be this year's Christmas trees, growing next to Loch Crunachden; the mountains beyond were lit by the setting sun. I would have appreciated everything more had the midges not invited their friends for dinner; a few handfuls of bog myrtle would have been helpful as I learned later that it is an excellent bug deterrent. In the fading light, as the situation became annoying, we lit a fire; its flickering light and mellow smell of burning wood not only dispersed the insects but mesmerized us – body and soul – soothing away the rigours of the day.

Day 3   Glen Shirra – Inshriach Forest

+250m -160m 20km

We woke to a gloriously cloudless day. The insects had not returned, allowing a leisurely breakfast and packing up. Today was to be an easy, low-level trek with many luxuries – even a short car drive to Kingussie, where we would replenish our supplies before proceeding to the foot of the Cairngorms. But first to Laggan and Strathspey, along Wade's Road.

The river Spey flows from the Monadhliath from the Corrieyairack Pass, cutting through the local shist and granite, into Speyside. There it continues over layers of sand/gravel deposited after the last ice sheets retreated – and therefore responsible for making Strathspey broader and deeper than other glens. The river has aided the local population's economic success but, along with the fertile deposits, Speyside is one of the most densely-populated areas of the Highlands. The river is now used more for pleasure and not, as from AD 800, for floating timber down from the gradually disappearing Caledonian Forest that once covered huge areas of Scotland. This was especially so around 1850, when much timber was sold off for ship-building, ceased only with the advent of iron-built ships.

Wood-cutting/logging was traditional for many families in this area for many years, a very dangerous job. Due to the river's slow course, dams or sluice gates were constructed and, when opened, created a huge wave. This pushed the fallen logs down towards the coast and here the loggers were greatly at risk, hanging on to the logs as they tried to guide them on their way. It was also probably the earliest type of 'roller coaster' ride!

This valley has been the scene of many disputes between clans – not only over the riches made from timber but also from the pasturelands, which can be used up to a height of 370m. One aspect of Speyside to which the clans did not object was the quantity of salmon in the river's rich waters, plus the wide variety of animal/bird life inhabiting its banks and in the hills which, now, attract many tourists to the area. But the real gem of the Strathspey is the whiskey. Since the 14th Century the value of the surrounding granite and the superior water draining off it (compared to that from sandstone or limestone) has resulted in some of the most famous distilleries in the area – Glenfiddich in Lower Strathspey and Black & White (created by James Buchanan) in Dalwinnie. Unfortunately our trip took us nowhere near either!

When planning this trip I was more concerned (as most hikers) with mountains, forever mountains. Yet as I learned more of the history and traditions of the area, my interest grew – especially of the Clan Macpherson, long established in this area. After the Jacobites' third uprising in 1719 and General Wade had built his military road to connect the highland forts, one clan leader (who joined forces with the followers of Bonnie Prince Charlie) was involved in the famous Battle of Culloden. For that act, along with most other clan chiefs, his estates were confiscated and he had to live under new laws; these prevented any possession of arms as well as the wearing of clan tartan. His name was Ewan Ban, son of the chief of the Macpherson Clan – more popularly known as Cluny Macpherson.

Spey dam

When his castle was burnt to the ground the Redcoats under Cumberland hunted him but, aided by his faithful Clansmen, he successfully hid for some years – before eventually sailing to France, where he died. One of his better-known hiding places is a cave on Creag Dhubh above the A86 and near his castle; this was later replaced by an elegant country house.

During our walk along Wade's Road, Mark's thoughts were not really on the Strathspey and its history, or the fact that – as we passed the Spey Dam – above us lay the remains of Dun-da-Lamh, situated on top of an excellent defensible position with views up and down the Spey. No, he was more concerned with food, more food and a new pair of socks! His, like mine, had almost solidified into cardboard. Most of our provisions were chosen for their high fat/energy content but, unfortunately, these factors do not include taste. We had only been walking for two days but, in the unexpected heat, would have given anything for a cold drink. We didn't know if there was a shop at Laggan but, as we neared the town, were relieved to see one.

Two cold drinks plus a quick visit to the insect/grass-free toilet later, we were resting against our rucksacks by the road awaiting our 'chariot' – from which we would appreciate this wide valley's attraction, driving past the junction of the Spey and the Truim, where one of the many clan battles for this paradise-amid-mountains occurred.

Ruthven Barracks

It happened around 1370, when the Cameron Clan had picked another fight with the Macintosh, Macpherson and Davidson Clans (who were small but, between them, more powerful). Before the battle began the Macpherson Clan claimed their right to hold the right wing, but were later told that the honour had been bestowed on the Davidson Clan. This angered them and they withdrew from the battle, watching as the Cameron Clan slowly beat their challengers. In desperation the Macintosh Chief sent a message to the Macpherson Chief accusing him of cowardice; this alone was bad enough but he made the message appear as if it had come from the enemy. In response to this insult the Macpherson Chief called his men to arms, pursued the victorious Camerons and surprised them as they celebrated their win, resulting in great losses for the Camerons.

On our way to Kingussie we passed through the small frontier town of Newtonmore, home not only to an interesting drink – 'Stag's breath' (made from whiskey and comb heather honey) – but also to a witch. She lived near Nuide House and so terrified the locals that they would pay her in money and kindness to keep her happy. Then an outsider moved into a local farm and just threw insults at her. She retaliated with spells but he continued, even after she cast a spell on him, said to cause him to choke to death. He ignored the old woman's threats and remained unconcerned until, whilst walking home one dark and stormy night, he was slightly alarmed when his dogs became agitated as he passed the Inverton burn. Gradually, in the darkness, he made out the shape of a huge grey hound and, before he could react, it was at his throat. His two faithful dogs retaliated and chased the hound. Soon afterwards he heard a terrified cry – "call off your dogs!" – but he was too exhausted and said nothing. After that night neither his dogs, nor the witch, were seen again.

Once in Kingussie we found the local café – and the sports shop for those all-important socks. Then, dismissing the attraction of B & B, we set off again towards Ruthven Castle, clearly visible as we left the town. The natural mound it was built on has been used for defensive positions for centuries. The first castle, built there in 1229 for the Lord of Badenoch, was of timber; it was later used as a power base by the 'Wolf of Badenoch', notorious for his wild raiding/plundering – including the burning of Elgin Cathedral (the result of a disagreement between himself and the Bishop of Moray).

The wooden castle was eventually burnt down and, over the years, replaced with stronger structures and used by both sides during the English Civil War – until eventually destroyed by fire. Next it was used as a strategic position for troop movements in the Highlands along Wade's Road. At the end of the Jacobite Rising barracks were built, as part of a line of fortifications intended to prevent further uprising; but, after several attacks, the soldiers were forced to surrender. The barracks were burnt down for the last time by Highlanders after the Battle of Culloden and the building no longer used. It had one final claim to fame, however, about 175 years ago – as the location of the last reported sighting of the mythical beasts, the 'green fairy dogs'. Many stories exist about these creatures, most of them reporting them as non-violent, but it is said if they follow you and are heard to bark three times, it is a death omen – unless the unfortunate victim manages to 'stone' them at the first bark…

Opposite the castle remains we struck out towards the distant Cairngorms via Tromie Glen, on an old path once used by Redcoat soldiers. As we strolled up the gentle slope I could imagine those soldiers marching rhythmically in perfect file, shouted at by their superiors to keep in step. And here *we* were, looking and smelling horrendous, just taking our time. We were back on a path of very short grass, so much easier to follow the footsteps of our predecessors. Our route into the Cairngorms may not have been the shortest or most well-known to the high plateau, but for us it formed part of the build-up.

From the highest point on the path, before descending into the Glen Tromie Wood, there was a wonderful panoramic view of the Monadhliath behind Kingussie. Even though the highest peak may only be 878km, their bulk appeared huge rising above the town. One of the highest (and probably most popular) summits could just be seen; it has the unusual name of 'Carn an Fhreiceadain' – meaning 'The Watchtower' and was used by the Black Watch when looking for cattle thieves. In the days when cattle theft was an accepted part of life, people lived according to the regional saying: *"the good old rule sufficed them, the simple plan that they should take who have the power – and they should keep who can"*.

Below us lay Glen Tromie Wood and, in the distance over more wood plantations, and the Cairngorms. From there the sight did not seem too impressive, but that would slowly change as we drew nearer. Mountains then disappeared from sight as we entered Glen Tromie Wood. Compared to earlier experiences, this Glen was really narrow and straight – excellent for lookouts high up on the ridges; even today, there is said to be a stone, somewhere along its length, that resembles a chair. It was apparently made, over a period, by a large farmer called Big Farquhar who, after a dispute with the local Baron, took to sitting up there overlooking the Glen – waiting for the Baron's men to come and get him. If we had arrived earlier in the day I might have been tempted to search for it but, as it was, we stopped for water in the Tromie river and made our way to Inshriach Forest. There we hoped for some relief from the sun but were soon invaded by millions of flies and, later, midges. When we emerged on the other side of the forest we were tired of the insects, increasing in number every hour; and my burning blisters added to the general discomfort. Our perfect camping spot of yesterday seemed a million miles away compared to our present site; the only consolation was the awesome sight of Carn Ban Mor and the start of the Cairngorms, looming ahead.

It seems that if I see a mountain, I get a blister – huge and always in the same spot; but, some years ago, I found salvation in a plaster that really works. You just drain the blister, rip the skin off and pop the plaster on. Simple – but damn painful! They don't come off whilst you're walking, even if immersed in water, and the pain is hardly felt; the only drawback is the smell when removed – a small price to pay for more comfortable walking.

CAIRNGORM MOUNTAINS

Day 4 Inshriach Forest – Loch Nan Stuirteag

+780m -210m   16km

I woke at sunrise, stiff but otherwise happy, and took a good look around outside. The blister kit had worked so maybe now I could walk without hobbling. It was the first time I'd woken at sunrise and the soft light of the new sun made the scenery appear magical. Light flickered on the stream as it flowed slowly into the pasture land spreading out towards a pine plantation surrounding the area. The Cairngorms rose majestically behind, looking slightly out of place set against wood and fields but, as the sun rose and the morning fog disappeared, they made a perfect frame for the images of strength and beauty now unfolding.

Early morning view towards Cairngorms

I took one of my better photographs during these few moments, made more impressive by the presence of the antler we had found the previous day and, after careful timing, the flight of an osprey as it took off from a dead tree trunk whose side glowed in the early light. Usually I take many photographs on my trips but only a few give me that smug, satisfied feeling; this was one of them. Of all those I took on the trip, no others captured the atmosphere of the place and my feelings at the time.

Briefly I laid inside the tent and watched the bird, then the sun slowly came up above the wood, dispersing the fog to reveal a clear, crisp view up Carn Mor and the visible line of the path we would take up to it. This I considered our first major haul up, partly dreading it yet wanting to set off. Would we finally see some of the unpredictable weather I had heard so much about? My thoughts were disturbed by Mark, stirring in his maggot coating. After his morning ritual of stretching/groaning we started to pack, deciding that the black flies' invasion made it advisable to depart as fast as possible and stop for breakfast somewhere less intrusive – *without* our persistently annoying neighbours.

Due to its bulk, Carn Ban Mor seemed closer than it actually was. In between it and us were remnants of the Great Caledonian Forest once covering this area. When I think of Scotland the forests and woods do not usually spring to mind, but the areas that still exist contain such a variety of wildlife that they must not be missed – particularly the birds of prey, which I have been lucky to see.

These remnant forests, descendants of the Caledonian Forest, are cared for by the Forestry Commission; whilst allowing people to enjoy them, they manage them in ways to promote growth and encourage the wildlife that would otherwise disappear. The first forest we walked through on the way to the Feshie river was quite dense, like the hoards of flies, so it didn't take long to reach the river due to our breaking all pace records. Crossing the river by a good solid bridge by Achlean, we set off towards another forest.

There are numerous mammals within the Cairngorm Nature Reserve, which I had hoped to see, but, being wild, they are experts in elusion – particularly when they hear the earth-shattering approach of human boots. Unfortunately I missed the deer, foxes and badgers – as well as others exclusive to the Reserve: the wild cat (said to be mostly established on this side of the Reserve), the otter (whose track I did not see) and the red squirrel. After spotting so many grey squirrels all over UK, it would have been good to see one of our native squirrels.

So far we had seen no one, which made no sense. The path up the mountain, and the bridge, bore signs of much use. We began worrying whether we had taken the wrong path – or *I* had (as Mark kept reminding me), then suddenly saw people – and a more established path up a waterfall. It was one of the best of the entire trip. Various routes of the river cascaded down past tall pine trees, revealing twisted roots and intermittent pools where the rock had been eroded until the river found an easier route. The waterfall may have had no name but the path up to it did – Moire Mhor; we would follow it as far as Loch nan Cnapan, from where we would strike off towards Glen Geusachan.

The walk up Carn Ban Mor was at gentle pace, dead slow. Unfortunately we ascended at high noon and it *was* hot. As we progressed higher, however, it began to cool and the wind increased; heather was replaced by cotton grass. More and more hikers joined us, their sacks smaller and they seemed to almost run past. By the time we reached the top – or at least the large expanse of sloping, shallow grassland, the wind was quite strong; we walked a little further until the plateau of the Western Cairngorms came into full view below. The majority of it is lower than its Eastern counterpart, but still looked vast; the land sloped down in front of us to a point where we could see tents; then it rose up to Carn Toul in the far distance, at 1291m the highest summit on this plateau. We couldn't see any corries – yet – except a few above Loch Einich; the remainder were still hidden.

Loch Einich

The Cairngorms form the largest tract of mountainous land over 900m in Britain, due to their being formed from an old block of granite – less susceptible to the forces of erosion and as old as the granite that makes up the Ben Nevis massif. Both the Cairngorms and Ben Nevis were pushed up eons ago when the Caledonian Mountains were first being formed; since then subsequent Ice Ages have contributed to the erosion, the last being only 10,000years ago. Before the Ice Ages, the Cairngorms area would have appeared similar to the rolling hills of the Monadhliath, but glaciers (and the way they grind away rocks) have played a major part in creating the high plateau's wide, undulating range with broad summits and vertical edges. These edges (or corries) include – amongst others – the cliffs above Loch Avon, the Lairig Ghru, whilst those between Cairn Toul and Braeriach hold the greatest attraction in this area for me. I looked forward to the amazing contrasts of cauldron corries, cliffs and pink rock.

On our descent towards Loch nan Cnapnan the plateau's size enlarged; shallow slopes and short distances suddenly increased and I recognized the true meaning of all the warnings I had heard about this area. Today we were safe but if we had encountered unpleasant weather conditions – low cloud, rain, strong wind – the situation would have been different. In a place with almost no good natural markers, getting lost was easy – even in perfect weather, as I found out. But on such a glorious day my thoughts were far from any likely dangers and, as we passed the tents, began our last leg of the day's hike up towards Loch nan Stuirteag. After a slight detour due to my walking up the wrong valley (nobody's perfect) we soon arrived. Because of the detour we first saw it from slightly higher than we would have at the 899m pass and we were impressed by the immense scale of Devil's Point. This was first called, in Gaelic, 'Bod an Deamhaim' or 'Demon's Penis'…. Suffice to say that it, and the surrounding hills, looked spectacular – along with the deep gorge below it to Glen Dee and the Loch that was to be home for the night; a welcome sight. It had, in our opinion, a little beach and, due to the Loch's shallowness, we nicknamed it 'Littlehampton'.

This was our highest camp so far and I expected to feel colder as we ambled around for a few hours before bed. But my expectations were dashed yet again – the weather was too good to be true. Something had to happen but not today; in this sheltered spot there was no wind and not a cloud in sight. Two hikers passed as we rested by the Loch and the looks on their faces summed up our situation – tanned and unshaven, we resembled scruffy sun-worshippers swopping the last of their bad jokes. We could almost have been having the time of our lives in a pub!

Up in this area conditions can become severe at any time of the year but especially in winter, when the Cairngorms experience Arctic conditions. Since this trip, I have walked near to Ben Macdui in the depths of winter, but only after feeling experienced enough to do so, where if I encountered trouble, there are numerous escape routes. On this side of the plateau, there is thankful bothies and huts; they offer very cosy and warm shelter. Near the Loch are two such shelters – one below Devil's Point in the Lairig Ghru plus a bivouac within the corries between Cairn Toul and Braeriach.

Day 5   Loch Nan Stuirteag – Lochan Buidhe

+900m   -650m   18km

We awoke next morning not to snowstorms, thankfully, nor rain or even cold wind – but to the same clear blue sky. No complaints. It was wonderful, even the purity of the air made me feel good – not stiff or stuffy as I usually do when I wake up, but wide-awake and eager to be off. Today we would be walking up to the summit of Ben Macdui, second highest to Ben Nevis by a mere 35m – not much when you consider they are both above 1300m. I wasn't concerned, however, as to how tall or steep this summit would be but more interested in the marvelous panoramic view there would be across the rest of the plateau into Lairig Ghru with its many corries and beyond – providing no cloud blocked it.

From the Loch we walked to the edge of the moraine and descended steeply into the gorge of Glen Geusachan where, at first, the cliffs of the surrounding mountains seemed close and high. Following the course of the stream Allt Glais an T-Sabhail, the gorge became wider lower down, making the high, steep mountains from the plateau around us more impressive – until we neared the end of this Glen and reached the beginning of Glen Dee. Directly ahead was the prominent Carn a Mhaim and, to the right, the much lower and rounded summit of Creagan nan Gabhar. In between lay the wide pass we would follow to Luibeg

Bridge. Before that were two rivers to cross on our route over the Glen and, due to the lack of rain, these were easily crossed by using visible rocks as stepping stones. If the rivers were in full spate it would have been more thrilling, but if excitement and a wet backside are not desired then the Allt Glais an T-Sabhail could be crossed back up in Glen Geusachan, where it is not so wide. The river Dee could be crossed by the Corrour Bridge near to the hut under Devil's Point where, I imagine, the extra effort would be rewarded by better views up the Lairig Ghru than we had – and a higher perspective of southern Glen Dee. It presents an inspiring view, especially after the narrow Glen we had just ascended.

Since reaching the 700m mark, the heather had begun to dominate the landscape and we again found ourselves struggling through it as we made our way across the river to the Lairig Ghru path. I expected to see more people on this well-used track but we were alone. It was a strange week – no rain or cloud, just heat, and hardly anyone up in the hills with us. Did the notoriously bad weather in this area only occur when sufficiently large numbers of hikers invaded it? Suspicions were soon confirmed as a large group of German walkers appeared from Luiberg – then two more such groups – followed by a dark cloud rapidly making its way towards us! "It's not raining, but pouring" (tourists) was the phrase that came to mind – all of them en route through the Lairig like thousands before them. I had read that, in past centuries, the Lairig Ghru had been regularly used by young girls carrying baskets of eggs on their heads from Braemar to Rothiemurchus. Numerous thieves must have used it too, judging by the name of the stream below the path we were on – 'Allt Preas nam Meirleach' ('The Stream of the Thieves'). But the most well-known and unfortunate tale about the route must be that of the three tailors. One Hogmanay, after drinking too much 'John Barleycorn', they coaxed each other into a 'risk and dare' – to dance at the dells of Abernethy, Rothiemurchus and Braemar, all within 24 hours. They managed the southern two easily but, when making their way through the Lairig towards Braemar, the cold and the effect of the drink overcame their merriment. They took shelter under a stone half way down, where they died. Today that stone is named after them, (The Tailors' Stone) probably more as a warning than a remembrance. Did the Germans making their way up towards it know this, I wondered? Not that they needed to worry – they were more likely to get sunstroke than freeze to death!

Track to Glen Luibeg

We were not planning to walk past the stone, unfortunately, but were proceeding to Ben Macdui via the route to Luibeg-Bridge. It was strange to see 'Men at Work' signs on the path, in places I considered as far from the M25 as it was possible to be! Their task was to repair erosion and make channels along the path to allow water to escape, avoiding further damage. The work looked hard and most of them were probably volunteers, making me feel slightly guilty as we stopped by the pine trees near Luibeg Burn for a rest before the major ascent up to Ben Macdui.

According to local legend, on the slopes of nearby Carn Crom stands an old gnarled fir tree – 'Craorn an Oir' (Tree of Gold) –

not because it is covered in gold but because gold was once buried there by a certain Laird of Dalmore, who acquired it after a raid in Lochaber. Unfortunately he removed it, to buy some land. I couldn't see the tree and wasn't planning to locate it. If the gold hadn't been removed, however...

Of all the stories about these mountains, one stands out for its spookiness – the tale of the 'Old Man of Macdui'. Since the 18th century, there have been many strange tales about this old character, most of them the result of over-active imagination – or just for profit. Nevertheless, strange noises can be heard up on the plateau, caused by the wind blowing through corries. This noise, I am told, is similar to music or voices. But what is more significant is that, in the dying light when the sun is low, a grayish distorted image can be spotted – silhouetted against any existing mist or cloud. This is actually just a person's shadow but I might be persuaded to think differently if it happened to us. Today was probably the best time for something to happen – or appear – there being two of us, not one, to tell the tale. On one occasion when something revealed itself to two brothers on the plateau while they were collecting stones just below the Ben, both witnessed a strange figure running down towards them. As it disappeared into a dip, both were overcome by a terrible fear and they ran for their lives away from the pursuing figure. Later it was stated that the figure could be explained by natural means, but does the fact that *both* of them were so afraid indicate that perhaps some things *are* beyond explanation?

Could there be some sort of 'presence' up on the Ben? Several explanations that partly answer this suggest that the Ben is a 'centre of cosmic intelligence' for visitors from outer space. Some Buddhists believe that the Ben is a holy place where a 'perfect being' exists, such as the 'perfect men' seen by a practicing Mahayana Buddhist in the Lairig Ghru. The local Mackenzies believe that the grey man is the ghost of an ancestor who once wrote in a poem that he would 'come again'. Whichever explanation is true, I'm sure the knowledge of there being something there will continue to attract hikers from everywhere – hoping to solve the mystery or at least have some sort of 'experience'.

Today we would test the stories as we made our way up the ridge of Sron Riach and on to the summit. The top was in cloud and my first thought was 'damn, no view' but this was quickly followed by the realization that we might see or feel 'something'. I hoped not – I wouldn't be able to run very fast with my pack on! If the extent of the fear was as severe as reported, however, then I doubted I'd think twice about dumping it…

Ben Macdui summit

We were climbing up on to the plateau at 1400 hours; there was no one to be seen. The clouds that had built up earlier were dispersing but the view remained darkened and hazy. Not far up the ridge the heather was replaced by cotton grass but this also began disappearing amongst increasing quantities of broken stones. Past the strange but tranquil Lochan Uaine far down below the ridge, the stones turned to slabs until the slope began to level out on our final approach to the summit. Thankfully the cloud had now completely dispersed, revealing spectacular views down Glen Luibeg, the Carn of Derry Cairngorm and past the ridge of Carn A' Mhaim to Devil's Point. Once on the plateau, the wind gathered pace and soon the heat and sweat built up on the hard climb was replaced by cold and freezing sweat, the first real cold we had experienced all week; my jacket finally saw daylight! If the wind – and the chill factor it brought with it – felt this cold when it was hot below, then I realized it must be a killer in the colder months, for both humans and plant life. Up here, there was only moss and lichen. Moss helps protect the scant amounts of underlying soil whilst the lichen, during its 10,000-year-plus lifetime, slowly breaks up the stones and boulders. By the surround evidence, it had done its job well. The presence of moss and lichen has enabled geologists to discover more about the ice fields that once covered this area and has proved equally useful to the locals in providing dyes used in Harris Tweed.

Camp at lochan buidhe

Once passed the old Sapper Bothy, last used by surveyors in 1847, we could see the high summit cairn, a wonderful sight; many photos were taken as we took turns standing on it – as many others had before us. The most rewarding part of reaching a summit like Ben Macdui is that there is no higher peak in the near vicinity, plus the 360 degree view when it is clear. You simply have to see it for yourself. From the cairn we left the rucksacks and made our way towards the Lairig Ghru for a better perspective of the corries on the other side and, apart from some haze, had a clear view. The large abyss of the Lairig made them seem quite small but still incredible – all amazingly created by the movement of ice, slowly but dramatically changing the shape of these mountains.

Our final destination was Lochan Buidhe, at 1300m the highest named stretch of water in Britain. Mark found this both amusing and pleasing – it would be the highest he had ever camped. The Loch lies in a very exposed area and probably not classed as an ideal place to camp overnight, especially with the opportunity of a rather better location nearby at Loch Etchachan, to the east. As the weather had been so good thus far, however, I decided the risk would justify the thrill.

Before I began this trip I decided to read up on the area, and discovered two interesting facts. The first, a real gem (literally) caused me to take more notice of the stones and rocks I stepped and tripped over. One could be a 'Cairngorm Stone', regarded as a precious stone; unfortunately this, like most gems, is hard to find and some have spent their whole lives searching for just one. The second fact concerned the colour of the pink granite; it is reported to be a weird and wonderful sight but, due to my colour blindness, I held little hope of seeing it. Then, just as we began our descent from the summit, the cloud cleared and the sun shone directly on to a patch of scree below us, for a while, I was amazed to actually be seeing bright pink. This made a change from the usual greens, browns and greys of the mountains and I quickly took photographs to capture it; fortunately, when processed, all the colour had been successfully captured.

Our tent's position was near to the Loch in a concave part of the plateau; we were sheltered from the wind off the summit and for a while everything was fine. I hoped it would stay that way and we wouldn't be woken in the night by strong wind, heavy rain or even strange ghostly sounds… Just before we disappeared into our maggots, however, I noticed that the cloud had descended and was lying just above us – trapping in all the warmth of the day and, at one point, forcing me to spend part of the night outside the sleeping bag. I remember thinking how improbable the weather had been all week – for here we were, tempting nature to do its worst – rain, even wind – but there was nothing. At every other time of the year this would definitely be a 'no camp' area but we seemed to have chosen the one week when it was hotter than Death Valley!

Day 6   Lochan Buidhe – Glenmore

+230m   -990m   12.5km

Next morning I rose early, hoping to reach Hells Lum in time to take some photographs of Loch Avon before the sun was too high. The clouds were abundant – thick and fluffy. Whether they would yield rain only time would tell but at the moment they were calm, only a light breeze nudging them across the sky. What seemed incredible was that the sun cast a kaleidoscope of colours on to the rock faces, mixing them with the swirling fog as it climbed out of the Lairig Ghru, creating a sense of peace. Turning away from it all was unattractive but if I wanted that photograph of Loch Avon I must make my way to Hells Lum, not too far from our tent. In reality, the ground between Hells Lum and me was full of soggy, boggy streams and moss! On arrival, as I looked down from the steep, almost vertical cliff into Loch Avon, the sun's soft early rays shone on the surface – making it appear especially radiant against the dark, steep slopes of Beinn Mheadhoin. To obtain my photograph I had to walk out on to a rock slab which, due to a long crack against the main rock face, appeared to be about to plunge into the valley. I felt very vulnerable, standing on the edge, but obtained some classic shots with which to bore the family.

If you look at the name 'Loch Avon' on the map, it has in brackets a different version – nothing unusual in this area. It was first known as Loch A'an, due to a delightful story involving the mythical warriors referred to as 'The Feinne' or 'Fianna'. The tale concerns their leader, Fionn and his wife Ath Fhinn (or A'an). One day they went hunting alone and came to a river in full spate. Fionn crossed it safely but when his wife attempted to cross she was dragged under by the strong current, and drowned. That river was the same one that runs out of the Loch. Before this event it is believed the river was called 'Uisage geal' or 'Uisage Ban nan Clachan Sleamhuinn' (White Water of the Slippery Stones) – until Fionn, full of remorse, renamed it after his wife, then 'A'an'. There is also another explanation for the name, this being that it derives from an Anglicised form of the Gaelic word 'Amhuinn' – meaning 'a river' but, for me, the second explanation doesn't have the appeal of the first.

Unfortunately, by the time I returned to base the wind had gathered speed, making packing up the tent almost impossible – including one moment when it was momentarily blown away when we let go of it by mistake. I knew, and always expected, that we would experience a change in the weather up on the plateau – but did it have to be at our last wild camp? I'd hoped to have a few moments to reminisce not only on our last few nights of isolation and total freedom (which seemed to have passed so quickly) but on our experiences along the way, away from the stresses of modern life, artificial lights at night – and the stars. No noise, except for running water, wonderful views of the hills and the animals living there – all beneath a blazing sun. Lastly, no more aches, pains and blisters – I would miss them the most…

Top of alladins crag

From the Loch we followed the well-defined track taking us to our last Munro – Cairn Gorm, which was reputedly one of the easiest to climb. We were making our way up by what could be called 'the back way', through what I considered the best possible area to see these mountains. Whether this made the ascent to Cairn Gorm easy or hard didn't really matter, for we just seemed on our own again and the views around us were amongst the best so far; they made the forthcoming climb seem trivial. Once up by the edge of the plateau, the waters of Loch Morlich and the silent old trees of Glenmore Forest (which surrounds it) were a wonderful sight. Behind us the unique panorama of the undulating ridges jutting up from Loch Avon perfectly matched the few lingering early morning clouds. How would these views compare with those on top of Cairn Gorm? The path along the edge of the corries towards Cairn Gorm is only about 2 miles, but due to endless gazing at the breath-taking scenery, it took us about 2 hours to reach the start of the climb. Sometimes you just *have* to take your time....

According to the map there was a structure of some sort on the summit; what it was I did not know. From first hazy sight, I thought it was a cross, like those found on summits in the Alps. In fact it was a weather station and mast, plus a base for rescue missions undertaken on the plateau. The weather station, for the past 20+ years, has taken weather readings every 3 minutes. During our stay, there was little wind and it was warm – a very pleasant, calm time compared to the highest wind speed of 140mph and low temperature of -10 Celsius recorded in the past. It amazed me that the mast and building – especially the mast – had stayed up for that long, considering the conditions. The rescue station was quite low and compact and, on looking at Mark, I thought he might need to be rescued. His facial hair had grown so fast during the last few days that he resembled an animal! We were not the cause of an expensive and dangerous rescue this time, although there was once a woman who would have welcomed it. Unfortunately she perished long before the station was built and rescuers operated in the hills. It began when a Mackintosh boy, with whom she was madly in love, was condemned to death by the Chief for some gross misdeed. At first she pleaded with the Chief to spare his life but was refused; after his death she lost her reason and began roaming endlessly – until she found her peace in a little hollow not far from Marquis Well, situated just below this summit. The hollow is called 'Cista Mearad' ('Margaret's Coffin')

Due to thickening haze the views from the summit were disappointing, it being our last day and on a high vantage point. We did not stay long and sadly began making our way down towards the Ptarmigan Restaurant via Marquis Well. This side of the Cairngorms would probably be quite crowded in the winter months, with skiers taking advantage of the 17 lifts giving access to 23 runs. In winter the ski slopes would look pretty, covered in snow, but as we neared the restaurant it looked quite different.

The unused chair lifts and endless fences, along with the pale colour of the granite and the swirling wind, made it seem like a ghost town; I half expected to see dead sage bushes blowing about and dreaded to think how the proposed rail link could add to all this (which, as of publication, is finished). The walk further on down to White Lady Shieling and on to the ski center did not improve matters; more chair lifts and fences adversely affected the true character of the mountains that we had come to love.

Weather station on cairn gorm summit.

The magnificent views weren't over yet, however; out in the thinning haze, in the far distance, the vast expanse of Rothiemurchus (in Gaelic meaning 'Plain of the Great Pine') and the Queen's Forest opened up – one of the remaining remnants of the once-grand Caledonian Forest. Ten square miles of glorious woodland that, somehow, was saved from the many fires, ship-builders and other circumstances that lead to the demise of forests in other areas. Today these trees, and the shimmering waters of Loch Morlich, are protected by the Forestry Commission; together they are home to an abundance of wildlife, some of which we later enjoyed from inside a café beside the camp-ground in Glenmore. For the present, however, our sights were set on the café by the ski center – decent food and a cool drink. By the amount of people now walking up past us, we decided it was just a day's stroll for most of them; but for us it marked the end of a glorious week's walking. To my surprise, neither of us wanted alcohol – as is usual at the end – but we were satisfied with a few Cokes and ploughman's lunches. It all went down well but I wondered how my body would react to this sudden large intake of real food…

View from camp site

We had hoped to catch a bus down to the Glenmore camp-site but, due to our feasting, we missed it. All turned out well, however, as we made our way on foot into the forest; the sun was still shining and the air was pleasantly warm as the gradient lowered. In the forest I heard birdsong – not unusual – unless you have been in the mountains for a while, hearing and seeing nothing in the skies. What I hadn't missed, and was once again traumatically pestered by, were the flies, several buzzing round my face until we reached the camp-site-the definite sign of journey's end. We rapidly made use of the facilities – shower, shop, and café – discovering that underneath all that hair we had acquired a reasonable tan.

Apart from the inhabitants of a normal wood, Glenmore has been – and may still be – home to the Fairies. One of the better known is the King of the Fairies, 'Domhnull Mor Bad an t-sithean' – or 'Big Donald' for short. Apparently he was larger than a normal fairy, and lived to the west of Loch Morlich on top of a small knoll called 'Sithean' or 'Fairy Knoll'. The reason he was so well remembered is due to the unpopular pranks he played on local people, although he did also help them sometimes by frightening off outsiders trying to use the local Laird's land for their own purposes. Past Glenmore Lodge there is a loch – Lochan Uaine – whose waters are green. These days the colour has been ascribed to scientific reasons but that is simply denying the fact that the water is green due to the King Fairy and all his followers constantly washing their clothes in it – a much more probable explanation…

During the night it rained – the first of the week. The subsequent view of the Cairngorms in the morning was free of haze; they were crisp and magnificent. If only the air had been that clear whilst we were up there! Nevertheless, we had no complaints – perfect climate, perfect scenery.

The images and impressions we were taking with us would remain with us forever – the air we breathed, the mountains we climbed, the brilliant stars at night… But, most of all, the overwhelming sense of timeless beauty and isolation.

Unforgettable.

UNITED STATES of AMERICA

California, Yosemite National Park

Hidden Treasure

If I had planned this trip to Yosemite Valley about 130 years ago, my expectations and length of stay would have been increased by a factor of 10. This would have been due partly to the amount of information available at that time, but mostly to the conditions of the journey. The latter would of proved a harder undertaking, initially involving a long skull -shattering coach trip from the coast to a town like Merced, followed by a rear-aching mule ride into the valley. Tourists, these days, are presented with a much more comfortable means of transport – due to the invention of rubber tyres, suspension and air conditioning. A few 'nutters' may regard these, as a tad less adventurous than a horse and cart but they are a lot kinder to my old bones!

So on a clear, hot sunny day (which, I was constantly informed, was the norm in California), I left the wide vineyard-covered central valley by Fresno, feeling a sense of wonder for the place I was about to enter. Millions of people had visited Yosemite before me and all had left with their own feelings and thoughts on the beauty of the place; some had even written about it. Of all the authors that came here there was only one whose words captured my imagination - those of the Scottish naturalist John Muir; his endless energy first was responsible for the creation of the Yosemite National Park. But even the most passionate and descriptive prose is no substitute for the real thing. Just as his adventures did not prepare me for what was to come (giving no hint of the paradise that these mountains held), neither did the surrounding scenery leading up to the valley. Not until I emerged from the Wawona Tunnel at Discovery view did I see it all for myself.. And what a view! I marvelled at what lay before me. Although the valley floor was shrouded in a fog-like haze, the steep cliffs of El Capitan and Half Dome were unmistakable even from ten miles away, their mass and

height rising majestically above the narrow, misty valley floor. They towered over a place whose entrance must have appeared to lead into an awe-inspiring green and fertile valley. So it must have seemed, at least to the first Indians (the Miwoks) or, specifically, to a group of the Southern Miwoks arriving here over 4,000 years ago as they travelled up the Merced River. The Valley entrance, which to them, resembled a gaping mouth (translated in their language to Awahni), gave rise to the name given to these first settlers, the Awahnichi - or 'people who live in Awahni'.

A quite different name was given to the Indians of Awahni in the 1800's after a fatal 'black disease' decimated their numbers. They left their valley, only to return years later under the leadership of an old Awahnichi chief's son called Tenaya. He sought his homeland after hearing, in his youth (along with other survivors of the original tribe), many stories of the deep green valley. During this time, despite their living a mostly peaceful life, they were given the name Yohemite, meaning 'some of them are killers'

Once there it probably did not take them long to revert back to their old, contented and uniquely fulfilling ways; Living off the land, reciting old stories of animals they feared and respected, places they had lived and events which had shaped their existence. There were the all-important thrilling fireside stories of their greatest hero, Wek-wek. He was a falcon, born out of a rock burnt in a fire; the rock was his mother and a condor, Yayil, was his father. The stories tell of his bravery in battle: the fight against Ki-Lak, a feared bird monster; of the magic Wek-wek possessed - and used on one occasion - to rise from the dead after allowing the underworld people believe they had cooked him, which gave him the opportunity to escape upon a magical arrow he had shot.

Six mountain hikes from around the world

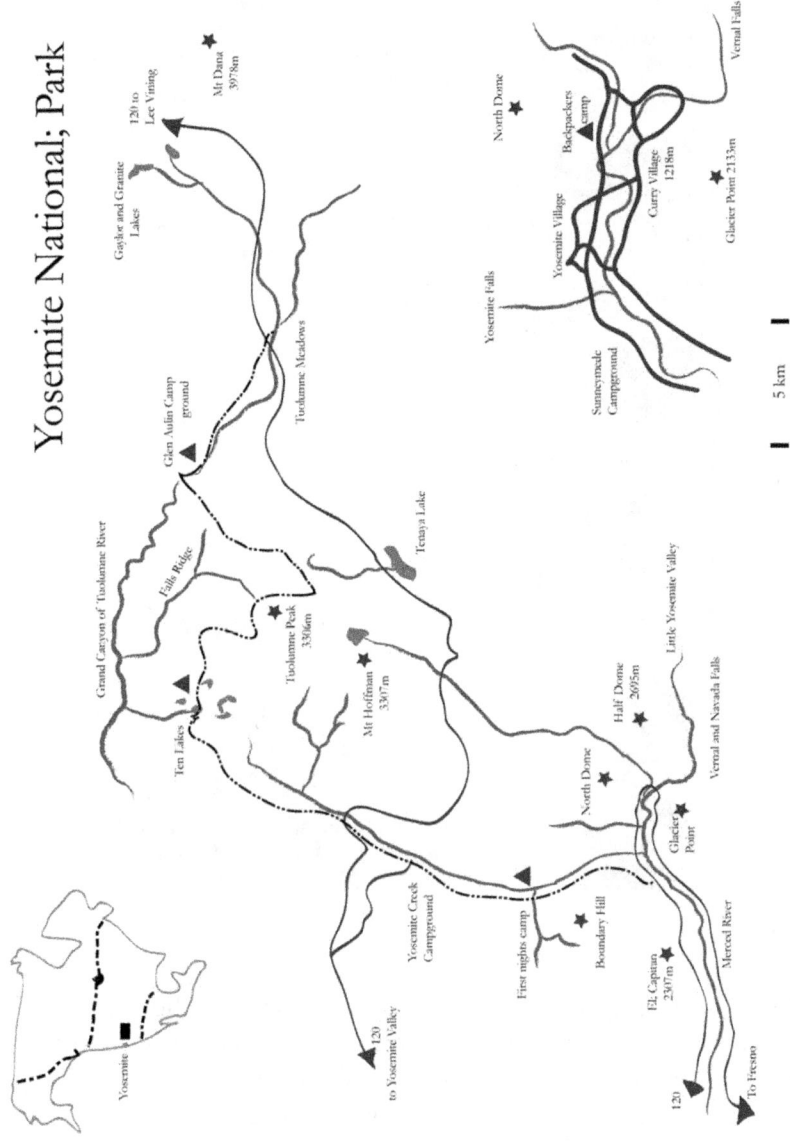

El Capitan

One day during my stay in the valley I visited the replica of an Indian village, behind the Museum in Yosemite Village, and stood over the central fireplace. I imagined the many still; warm nights with them all gathered round it, listening excitedly to the elders telling endless stories. Unfortunately even these jovial occasions came to an end for Tenaya and his band with the arrival of the

White man: prospectors, ranchers and traders. One, James D.Savage, befriended the Awahnichi through the work they did for him - collecting gold from Big Oat Flats in exchange for goods from his trading post on the south fork of the Merced River. Savage knew more than most about the surrounding Indians at that time and tried hard to protect his friends and their land. But he was just one man against an ever-increasing number of whites gradually entering the area. He was, unfortunately, killed for his efforts - but not before he saw the struggle between the Awahnichi and the whites start in earnest.

The valley offered the Indians some protection but, eventually, a group of soldiers, the Mariposa Battalion, found their way in. Once most of the Indians had been caught, including their chief, they were all relocated to reservations - only to be returned later to the valley under the promise that they would live peacefully. The struggle throughout America between the Whites and the Indians was not one of mutual acceptance, so it was inevitable that trouble would break out again. The Mariposa Battalion were again despatched to capture the Indians, but Tenaya's group had already dispersed. He joined the Mono Tribe, with whom he had once lived, only to be killed whilst playing an Indian board game - taking with him the last hope of the Awahnichi Indians.

Shortly after Tenaya's death people began to realize that the valley was an ideal tourist attraction. Very soon the first reports reached them, from Land Surveyors and men of the Mariposa Battalion, urging them to come and see for themselves the awe-inspiring sheer granite cliffs and huge waterfalls. One of the first men to foresee the possibilities of the valley was an Englishman, a Mr. Hutchings; Hutchings did not just spread the word about Yosemite through his own magazine, but he also built the first Hotel there. It was at this hotel where John Muir first stayed, amid his 'Range of Light' (as he called to the Sierra Nevada Mountains). Funny enough, it was the environmentally unfriendly hoofed sheep, which first brought Muir to the Yosemite area that finally brought about his efforts to put the area under national park status protection.

The story of the valley and the park since that time is one of steady growth; rough trails becoming tracks, tracks become roads; more hotels were built. Increase numbers of wealthy travellers on isolated tracks attracted the occasional highway robber, such as Black Bart. He, despite using an unloaded gun, bluffed his way thought 27 robberies before he was caught. His capture was due to his gentlemanly manners and impeccable dress sense - he left behind a tailor's tag after one robbery! There was also the notorious 'Lone highwayman', who held up 5 wagons on the Chowchilla Road with his 'Big 44'.

I was first attracted to Yosemite by stories of colorful characters like these, of the Indians and John Muir. I knew that, in great American style, their lives would only really come alive in the Valley. After driving past discovery view I wondered if – perhaps - the guardians of this paradise had a re-enactment of a highway robbery waiting for us around the next corner.

YOSEMITE VALLEY

During the 2 to 3 days I spent wandering around the valley floor, before and after the hike, I was never once in doubt of the incredibly solid, yet fragile, structure of the valley walls. By day I admired their natural beauty; by night, hearing the thunderous roar of rockslides, my admiration turned to respect. One night a slide felt so close that – briefly - I imagined countless boulders hurtling towards the camp; this fear greatly increased on hearing from two climbers that a slab of rock sheered off on a nearby slope during their climb up El Capitan.

I regarded the services available in the two main villages of the valley as equal to the surrounding scenery - out of this world. The free shuttle bus running around the eastern end of the valley in particular saved much footwork after hiking; it took me, effortlessly, to food, and to the two campsites I used during my stay. The first - Backpackers campground – was tucked behind the North pines campground near to the Merced river, whose clear waters were regularly fished by the diving American dipper.

Valley view towards el capitan

The backpackers was situated across the river in a quiet, isolated spot away from the larger-than-life mobile home campers, close to the site of the old Awahnichi village called Wis-Kul-La. The thin canopy of tall conifers only slightly masked the beautifully sculptured examples of how the granite in this area breaks off in huge slabs, like blocks of snow in an avalanche. Its name, Royal Arches, hints at its majesty, but not so definitively as the name given to it by an early visitor – Winged Lion.

My second campsite stay was at Sunnymede walk-in campsite, much noisier then backpackers, but warmer for the experience as it throbbed with the noise and activity of rock climbers from all over the world. Hair-raising stories abound, true or otherwise were immaterial, but I appreciated the readily extended comradeship from strangers who treated me as though we had been friends for years.

Soon after arriving in the valley night fell, I finished dinner in darkness, not an unusual occurrence. But that night, in that particular location, somehow it felt different. I was in an area frequented by large animals, but had been assured that the three resident female Black bears, their cubs and a Mountain lion were of no real threat. So many contradicting tales, however, did not help. I had hoped to see some wild life, but on *my* terms - and not whilst I was eating! Always on the alert, I reacted to the slightest noise or movement.

Royal Arches

To my relief next morning the tent and I were still in the belly of the valley and not in that of a mountain lion! It was a bright, clear and potentially hot day but I remained watchful as I set off for Yosemite village via a section of the 17km Valley circular walk. This walk veered away from the noise and bustle of the mobile homes, under conifers and oak, into an area thronged with wild life. In the calm of the early morning I heard birds gossiping, saw Californian ground squirrels, colourful striped golden-mantled ground squirrel and a few mule deer. They appeared undisturbed by my presence, making me feel part of their wilderness. Then I reached the village - and town life was thrust upon me.

Due to the park being visited by millions of people annually, there were a few things I needed before I headed out into the high country surrounding the Valley - the most important a wilderness permit. These help restrict the numbers of hikers on the trails at the height of the season. It being the end of September, I had no worry about overcrowding but had to be wary of forest fires; these were extensive during my stay due to a drought, ongoing for several weeks. Unfortunately, too, both Yosemite and Bridal waterfalls - and most of the smaller rivers – had tried up. Most of these fires were in the center of the areas where I planned to hike, resulting in all my plans being changed. The warden at the Wilderness centre happily pointed out that I could still do the John Muir trail, but I had not come prepared for a 220-mile hike to Mt Whitney! Eventually I chose a 5-day hike to Ten Lakes, including a day by the lakes, finishing at Tuolumne Meadows. I had not read a lot about this area but the 'nature watch day' by the lakes was inviting in such wonderful scenery.

Permit in pocket, I needed important supplies - and bear canister. This devise I found a useful defence against those big animals taking my food, but very heavy in the rucksack. This was, at times, of more concerned then animals themselves, specially during the first few days of the hike when I would be acquiring a lot of altitude (3,000ft on the first day) and needed to consider the possible lack of water sources. Perhaps the appeal of the alien landscape I would be walking though would cancel out any fatigue I felt – but maybe not!

Sentinal Rock from Merced river

Back on the valley floor I had no such worries, just many rolls of film to use and an overwhelming enthusiasm to see everything. Despite the absence of the main waterfalls, the scenery was breathtaking. Every season here has it's own silent wonder; autumn in the valley is spectacular.

El Capitan is not far from Sunnymede, especially if you are given a lift. The sun was just rising above the valley rim as I arrived; I saw two climbers making their way up the mountain, resembling tiny ants on the huge rock face. Naturally I would have liked to say I would join them at the drop of a hat (or an increase in my bank account by over 6 digits) but was satisfied with the isolation of the meadow fronting the mountain. A golden hint of autumn was just developing, a fascinating contrast to the creamy white of the granite mountains.

Half dome

I sat in the tall grass and wild flowers of the meadow for some time, watching the changing face of El Capitan. The sun moved across it, casting different colors and shadows on its surface. I could check the progress of the two climbers and wondered if, during their climb, they also pondered on the significance of the rock they were climbing. Not only has it witnessed millions of camera flashes but has also been given many exotic names: Giant's tower, Monarch of the vale, Crouching Lion of Yosemite. The climbers were probably more familiar with the titanic geological facts surrounding the origins of the mountain and the valley - which present-day geologist ascribe to erosion, initiated by the Merced river and then speeded up by those great white giants – glaciers

Somehow, on such a beautiful day, such scientific explanations did not compare to the old Indian tale of El Capitan, which originated in a time when only black bears inhabited the valley; when their young played and swim happily in the Merced. A time even before El Capitan (or Tu-tok-a-nu-la) existed. According to the story, two young black bears were playing in their favorite part of the river then, tired, rested on a boulder bordering the river. Sleeping deeply, they did not feel the boulder rising slowly and remained asleep for days as it carried on climbing above the clouds. Down in the valley their family and friends missed them. Then the Hawk spotted their position and all the Valley animals took turns attempting to ascend the towering rock face. Each climbed further than the last, but all failed; the mountain lion made the most progress. Then Tul-tak-a-na arrived, a small measuring worm. All the other animals thought he had no hope but as he ascended - and passed - all the levels *they* had achieved, their scorn changed to amazement.

For days the little worm struggled up wards, frightened as he saw the valley below and all the other animals getting smaller. Then he reached the top, exhausted, and was thankful to see the two young black bears, still asleep. He wake them, guided them back down the route up which he had come and was proclaimed a hero for their safe rescue. For his courage the animals decided it was only right that the new mountain be named after the small worm, Tu-tok-a-nu-la. In the Miwok language this also means Rock Chief as, from certain angles, the face of an old chief can be seen on the rock face.

I was unable to make out the figure of this man nor, the dark patch of Diorite rock on the cliff face, which set against the lighter granite is supposed to look like a crude map of North America. All I saw was the reason why this rock face had inspired so many before me; it towered over me as I made my way across the meadow towards Devils Elbow. This was the Indian name given to a certain part of the Merced, which I wanted to follow back into the valley. Despite the lack of water elsewhere, the area appeared fertile. In some of the few remaining deep parts of the river, there was the chance of seeing some of the fish that attract many fishermen to this area, but also the possibility of spotting river mermaids or water women - called Ho-ha-pe by the locals; they had, reputedly, seen them in parts of the river. At the time I knew very little about these legendary creatures but, when I fully investigated the local myths, realized that my search, long ago, would have been regarded as foolhardy; these mermaids loved to entice men into the water to their deaths!

But that day my life was spared; not even a breeze disturbed the mirror-smooth surface of the river with its wonderfully reflected double images of the valley. It twisted its way along the valley far from any of roads, through isolated patches of wild flowers and dense, tall conifers. It was difficult to identify most of the flowers as many were past their best. Some stalks were still as tall as the long grass; I touched them tenderly, unsure whether I was passing through Deerbrush - a plant much loved by the deer, thence it's name. Its leaves served as good hand soap. I would probably have recognized any Cowslips, by their size; some reach 12 ft, with 12 in. leaves - good shelter in the rain! I did see the remains of a few Mountain Ladies Slippers - their 3 purple and 1 white central petals; during spring they are apparently a stunning sight.

I felt disappointed that I had come too late to see the valley covered in these and other colorful plants, blooming under the spray of the two waterfalls. But even in decay and relative quiet, the whole valley remained vibrant - from the bronze and gold leaves below to the lofty deep blue sky above, the rugged valley walls in between – and everything radiant under the brilliance of an unobstructed sun. One spectacular example was Half Dome, its shining craggy rock face superbly reflected in the river.

I took many photographs of this peak, from all angles and different locations, but that first double image remains my favorite. Of all the spectacular peaks here, Half Dome was the one I always felt most drawn to. There was something inexplicable about it - like a beautiful woman; I could not get enough of her. According to legend, the mountain actually represents a woman who traveled here long ago with her husband and child. They, unlike the mountain, were not silent. Tired and thirsty on arrival, they headed straight towards Ah-wi-yah (or Mirror Lake) but Tis-se-yak, the wife, got there first and in her haste drank the lake dry. This angered her husband Nangas, so much that he struck her with his staff, causing her to drop the basket she was carrying - along with the seeds and acorns that produced the trees and plants existing in the valley today. The wife was enraged by his outburst and together they shattered the peace of the valley. The furious gods, as a punishment, turned them to stone. Tis-se-yak became Half Dome, whose tears are said to represent the dark streaks; Nangas became Washington Column, the basket was turned into Basket Dome and the child became Royal arches.

Another rock face, or pinnacle, shares a similar story. Called Lost Arrow, it is in reality a huge pillar of rock 1,500 ft. high - split away from the main rock face. It still continues to split in winter when spray from nearby Yosemite falls freezes inside it. In mythological terms it's Miwok history is much more romantic; it is said to have been created by the spirits in recognition of two lovers (Kos-soo-kah and Tee-hee-neh), who died on their wedding day. He fell from a cliff edge whilst attempting to shoot an arrow representing a message to his loved one and she due to a broken heart as she knelt over her dead husband-to-be.

Vernal falls

Stories like these made me look closer at most of the mountains, attempting to see the faces or features that inspired the stories around them. In most cases I saw something entirely different, the only exception being Mirror Lake, which I reached by another part of the Circular Path. It was very pleasant away from the hoards, seeing a few Squirrels and a particularly noisy Acorn Woodpecker - so named by his habit of storing acorns in the bark of trees. Then I passed warning signs of the possible presence of a Mountain lion in the surrounding woods; there were boulders scattered everywhere from rockslides, where any thing could easily have hidden. I was very relieved to reach the lake or - according to the map – where it *should* have been. There were only banks of white sand - and no water - yet another example of the whole valley, which used to be a giant lake but has slowly turned into meadows. Hopefully this lake will still have a few more years in it before it too becomes a meadow. I had hoped that, against all odds, there would still be water present in it - so I could see for myself the overwhelming beauty of it and appreciate the reasons, which persuaded early visitors to camp on its shore.

I felt disappointed. Even the high rock face of Half Dome opposite the lake did not cheer me; if it had not been for the lakes excellent sunbathing potential I doubt I would have stayed for long. But thankfully my lust for the wonders of water was gratified a few days after the hiking trip when I visited Vernal and Nevada falls. I had been told they were still running and, even though Vernal was not running at full strength, it retained the famous rainbow at its base, the fantastic colors mingling with the surrounding deep green grass and wonderful flowers. Lafayette H. Bunnell named both falls in around 1851, when he saw them on one of the Mariposa Battalions excursions into the valley. Both of course, have Indian names but Bunnell strongly rejected the name of Yo-wi-we (meaning 'give it a twist'), deciding that the slight sexual interpretation of it could not be tolerated at that time.

The climb to the top of Nevada falls was quite steep and high, gaining over 3,000 ft. and mostly followed the John Muir Trail - returning on the Misty Trail, whose track meanders much closer to the falls. Near the junction of both trails is a rock, which is named after Lady Franklin -wife of the famous Arctic explorer Sir John Franklin, in admiration for her efforts in solving the mysteries surrounding her husband's disappearance during his search for the North West passage. The rock in question is where she sat and viewed Vernal Falls.

The climb up to the top of these falls was relatively easy as I had finally acclimatized to the environment; Carrying only a daypack helped. Following the John Muir trail, the Vernal falls were completely hidden from view, whereas the Nevada falls impressive size and height - lying under the imposing Cathedral Peak - was very impressive. At first the falls looked tiny under this peak but, moving nearer, the falls real size opened up - especially when I could make out the people standing on its rim; then I *really* appreciate its 594 ft. drop. The area to the rear of the waterfall was quite level, covered by bare rock, bushes, conifers and a small lagoon in whose cool water I soaked my hot feet. On the left side of the river I could see scattered conifers that appeared to be rooted to solid rock. Conifers on the right side were denser and surrounded by much more vegetation, providing food and shelter for the many birds (I saw Violet-green swallows and Stellar jays) and a handful of butterflies and large dragonflies, all of which seemed to enjoy short glides over the lagoon. There was also a large pool just before the Vernal falls where the river flowed into it over smooth concave rock. It formed what had obviously once been used as an excellent water slide into the pool, before being made illegal; but that did not deter visitors, who still came to sunbathe.

The track down alongside Vernal falls was narrow, steep and made by giants judging by the distance between steps. They were neither slippery nor shrouded in mist, as happens when the falls are at full tilt. Thankfully the rainbow exploded into an array of colors that added brilliance to a landscape, which, until now, had been mostly an assortment of greys. The area around the falls resembled a small patch of paradise, a place that was not only good for the soul but in spring give a free shower too.

There was one other form of a fall in the valley that I would of liked to see but it was discontinued when I was but an adventurous 4-year-old. Called the Fireball, it was man-made from burnt coals from a fire that were pushed over the edge of Glacier point, falling 3,000 ft. on to a ledge just above Camp Curry. Begun in 1871 –2 by James McCauley, who built the 4-mile trail to Glacier point, it must have been a source of wonder for the people of the time during its brief but momentous career, resembling thousand of stars falling from the heavens above in the darkness of night. The appeal of throwing things off from the Valley's rim seemed at one point to become an addiction; items such as rocks, handkerchief and empty boxes were thrown but the most bizarre object was thrown by a certain Derrick Dobbs – who throw an old hen! This act would no doubt outrage present-day animal lovers but apparently the loud cackle that onlookers heard, on most subsequent days, was from the *same* hen!....

On the night preceding the hike I felt far away from the crowds I had seen during the day, camped in the almost empty Backpackers Campground. Alone with my thoughts, I stared up at the stars as numerous hopes and fears about the 5 days ahead filled my mind. Would the extra weight of excess water and the black bear canister break my back? Would I see any black bears? (That being more a hope then a fear). When I tried to sleep these thoughts continued and I could not rest; as soon as I dismissed one worry, another arrived. At least it wasn't the thought of getting up for work, my normal cause of sleepless nights; this time it was of 5 glorious free days where everything and anything could - and hopefully would - happen. This was natural therapy - sweeter than chocolate!

Day 1   Yosemite Valley – First Camp (Yosemite Creek)

+930m   8.9km

Transition from night to day unfolded. The long shadows of the surrounding tree's dissipated in the light of the full moon to the west and encroaching light from the sun in the east, highlighting the towering ridges around the campground. At least that how I imagine dawn greeted the valley that day as I didn't surface from my dream world until much later. The hike may have involved much height gain but the distance was small and I wasn't planning to start too early; I had time for a long stretch, to smell the air and slowly make my way to the start of the Yosemite Falls track, stopping in the village for a rather nice breakfast.

Half dome

In the heart of Spring and Summer the Yosemite falls are seen, photographed and climbed daily by hundreds of bustling tourist, all spending their designated 30 minutes looking up, across and down as thousands of tons of white water descend in thundering cascades down the sheer cliff. In John Muir's day there were far fewer tourists; he usually saw the falls magical appeal from his cabin nearby, which

to him must have seemed an ideal place in an area full with ideal locations. The Awahnichi, however, generally avoided areas near to Yosemite and Bridal Vail falls - or at least treated these masters of illusion, and the spirits they believed lived within them, with respect.
At Bridal Vail, or Po-ho-no, spirits are reputedly more playful then harmful, tending only to blow water out from the falls onto passing visitor who venture too close. The spirits of Yosemite, or Cho-lok, are different. Many years ago, according to legend, there was an Indian village near to the falls; one day, when a women was fetching water, she fell into the river below the falls; there the spirits impregnated her. When she gave birth a great wind suddenly swept through the village, pushing it and its people into the river.

As there was no falls - or river – when I visited, I did not meet with the same fate as the village people; but still felt deprived. Looking up at a silent, dry rock face, I could only imagine the falls and take photographs, but they meant nothing without the cascading water, merely recorded my route up. Lack of water, however, meant fewer tourists – a bonus. On the entire route I saw but a handful of people, who enjoyed the 3 miles of 60 or more switchbacks and 2,700 ft. ascent with me.

I set off happily, arms swinging, appreciating the shade from the hot sun provided by the gold-cup oaks, an increasing advantage as the track gradient steepened. The disadvantage of this cover, however, was having no views during the first part of the walk, something, which in its own way, made the whole effort of climbing, worse. The sandy gravel on the trail didn't help, causing my feet to slip occasionally. My first goal was Columbia Rock, reputably a good viewpoint over the Valley, 600 ft. below: this I hoped would compensate for the sweat pouring out of every pore on my body, which greatly increased whenever I left the shelter of the trees and stepped into the full powers of the sun. I swear I heard it taunting me: "If I can dry up a waterfall I can dry up you too". At times I'm sure I sweated a litre of water for every mouthful I drank.

Eventually I stopped and took shelter under a bay tree. Goal or no goal, sometimes it's better just to rest - preferably before you collapse. This trek *was* supposed to be fun! At least from where I was sitting I could see the valley below. Several people passed me but I didn't ask them the location of Columbia rock. I should have - it was only a short distance away.

It is said that an ascent of Cathedral Rock is "a magnificent feat in it's self" and, for most walkers, the superb panoramic view of the valley could be classed as unbeatable - and therefore a reason not to go on. My eyes were drawn immediately towards half dome; its beauty was far more impressive from this height, standing out from the other peaks around the Valley. Their combined size and mass distorted the size of the Valley floor, which seemed more then its actual 600 ft. below me, quiet and still under its dense canopy of conifers and oak. One could imagine how it looked long ago, classed then as real wilderness; even the odd treeless areas would not necessarily have been meadows, but more likely areas where the giant 'U-wu-lin' of Awahni had walked - taller then most conifers, possessing neither brain or blood, he roamed the earth catching and eating people as if they were ants.

The giant had only one weak spot - his heart -, which the fly, so loathed by summer hikers, discovered was in his heel! The Valley people took advantage of this information by burying hundreds of spears in the ground wherever the giant was known to walk; many were broken or pushed further in by the giant but eventually one hit the vital spot and he fell dead. The Valley scavengers must have had quite a party that day!

The next stage of the walk proved relatively easy, mainly level, following a wide ledge around the side of the mountain until the fall - or where it would have been - came into view; then the track climbed up again. With the attractive sights and sounds of the falls close by, the next stages would normally be climbed slowly, without realising the efforts involved. But on this occasion there was no diversions to marvel at - just heat, sun and mountain sand to cope with; everyone was affected, constantly stopping - especially on the final, exposed and difficult push up. Passing and being overtaken by, the same people was amusing and the day-trippers found the size of my rucksack fascinating. I wish I could have found theirs, just as humorous!

The elation on reaching the summit was exhilarating, though the lack of a view back down into the Valley was rather disappointing. The climb took 3 hours, including an hour's rest, which I considered good going, faster then I had anticipated. I had plenty of time to carry on along Yosemite creek and find a suitable place for the night.

I rested on a large fallen trunk, surrounded by many others towering above me, maybe up to 150 ft. (the average height of most Jeffrey pine and White fir). They looked higher than that - possibly due to *my* feeling a few inches shorter after the climb! I was tempted to pick up a few Jeffrey pine needles – a reputedly good treatment against black spider bites – as these where likely to be active in the heat; or maybe I should take one of the grapefruit-sized cones with which to squash them... Later one of them nearly squashed *me* when it tumbled out of a tree in front of me, landing with such a hard thud that - had it hit me - would have immediately cut my adventure short!

A little further along the Valley rim, is the point where Yosemite creek begins its long descent into the Valley. There, on the narrowest of ledges, John Muir first sighted the Valley and the Falls. The daredevil climb out over the Falls would have been routine behaviour for the adventurous Mr. Muir but, like the water slide above Vernal falls, is probably forbidden now, but it remains as tempting.

Above Ten Lakes

To see the ledge he walked on, and the valley from it were thrills I must leave for another time. Now my main aim was to use the extra time I'd gained to explore Yosemite Creek as far as possible. Also, I had also run out of water, which must now be sterilized against Giardia. I was using Iodine, which I had avoided as long as possible due to tales of its lingering taste; but tests proved it not dissimilar to normal tap water. My required fluid intake in the days ahead would be approximately 3.5 litres daily.

Approaching the creek the slopes on either side were close, and covered by the usual dull-colored trees and rocks but once into it, the changes in colour and character of the flora nearest to the river banks were amazing. Conifers and bushes seemed denser and greener, giving off a wonderful fragrance; collecting water here was very rewarding. Unfortunately this rich zone rapidly diminished as slopes fanned out to reveal sparse conifer covered white rock slopes; a harsh landscape that would produce a love/hate relationship in the coming days - hate for the reflection of heat and glare off the rock, love for it's unique physical beauty and many treasures.

In the quiet, isolated areas of these slopes I imagined I would dread seeing black bears or lions but instead, found myself looking around my new back yard in an effort to imprint the images forever in the pleasure zones of my brain - Such as squirrels and colorful striped chipmunks, who occasionally stopped running and climbing to investigate this intruder. The creek was not exciting as in seasons past, but silent as the surrounding rock. If there had been some ripe berries left on the Manzanita bushes I might have been tempted to pick them, as the Indians did, to make cider. Their recipe was apparently easy and would have certainly tasted better then Iodine water.

The berries were initially winnowed, or tossed in the air and the dirt blown from them; once boiled they were ground to a coarse meal, placed in a sieve-type basket over a waterproof cooking basket. Water was then passed through the meal until all the flavour of the meal was washed out; then the liquid was decanted. What could be simpler? The Indians drank the cider through a plume stick (a stick with hawk feathers stuck to one end) but I would have preferred the normal way and it would have been interesting to discover if it really *did* increase the appetite. I tend to lose mine whilst hiking.

My chosen spot for the night (one the guide book described) was not far from the Valley rim, near to Bluejay creek with brilliant views up to Boundary hill, backlit by the full moon. I searched for an existing fire ring, which wardens prefer hikers to use preference to making new ones, but was unlucky. No matter; last light comes early this time of year and there was little time left to search for firewood, and finish my chores.

The ground resembled the shoreline of a sandy beach, although loose and dry. It held the pegs of the tent but one good breeze would have blown it away. Near the river bank the sand sometimes gave way under foot, causing me to spill water, but this probably annoyed the ants more as I was destroying their homes. It was unavoidable, they were everywhere and I wondered if, after a visit to this 'ant city', an employee of Walt Disney had produced the idea for 'A Bugs Life'...Apart from ants, the only other sign of life was a frog; it hopped down the river side when I was collecting water; small but not necessarily insignificant. Could it have been a descendant of the frog that helped 'Ah-ha-la' the coyote to create people, and the land on which they lived, back in the time when the earth was covered with water and only inhabited by mammals and bird-like people?

Before the coyote could create people he had to make the land that they would need to live on. So he asked a few divers to collect sand from the depths of the water and here the frog excelled, being the only one who could find sand. The coyote scattered the sand to create land but, before he could make the people, must decide what form they would take. He had already made seeds for them to eat, bows and arrows for their use in hunting. He studied all the other animals, considering which had the best hands and feet for gripping. Eventually he decided that the lizard's limbs were the best and, after a few modifications, created man and set him upon the sandy earth.

After seeing the frog - and considering my location - I wondered if I'd be lucky enough to see a coyote. Such cunning graceful beast, which going by their many tales, was well known by the Indians. But that evening the mountains were quiet. The noise of fellow campers I did not miss, but a few chirps would have been welcome, even the car alarm call of the stellar jay or the rattlesnake sounds of grasshoppers. Nothing. Just silence. It felt really spooky, a few times I thought I could hear human voices, but I think that it was just my imagination. Maybe by some incredible coincidence a decoction of Tolguacha root had found it's way into my water? This gave Miwok shamans or witch doctors the appearance of possessing super human powers and took the form of a delirium, in which they sang, danced and then sucked on the bodies of the sick or injured.

No so, I had no strength left, let alone super human strength. But during the eerie silence I would have appreciated a small necklace made of small balls of wormwood and other medicinal plants. Apart from being worn during mourning for the deceased, it reputedly allowed the wearer to move about at night with out fear of ghosts. I wasn't in the habit of walking around unknown areas at night but, with the full moon casting so many shadows, any of them could have appeared to move - if I had looked long enough.

But I had no necklace. Instead I just kept busy around camp and, as light faded, descended into my sleeping bag – possibly as early as 19.00. I did not remember much after that...

Day 2   First camp – Ten Lakes

+610m   22.5km

Last night I camped under another glorious clear night sky. Having gained 3,000 ft. during the day, the stars somehow looked larger and brighter. The night temperature, however, was much lower - so low I had to wear extra layers in the sleeping bag. But the Californian sun would warm me during the day, if I had patience enough to wait for it. Now a good distance lay ahead and I was anxious to be up and moving - unlike the local wild life, who revealed their presence only when I was leaving; leading me to believe that their appearance was probably due to relief at my departure rather then habit!

Once again I started to feel that familiar adventurous feeling upon entering pastures new. The map, like most, was good enough to show me the various up and downs I would encounter, but it failed to give any hint as to the look of the land, or any thing unusual likely to remain in the memory. For instance, another camping spot (much smaller then last night's) snugly tucked in around fallen trunks, with a superb view of Yosemite creek and its now dry bed running over a beautiful example of concave granite, to which I would gladly have walked had I known of it.

Next I came upon sheer granite boulders that rose suddenly up from the surrounding rock, upon whose bare slopes saw my first deer, which reacted a lot different to those in the valley and soon disappeared into the woods. Possibly from habit when they used to be hunted, especially by the local Indians. Their preparations for the hunt, long and arduous, not only gave them perfect means of concealment but also seemed quite symbolic to these beautiful animals. This reminded me of the story of Kah-kool the raven, who was the first to see and hunt the deer in the valley long ago. The deer then were little different from today, but the raven had one disadvantage to mar his hunting efforts - he was white. So, after many failed attempts to catch the deer, he covered himself in charcoal. He and his ancestors have been black ever since! The Indians method of concealment was more one of purification then disguises; it was conducted in a sweat house (similar to a sauna) ;on leaving, they jump into cold water, then rubbed themselves with Wormwood and other aromatic plants to conceal their natural odour. Then they gather their weapons - a bow called Tanuka, of about 3 ft. long and made of spruce or incense cedar, stringed with the twisted fibres of Milkweed or sinew. The arrows, constructed in two parts, were made from young tree shoots of the Gilme tree (similar to elder or white oak); these were glued together with a type of adhesive that the animals body heat would loosen. The actual arrowhead was made of Obsidian (dark glassy volcanic rock) or flint, and the feathers of the Western red-tailed hawk or those of the Roadrunner - said to guarantee a kill.

The hunt was normally conducted in groups deploying various hunting methods; for instance, large nets that the deer were driven into, or use the deer's favorite food as bait (young oak, mistletoe or deer brush). Sometimes the animals were driven over precipices or attacked by their watering holes. But the most bizarre was when the Indians imitated the deer by wearing masks and oak sticks as antlers. This method produced a few successful kills but also attracted attention of other animals and it was not uncommon for some of them to be attacked by bears.

The best part of the whole hunt must have been the kill, then the sharing of meat amongst the villagers. Each hunter would have little meat left after the sharing but due to all the other hunters' generosity, he was always repaid in kindness. For the hunter who did not share, he was looked down upon. The Roe deer was the favorite food of the Miwoks; infinitely more appetizing then acorn mush and, had conditions not been favourable, I might have been sampling it myself. But my only major problem was availability of water, which I hoped to find at a permanent campground along the Yosemite creek not far away.

My hopes of obtaining water were initially dashed on reaching the camp when I saw a dark-colored bug and dead fish ridden, smelly pool. The camp was deserted and the clouds of dust I kicked up weren't encouraging. The presence of a telephone I found humourous, but would anyone deliver a pizza this far out?... This *was* America after all! I did not dwell on that for long, the thought of food made my mouth dryer: I wasn't at deaths door yet but being thirsty is no joke in this heat. Relief came with the discovery of cool running water not far from the camp. I climbed the next few miles over the slightest of inclines totally refreshed - where the track I was following crossed over the main 120 road, that runs the length of the park.

Half Moon meadow

At first it felt weird, exchanging conifer woods and exposed mountains slopes for road tarmac. How dare they put it here, I thought! But this same road would take me back to the valley in few days when I would see that the many forest fires that covered the park had made their way to the wood I had just walked through. No surprise really, the wood had been scorched dry as where all the others I past through, which at this time of year, I imagine would only need a small spark to set alight.

On the other side of the road, the going proved to be very easy over level ground, through woods of Jeffrey pine and huckleberry oak; I walking much slower now and their dense canopy offered good shelter. Past arrays of flowers and grasses, mostly long past their prime, but whose pungent odours seemed to clear my clogged tubes and brain.

It did not last, I soon started climbing again out of the woods on to a large exposed area I had been dreading all day. The sun was blazing and only a few juniper trees diverted the raging weight of the sun's heat from my back. Here, feeling and looking worsted for the wear, I unfortunately passed most of the hikers I saw during the entire trip, returning from a weekend at Ten Lakes. Their smiles, happy talk and small rucksacks only slightly eased my breathlessness, along with the first major view of the day – Mt. Hoffman. At a height of 2 miles it provides excellent 360 degrees views of the park and is considered a 'must'. But I was destined to spy upon the land at lower altitudes and in less crowded locations, a preference I preferred here – not so on other summits when I've been too windswept, tired, wet or freezing to care about the view. If the weather remained good there would be no low points, although a few approaching clouds might help. Being used to the more familiar cloud ridden, damp hills and mountains of Europe, I found it difficult to acclimatise to these conditions, refreshing though they may be. The few days I had spent in the valley proved inadequate acclimatization time. The Americans I met told me I was doing well, considering my disadvantage of coming from a land where it rains every day!! Sometimes I wished I 'd brought some with me, even a few clouds would have darkened the intermittent tree-less areas I found myself on.

Thankfully, salvation was near in the form of another wood, where also the gradient slacked off. Ten minutes, there after my panting finally stopped but I felt I had to stop, if only to take advantage of a small running stream. I rested under a huge Red fir while the iodine did its work and allowed me a cool drink. Not quite Coca-Cola with crushed ice but champagne, being drunk in the best of dining establishments; I was bathed in hazy light descending through the trees similar to that into a church and surrounded by the most charming and peaceful of decors... I could easily have fallen asleep but for the nagging thought of the climb to come. At least I had all the next day to look forward to; once I had found a good spot I could laze around all day and watch the wild life go by, maybe even swim or do some fishing. Normally I never considered resting for a whole day but here it felt different, almost a necessity. Those pleasant thoughts made the immediate climbs easier to bare, helped also by more stunning views and the discovery of the largest, lushest meadow I'd seen so far - Called half moon meadows because of its shape.

I crossed the meadow at a time when the Corn lilies along it's northern edge still stood tall above thick matted grass; a doe and her two foes were feeding not far from me. I knelt down quietly behind the lilies in an attempt to hide my presence before they ran further away like previous deer had done, hoping for a few photos. The Miwok used many animals for their stories, such as these Deer.

View from camp at ten lakes

One involves a black bear called Oo-soo-ma-te, who invited his sister in law, O-woo-yah the deer, to pick clovers in the meadows. The deer agreed but knew the black bear was not always to be trusted so, before she left her fawns, she told them that if a particular bag in their den fell to the floor then they must suspect the worse had happened. Why the deer decided to go when all along she must have known what was going to happen is a mystery.

The black bear, with all his strength, was destined to bring down the deer where as the sharp brain of the deer allowed her offspring to survive, hence the warning, which she probably hoped would give her young time to escape the black bear. But on seeing the bag fall, the fawns had other intentions in mind. They went to see the black bear's cubs and invited them to play a game - a game the fawns said that they had just invented and thought would be a real scream. Unfortunately the game brought about the death of the bear cub. Naturally the mother black bear tried to retaliate but found that all the other animals protected the young fawns and she could not find them.

I wondered if this sad tale had, down the ages, made black bears wary of deer. If there were any around the meadow watching the same deer as me then it was probably to protecting their own young, being mainly herbivores. It was unlikely they (unlike the mountain lion) would, out of hunger, regard me as food. A black bear would probably be more interested in the contents of my rucksack; I was told even the smell of toothpaste can attract their attention.

After a short rest I began the last climb of the day just beyond the meadow - all 350 ft. of it. At the time it felt more like 350 metres, up through thick forest and tall grasses leading to a broad flat top where only a few dwarf conifers survived amongst clumps of short grass and bare rock. The setting sun cast long dark shadows across the plateau, indicating I had made it in time and now had just enough daylight left to set up camp. Before doing so I took in the great panoramic view - the rugged, rolling Sierra Nevada, whose hard bright rock was only offset by alternating dense and thin coverings of conifers. The varying colours that the rock of these mountains reflected at different times of the day constantly amazed me, as now, especially across the rugged slopes of Ten lakes. I could see a couple of the lakes from the plateau as I looked into The Hollow – the name John Muir gave the basin containing these wonderful pools. One in particular, dark yet inviting, jutted out - surrounded by a rich mixture of hemlock, lodge pole and white fir, towering over boulder sprawled slopes. A few bare earth patches remained where a variety of plants survived, i.e. Red heather, Labrador tea; the latter, despite its name, is poisonous. In the months preceding August I was told this area is a mosquito hell but during September I found it quite free of all airborne suckers, even by the lakeside.

On my journey down into the Hollow I only saw the same two lakes as I had from higher up, both of which I imagined must offer plenty of isolated camping spots; but I would not be able to explore them until the morning. For now I would have to accept the first flat area available and I soon found it, along the track just above the main lake. Sleep rapidly overtook my tired but fulfilled body.

Day 3

Day Camp At Ten Lakes

Before setting up camp last night, I knew I was near a couple of other campers. With more time I'd have respected their want of isolation and privacy, the main reasons why people take occasional weekends here. In the light of day I decided they were probably not bothered as they, like me, were near to the track and not in one of the isolated spots - so I said hello. Most of the hikers I had encountered so far were Americans and if these two were regulars to the park, I might pick up some useful tips. Unfortunately they weren't but their spot looked perfect, flat, with a fire ring and great views down on to the lake – and they were leaving. Although near to the track, it mattered little, there wasn't hordes of people around the lake so until they left time passed quickly as we all swapped boastful stories. I've always found a few tall or short tales create a friendly atmosphere. That day, they also took the edge off the cool, crisp morning, warming body and soul: such tales told in the darkness of night can produce nightmares, especially if they feature mountain lions and black bears as ours did. Such tales excite an audience, even if they are sometimes misleading about the true nature of these beauties.

Once I'd set up camp I decided on a walk along the lake below. On a windless day its smooth undisturbed surface sparkled under the bright sun, producing wonderful double images of the surrounding slopes and trees. Looking back now, maybe I should have gone swimming but at the time felt it wrong to shatter the silence. Had I bothered to collect some White fir leaves and used them, as the Indians did, as a deodorant. I could have had a wonderful wash in my own private open-air bath! I might have caught some fish too which, though small, would have been a welcome addition to my food stock. Naturally I would have caught them by using the local Indian method, using a mixture of mushed buckeye and soaproot, which poisoned the fish. Later on I regretted not trying it.

This was my 3rd day out and I was starting to dream of sweeter cuisine - sad, but normal for me. Usually I go for a Sunday roast or fillet steak, but now seemed to be developing a worrying yen for fricadella with mustard and iced jack Daniels - not a drink to mix well with my current meal, even the food the Miwoks ate appealed more to me than that. According to one myth, their traditional foods only became available by courtesy of four certain creatures.

The first was Ol-lus-muk-ki-e, the toad woman, who was kidnapped and married to Yel-lo-kin, a giant bird who passed his time catching teenage boys and girls and eating them in his home on top of the sky. He had been doing this for some time, from the security of his home, making it almost impossible for any body to stop him - except for the toad woman, who one day managed to catch We-pi-ahk, the eagle. Being one of her relatives, he listened intently as she told him of a way to kill the bird. But once they had rid the world of Yel-lo-kin they must decide how to dispose of the body. The wrong decision could bring him back to life to haunt them again... this is where the final character comes appears - Ah-ha-le, the coyote, who suggested the best solution.

He took the birds feathers and planted them. These grew into many plants and trees – which still exist today - and provided seeds and nuts for the people to eat. Finally the coyote planted other parts of the bird, which grew into people, replacing those the bird had eaten. It may have been one of these people who first discovered how to use the versatile acorn to make soups, biscuits and bread?...

Like most indigenous people, the Awahni used many of the surrounding plants, trees and fungi in their day-to-day living. I have always thought that indigenous people must have had courage and a healthy appetite in order to survival - especially those who were the first to experiment with the local vegetation in order to discover what was or wasn't edible. They had only their senses to guide them, not highly informative packaging! Sampling fungi was probably the most risky; many a life must have been lost trying them, and the other sources of food, until it was clear which ones were edible.

The abundant acorn would have been an obvious food source; its method of use was perfected centuries ago and is little changed today. After being collected in open twined burden baskets (made mostly of willow and coated in soaproot juice to prevent any of the seeds from falling out), they were then ground to a fine meal, firstly by a stone mortar and then sifted, using a coarse twined basket. The meal was then leached in open sand pits lined with boughs, fine grass and covered with green conifer twigs; these broke the fall of water that was poured continuously over the meal, until the yellow of the acidic tannin disappeared. The meal was then ready to be made into a mush, and then cooked in cooking baskets on hot steatite stones. This would be used to make soups, biscuits or bread; the latter could be leavened and sweetened by adding the ashes of water oak bark. One cannot imagine the taste but obviously they survive on it! It would have been accompanied by greens, such as milkweed, rose lupine and miner's lettuce, plus meat.

All sounds quite mouth-watering but, if it had not been for many finely twined fibers, none of it could have been made - at least not by the above method. Back in the valley I visited to the Indian cultural museum several times; there, apart from seeing several of the baskets used, I also saw local demonstrators at work. The first was making baskets, the second the twine to make the baskets; I found all this greatly enhanced my appreciation of the information gathered. They made it look amazing easy. Accustomed to reliance on modern, machinery to produce such items, it was difficult to believe that these beautifully patterned and finely woven finished baskets on display could be handmade. No machine could duplicate them.

Back at camp, with time to prepare it properly, I ate the largest meal I'd had since starting the trip. After collected plenty of dead wood, I settled down against a rock near the fire and, armed with a fresh flask of tea, waited to see what the next few hours might bring.

On a scale of 1 to 10 for good nature watching spots, sitting next to the fire and upwind from the lake probably rated somewhere between 0 and −10; but the fire *did* provide warmth from the cold that came with being at 9,000 ft. in the shade! Despite my position I had some excellent views of a doe and her two fawns as they crossed my path several times, a few Californian ground squirrels and some smaller lodgepole chipmunks; the latter's interest in my tea was annoying at one point.

The best encounter by far of the whole day was not with black bears but three Californian or Blue grouse; just as I was rummaging around in the tent they strolled into my camp, heads held high as if they owned the whole woods. One came right up to the tent entrance, looked around inside and then at me, as if searching for something he had lost; his eyes seemed to be saying "so, where is it then?" My presence didn't bother them and they soon went on their way, apparently satisfied that I did not have what they were looking for.

The larger animals I hoped to see didn't materialise though I suspect my position didn't help; but I had passed a peaceful, relaxing and thought provoking few hours. Sometimes I laid on my back, gazing up into the high branches of the conifers - an excellent alternative view of any tree. It seems to block out all the other sounds whilst at the same time amplifying not only the wind but the tree's pleasant sounds as branches hit or brushed against each other in a kind of natural chaotic rhythm. This usually lulls me into a kind of a trance, slowing everything down and draining my body of stress - a magical experience that not everyone can enjoy. A horizontal position was also the most rewarding for reviewing the stars.

When the trees and wind came into their own again, certain sounds - to quiet to be heard in daylight – become clear. At night the movements of the trees branches defied wonder, seeming to join together and move about the high canopy - or perhaps it was a few little brown Myotis bats I could see flitting from tree to tree in the darkness... Whatever it mattered little, day or night, for not only did I feel closer to the woods but also to myself and there are few places in the world these days where there is sufficient peace to do that.

After having felt so relaxed I was naturally overcome by the '40 winks' syndrome, then when I woke up, could not immediately remember quite where I was - until I felt the warm sun on my body. It had finally found its way through the trees, to bathe me in welcoming heat. What had been a misgiving whilst hiking had now become a blessing, tempting me to close my eyes again. But a camp is not like at home, not mine anyway. There were things to do and I had to force myself to wake up and do them - cook another meal, collect more water, and gather wood for the fire. It had gone out during my snooze but was easily restarted by my blowing over the hot embers.

Fire is a major survival aid. The Indians had to devise a means of making it and the Miwoks used two methods, both common throughout the world. They used fire drills to produce heat under friction, and flint's (called Sitikwina or Kolubu) to produce sparks. I still rely on the all-important mobile flamethrower, or a lighter. If I'd had a whole week, even a day, I might have tried their way but if the worst happen and I lost the lighter - I'd probably be better waiting for Ah-ha-la, the coyote, to come along. He might have helped me to make fire, as he did the Indians.

There was a time when the people of the Yosemite Valley had no fire, not even a sun to give them daylight. Therefore they could neither hunt nor gather food until, during one of his trips, the coyote met a different group of Indians - who sat around fires, hunted and gathered food. This, thought the coyote, was what was needed back in the Valley and he asked the Indians if they would sell him the sun. They told him it was not for sale. He realised that if he wanted the sun he would have to steal it, but to do so, he would first have to get past the guardian of the sun. The guardian was a Turtle; it only slept for a few minutes each day but, even then, kept one eye open. Fortunately the Coyote had the power to turn himself into different objects so the he became a stick - first ensuring that he was on a path the turtle used. Luckily, the turtle did pick the stick up and so the coyote gained easy entry into the turtle's cave. Once there he waited until the turtle feel asleep before turning back into his normal shape - and so escaped with the sun.

At first the Valley Indians did not want the sudden brightness of the sun and told the coyote to remove it but, after all the risks he had taken, he was not about to return it. Instead he instructed the sun to move, much as it does now, from East to West; there, just below the horizon, he showed the sun some holes in the earth and instructed it to go into and out of them. This way, thought the coyote, the two groups of Indians could share the sun. Both could then hunt by day and sleep by night - something I planned to do as soon as the sun headed closer towards the Western hole!

It had been a superb day, short but with a great insight into the silent appeal of this mountain range and disrupted only by a few passing hikers. Despite walking close to the camp they noticed neither me nor, amazingly, the fire. I wasn't disappointment; I preferred my peaceful acquaintance with my surroundings to remain undisturbed.

Day 4   Ten Lakes – Glen Aulin

+540m   -335m   25.7km

Woke up early, drowsy and stiff after another cold night. Last night I could have wished for cloud cover more than at any other time this trip; I'd never experienced such temperature extremes over 24 hours before and any acclimatization I'd acquired during my stay had been thrown into confusion. But at least I'd be camping lower down from now on.

My next destination was Glen Aulin High Sierra campground, one of 5 such camps around the mountains of Tuolumne Meadows. During the summer months food and shelter is available at each camp, allowing hikers to walk the hills without struggling around with heavy rucksacks. I, on the other hand, had a hike of 16 miles - and an ascent of over 500m - over more dusty, rock and boulder laden tracks to take me up to the dizzy height of almost 10,000 ft. during yet another scorcher of a day.

That was to come, however. My first thoughts were not of any hardships but of the lake, which I was about to leave behind. I was sure that I 'd see and experience its wilderness again, maybe not here but in the many other similar areas that lie out there, somewhere, just waiting to be found. I would at least see it for a while longer as I followed the track along its shore into the woods, past a small but lush meadow; the frosted tips of long grass bore witness to last night's freezing temperature. Before I climbed out of the hollow I was treated to some fine views over the lake and its surrounding slopes and, finally, part way down into the Grand Canyon of the Tuolumne River. The only disadvantage now was that the sun was up again; its heat soon started to drain me of all energy and this diminished my enthusiasm for another of the ten lakes I found on reaching the top. It was more exposed and possessed almost no views so, eager to be on my way, I didn't stay long; I started my descent under a lovely stretch of shade, towards the deep V-shaped and picturesque Crest canyon. Stretching all the way from the slopes of Mt. Hoffman, to the slopes off Falls Ridge, it terminates - out of sight - into darkness.

If I'd been inclined to ignore local advice and leave the track to take one of my famous short cuts, that dark spot would have been my destination. But what would I find there? Maybe I'd have discovered not a way out but the entrance to a cave – perhaps the very one that led to the Thereafter, where legend says all deceased Awahnichi go… The story tells of an old man, Hoo-meh-let-kee, who after seeing his wife Aw-naw-haut-kee rise from her grave, followed her to the thereafter and went right into it. There he was told to return to the living and await his own death. Naturally if there was a thereafter there had to be mortal souls to inhabit it. After the coyote created people he made them immortal - and it was not until the meadowlark invented death that these people began to die. I wonder how many people there would be on this earth if he had not?...

From the crest of the canyon, I started on down the long exposed track, along the many switchbacks dotted with junipers. The views that unraveled around me may have been on a par with those in Yosemite Valley but I was still very relieved to see the canyon bottom - a narrow stretch of wood, dark green meadows and running water. Further up, on the opposite ridge, I could also see where I would climb up to and out of the canyon. This was a good couple of hours ahead and my main concern now was to reach the valley floor and find shelter from the suns merciless heat.

Once there I found the shade very cold but it and the frost-covered grass were a blessing. From what had felt like total silence on the high slopes the contrasting sounds of running water, and the reassuring colours the river brought to life, provided a welcome change. The river, whose sounds seemed to turn to honey in my parched mouth, looked more like a stream; it was very narrow and easy to cross. Yet judging by the amount of weathered boulders and strips of dry riverbed I crossed over, the river must be considerably wider in wetter climates and during times of snow melt. I considered that this canyon, more then any other place I had visited during the trip, was probably the most isolated and less frequented - by humans, anyway. But if I thought this meant there might be black bears amongst the richly vegetated spots amongst the conifers, I was wrong. Ideally, there might have a better chance of seeing some had I spent the day here but this was just a flying visit to the canyon. An hour later I reached the point where I would start my climb out.

Towards falls ridge

Because I wasn't looking forward to the ascent, I naturally presumed that it would be hard – one to definitely break my back, induce shooting pains through my bad knee and generally exhaust me. To my surprise (and relief) it was quite easy. Massive conifers provided plenty of cover for most of the climb and the switchbacks offered lovely gentle ascents; at times the track traversed below great vertical slabs of granite, which I hoped I wouldn't need to climb. So I didn't experience my usual urge to stop every 5 minutes and still had some wonderful views back down the canyon.

On climbing up and around the slopes off Tuolumne peak, I continued through a maze of isolated meadows separated by a jumble of moraine-like mounds; these hid small areas that looked perfect for those all-important wild camps. Water is scarce this time of year but the views are magnificent and exploring possibilities endless. Water *was* available but involved a long trek from the moraines each time. I made my way towards one particular cool pool that, according to the map, I should have been close to but every time I rounded or topped another mound, I only saw more mounds – this combined with being near 10,000 ft. Started to make me feel agitated as the air thinned.

After climbing a particularly steep open slope I saw the small pool, one of two, marked on the map as two small blue oasis just under the thick 10,000-ft. line. I planned an hour-long lunch there, well-deserved reward after the breathlessness I'd felt during the last ascent. Having found the idea spot, I let my rucksack fall with such a force that it literally shook the ground, leaving a rectangle imprint. It might be there still – and tripped over if, like me, you were more interested in the panoramic views of the Sierra Mountains then the track beneath your feet! Describing the mountains as bright, lumpy and dark dotted mounds does not do them justice but, during the first half hour of my rest, that was my opinion. It wasn't until I'd had a little splash in the pool that I fully appreciated these predominantly granite mountains. Today they contain only small, sporadic amounts of sedimentary and volcanic rocks – remains from when the whole area was volcanic - like the Cascade range to the north is today and caused by the subduction of the Pacific Oceanic plate under the Continental plate of North America. At some point the volcanoes of this area were shut off and the magma remaining deep in the ground hardened, producing plutons. These merged and were exposed to the air, once the overlaying rock was eroded away. Then uplifting from the East started, giving the range its characteristic slant to the West. Glaciers then shaped the rounded mounds of plutons into the range we see today, aided by a few rivers. Yet the weather cannot be the only earthly element rewarded for creating such a magnificent landscape; vegetation also played its part - not so much by any erosion but by its ability to penetrate this hardwearing rock and add that aspect to this landscape that identifies it only as the uniquely beautiful Californian Sierra

Nevada. Feeling refreshed and fairly strong towards the end of my rest, I wondered if the walk along the John Muir trail to Mt Whitney would have been worth it - if only to see these mountains from 14,000 ft. After a 200-mile trek it would have to be good, if not breath taking!

Not far past the pool, I reached the point at which my excessive ascending for the day was over and the descending started. Gentle at first, under the dense cover of my friends the lodge pole and red fir; they revealed several views of cathedral peak (so called after John Muir climbed it and compared it to a church). The next good views did not appear until I was back on the canyon floor. Near Cathedral Creek of the giants that guard the Eastern bounder of the park - like Mt Connes at 12,590 ft. and Sheep Peak. These views were not as good as those higher up, due to a thick haze and the surrounding conifers obstructed most of them. Even so, these few glimpses of my environment were a welcome distraction from the heavily dust-laden mule track I was following. I 'd been looking forward to the rewards of descending 1,300 ft. and the subsequent increase in oxygen but unfortunately the thick clouds of dust I kick up cancelled out any advantages to my lungs and throat. My throat was sore, as if I'd been smoking heavily, but I avoided the emetic effects the Indians suffered when they used the local tobacco plant, called coyote tobacco - so called because the coyote represents evil. Obviously the pleasure gained by smoking and drinking the leaves and stems of this sticky, smelly and repulsive plant were regarded as evil - or maybe the coyotes name was associated with it along with a certain small stone mortar, believed to have been created by the coyote...

The mortar was used to pulverize and mix together the tobacco plant and calcined shells, a mixture the Indians would drink to make themselves sick - especially after eating too much. Smoked like normal cigarette, they used a hollowed-out elder tube as a pipe; with sticks stuck in one end, which I presume acted like a filter. Men smoked for pleasure, women to cure colds. I would have liked proof of the latter - smoking has always made *my* colds worse!

Once across the shallow Cathedral Creek, I had another short rest. I had covered a long distance, it certainly felt like it and this rest was what I hoped represented the last. McGee Lake wasn't far and apart from marking the last of the days ascends; it was also the point from which I would see some outstanding views. Tired and exhausted, I was glad to reach the deep drop down into Glen Aulin - journeys end. The sight of a fairly well supplied Tuolumne River comforted me, forming a spectacular waterfall; it flowed gracefully under the wooden bridge I used to cross it, then swept on and disappeared into the steep-sided Grand Canyon beyond. I'd like to say it looked awesome, in a way that only certain mountain views can when reached the hard way, but somehow a description far poetic than mine would seem more fitting. I was speechless, but happy in the knowledge that for the first time during my trip - I would fall asleep to the sound of running water.

Day 5   Glen Aulin – Tuolumne Meadows

+275m   9.7km

Frost-covered ground, tall dead stems of corn lilies and extremely cold nights - all sure signs that the summer was truly coming to an end in the High Sierra, and so was my time in the wilderness. Until I went down to the river in the morning for water, I thought I would only have the freezing night of this camp to remember. But, just when least expected, I saw the fresh paw print of a black bear along the riverbank. At first fear gripped me with fright, but as I slowly scanned up and down the river my fear was overcome by curiosity - and hope.

After this chance sighting I asked a few other hikers if they had encountered any black bears but, just as in the valley, bears only seemed active around humans during the night. During my stay at Sunnymede campground a climber on the same plot as me spent a night sleeping in the open - and woke during the night to see a black bear sniffing around his sleeping bag! According to the guidebook, Pates Valley - situated at the other end of Tuolumne River Grand Canyon - is the place for bear spotting; unfortunately it was also the location of a forest fire. This prevented me from hiking there, but I'd hoped it would mean the black bears would make the trip from there up the Grand Canyon to Glen Aulin.

Glen Aulin

Sorry to say, as far as black bear sightings went, I was destined to finish my trip as unlucky as I had started it. I had arrived with a few fears of them but also a desire to see them in their true environment; now it seemed unlikely. Would I see them during my last 6-mile trek to the meadow? My hopes weren't high. With this disappointment and knowing it was my last day, I didn't looking forward to the uphill climb out to the meadow; it seemed more of a chore then a pleasure.

Oh, I'm such a winger! Sometimes I wonder why I venture into areas abound with hardships, massive ups and downs and unpredictable weather conditions! But regardless of my feelings at that moment, I knew I'd jump at the chance to do today's hike all over again, take the same photos of wonderful sights such as the Cascade and Tuolumne Falls at the start of the hike, separated by quaint pools of water. Then, later on, superb views up Cold Canyon beyond Glen Aulin and the oddly shaped column of basalt rock at Little Devil Postpile. This was a very old remnant of a volcanic conduit located near a short gorge, whose smooth river-warn surface trapped a little pool of water just beyond it, surrounded by conifers with the start of Tuolumne meadows in the back ground. The meadows wide, flat garden of grass and flowers indicated that the climb was nearly over, plus also opened up panoramic views of the Meadows rim, of peaks such as Cathedral, Unicorn and Johnson, to name but a few. The slow meandering of the river enhanced the beauty of the meadows, whose elegance and serenity I could only compare to the Merced River. In all, definitely a place to have chow time in.

It was pleasant to spend time near a river that possessed that certain magical quality only large rivers possess - something I'd missed amongst the dried-up rivers of the high country. It's flowed like silk in a breeze; the surface sparkled like diamonds. It was by a similar river that, 150 years earlier, one man's eyes caught the glint of something shining – a substance that would change these mountains, and the lives of the Indians living within them, forever. James W. Marshall's discovery of gold along the American river may not have been anything new to the locals but, when he took the news down out of the mountains, certain businessman rapidly picked it up. Together they voiced "the shout that was heard around the world". This, naturally, attracted a wide variety of people and it was they who created the legend of the 49's (the Forty-Niners). Initially they found gold in such huge amounts that they soon had to meet food and supplies prices that could still, in today's money, be considered expensive but there was plenty for all, at least at the start, when also crime was unheard of. When it *was*, the "Miners Law" stopped it by introducing punishments, i.e. tying a man to a tree, stark naked, at the height of mosquito season!

Yet, despite the thousands who flocked here, certain Geologists estimate that they found only 30 % of the gold in the mountains. Others believe that, because of the unique rock formations of the Sierra Nevada, there was no Mother Lobe within them. Yet could over 100,000 men and women – who left lives and homes behind them to harvest roughly 400 million dollars worth of gold between 1849 and 1855 - be wrong? I don't think so. For all the lucky ones who *did* find gold, thousands didn't strike it rich or pan out.

One such prospector was James M. Hutchings who, despite failure at gold digging, made a fortune by taking up his pen and writing the humorous "Miners Ten Commandments". Subsequent profits did not disappear behind a bar or in a gambling house; instead he invested them by founding the Californian Magazine and building the first hotel in the Yosemite Valley.
Apart from this connection with the gold rush, the Valley has only one other claim to fame associated with the gold obsession - that promising possibility of a mother lode (or 'great silver belt') existing in the Tioga hill area, encompassing present-day Gaylor Peak and the ridge west of Bennetville. Thousands of dollars and man-hours were concentrated on a project involving cutting a tunnel through some of the world's hardest rock - to where the lode was supposed to be.

The estimates of the lodes monetary value, was huge; this attracted many shareholders wishing to stake their claim and invest their money. This cash was used - and wasted - for years as man and machine ground away at the mountain. They built such towns as Bennetville and the Tioga road to help haul the heavy equipment to the site. But, eventually, the shareholders patients – as well as their money - ran out; all work on the tunnel ceased and the Great Sierra Consolidated Silver Mine was closed.

Near little devils Postpile

Others have subsequently tried but still the estimated $ 9,642,840 lode of silver lies undiscovered. Apart from the road - the present 120 - all that remains of the miner's efforts are a few Bennetville buildings and their machinery. Very few stories of their hardship and suffering survive, such as the tale of the man who carried 8 tons of equipment over rugged mountains, before the road was built; or the many who perished during the work or, even worse, in avalanches and terrible snowstorms. What drove these men on? Was it just the thought of the monetary gain - or simply because they could not imagine doing anything else? It certainly wasn't for fear or isolation they would have felt around 11pm on dark winter nights, for this was often when avalanches would strike, sweeping away cabins and occupants. Some survived through their own strength or with the help of others. The Bagby brothers and another man in their cabin survived; he was found, still in bed and with a kitten purring beside him, after an avalanche. During one avalanche on March 15th, 1882 a horse was rescued, after being found still standing upright.

Not all tales of hardship involved snow – nor any weather conditions – but acts of near-sanity. For instance, such as the story of some frozen nitro that was placed near a fire to thaw; it exploded, severely injuring three men near to it. Or when the mining companies bookkeeper experienced a lapse of insanity and began shoot up the town having what in those days was described as 'a high old time'.

Details of the many events that must have taken place in a mining town housing 50,000 are as lost now as the treasure they sought but I can imagine how all those hard-working, hard-playing, folk spent their time. It's strange now to think that most the stories from around the world about gold mining, started from the find of one little nugget, which could have really been found anywhere, in any river. Maybe even a tributary of *this* river, the one I was looking into, as it originated in the area directly off Tioga hill. Luckily for the surrounding mountains and wildlife, no nuggets where found here; maybe I should be thankful for that and not wonder if there was wealth to be found under the surface… but concentrate on admiring the scenery instead.

Once into the meadow, the track led mostly through sheltering woods over many undulating hills. These were, I thought, the cause of my sudden fatigue and slower pace but then realized it was due to my gradual awareness that the distance to come was much less than that, which lay behind, i.e. the trip was almost over. I'm sure that if any Indians had used the track I was presently on, years ago, they would have thought it had been made by a horde of Elephants (had they known what they were), compared to their own tracks. Only a few of these are still used by hikers and tourist today - those to Vernal falls and Inspiration Point for instance. Before the Indians introduced their trails to the Whites they were a lot less obvious than today, only marked with pine needles or sticks. They sometimes hung up dead skunks along a track, which even to us would make it obvious. Most tracks did not have that well-beaten look, as they do now, nor any switchbacks. They went as straight as an arrow, like Roman roads, even on slopes - straight up, straight down. Obviously the Indians were very fit and if they could see me now would probably think I was much older then I looked - hunched up under the rucksack weight and puffing like air was going out of fashion! I dreaded seeing anyone on the last few miles but, going so slowly, it had to happen – and I met two hikers.

They were two Americans, returning after a weekend bird watching, and they admitted to being equally exhausted. This somehow took a chunk of weight off of my back - or maybe it was just because they kept me company over the last few miles and offered a lift back to the Valley; but I don't think they realize just how thankful I was. Without their generosity, I might have had a long wait ahead - tiring my thumb whilst wondering if anyone would be willing to give a hairy, dusty smelly hiker a lift for the near 2-hour ride back to the valley.

I don't remember saying much during that ride back, but watching the scenery and mountains that had been home for the last 5 days rush past - especially the Tuolumne Meadows, whose expanse and serenity had been hidden from me on the track, but was now in full view. During Spring, with the wild flowers in bloom, they must be a spectacular sight and I regretted not spending more time there. But we started the descent down into the valley these feeling faded - there was nothing I could do about them now. For some inexplicable reason I expected the Valley to have changed, but my friends the mountains were all just as I remembered them, their majestic beauty seeming even more impressive after my excursion in their interior.

One in particular I had to check up on and I was thankful to find it just as I'd last seen it, high above the rest – remote and powerful.

Most days during my days spent in the Valley I had felt drawn towards this same peak, especially during my last sunset in my own special peaceful place on the banks of the Merced River, just behind Yosemite lodge. It wasn't just the majesty and another perfect reflection of Half Dome that I wanted to see for the last time, but also the true marvel of a natural phenomenon that I had witnessed earlier on its slopes - and had been too slow to capture on film. Now, with camera ready, perhaps I *would* capture it as I sat watching the mountain, not taking my eye off it for a second.

I didn't know exactly when this phenomenon would appear but I knew it was near, when the sun began its long descent. The slopes around me darkened, leaving the slopes of the much more distant and higher half dome burning under the suns last rays, brilliantly silhouetting it against silent tall trees. Any second I hoped that the last dying light of the sun would perform this miracle of nature when, for only a few seconds, the sunlight would reflect off the mountains surface at a certain angle, twisting the colour of the rock and the sparkle from it, to produce a shade of orange which is the brightest and most vivid I had ever seen. This breathtaking sight seemed a last act of defiance before the Dome, too, was overtaken by darkness.

Was my vigil rewarded? Did I see it? Oh no, Mother Nature is not like that – she tantalizes, but she never performs to order! Yet at least I was leaving with the knowledge of its existence. My memories of it – and the sheer unforgettable beauty of the valley – were mine forever.

Six mountain hikes from around the world